John Peter Altgeld

Live Questions

Including Our Penal Machinery and its Victims

John Peter Altgeld

Live Questions
Including Our Penal Machinery and its Victims

ISBN/EAN: 9783337165352

Printed in Europe, USA, Canada, Australia, Japan

Cover: Foto ©ninafisch / pixelio.de

More available books at **www.hansebooks.com**

LIVE QUESTIONS:

INCLUDING

OUR PENAL MACHINERY

AND

ITS VICTIMS.

———

BY

JOHN P. ALTGELD.

———

CHICAGO:
DONOHUE & HENNEBERRY,
1890.

CONTENTS.

PREFACE.

The questions treated in this book are not only questions of the day — pressing for solution—but many of them vitally affect the welfare and happiness of mankind, and can only be intelligently settled by a thorough investigation and wide discussion.　　　　J. P. A.

Chicago, April, 1890.

LIVE QUESTIONS.

PROTECTION OF NON-COMBATANTS;

OR,

ARBITRATION OF STRIKES.

[*Published in the Chicago Evening Mail of April 26, 1886.*]

Can the State enforce arbitration in a strike?

This question at once resolves itself into two:

First: *Has the State the right or the constitutional power to compel arbitration independent of the will of the contending parties?*

Secondly: *If it has the right, is it feasible to exercise it, and in what manner and how far can it enforce its award?*

It is assumed by many in this country that in a strike the State is powerless as a mediator; that its sole function in such a time is to keep the public peace, and that so long as the latter is not disturbed the State must remain an idle spectator; that every person has the right to do as he likes with his property or with his labor; that the employer has the right in all cases to employ and to discharge whom he thinks proper, and when he thinks proper, and to pay what wages he pleases; and that the laborer has the right in all cases to work when, and for whom he thinks best; and that neither employer nor employe stands in such a relation to society at large as to give the State, as the conservator of all classes

and interests, any right in case of a strike to interfere without the express consent of the parties to the
dispute. As strikes are often of such magnitude as
to affect the entire country, if long continued, this doctrine in effect affirms the following propositions:

1. That the rights which a man has in a state of
nature are not greatly modified or limited by his becoming a member of our complex society; that although all
of the members of the latter are interdependent, each
being affected by the conduct of the others, yet that a
limited number of these members have the constitutional right to pursue a course which is not only injurious to the whole, but which, if persisted in sufficiently
long, must result in a dissolution of society; that the
remainder, although they may constitute ninety per
cent. of the whole, have no constitutional right to protect themselves from the consequences of such conduct.
In short, that the State, as the embodiment of society,
has no power to prevent or to remove those conditions
which, if left alone, would lead to its own overthrow.

2. That although great changes in the method of
production and of transportation in this country have
altered the natural order of things, as it existed one
hundred years ago; have already destroyed and tend
more and more to destroy independent occupations;
and although great corporations have grown up with
thousands of men in their employ, who are almost at
their mercy; and although business is tending more and
more to be centralized and controlled by a few; and
although it is vital to the very existence of society, as
now constituted, that business in its various forms

should go on regularly and without great interruption; and that these corporations, particularly public carriers, should be not only required, but also enabled to do their work without delay, for every interruption of their operations subjects the public to serious loss and inconvenience; yet, as the relation between employer and employé is one of contract, the State can in no case interfere to protect the interests of the public at large, notwithstanding the fact that the highest courts of the land have, in other cases of contract, held that the State can interfere for the protection of the public. For example, in those cases relating to the rate of interest which may be charged, the amount of toll which may be charged, the rate of fare which may be charged, and the rate which may be charged for storing grain.

3. That although this is an age of great division of labor, by reason of which thousands of men in one line of industry are dependent for work, and consequently for the means of subsistence, on the industry of others, yet, if in consequence of a dispute between employer and employe in any one line all other industries should become paralyzed, (for example, during the recent strike of the coke makers in Pennsylvania, many large iron mills had to shut down for want of coke, thus throwing the ironworkers out of employment, while through these in turn other industries were affected,) * the State has no power to inquire into the nature of the difficulty, and dare, under no circumstances, interfere for the protection

* Note—Since publishing the above there has been a number of instances of whole communities of non-combatants being almost paralyzed, because the regular operations of great corporations were interrupted by strikes—notably the strikes on the Gould and on the Burlington systems of railroads.

of the non-combatants, but must stand by idle and helpless while its very existence is being jeopardized. In short, that the doctrine that was supposed to lie at the foundation of all civil society, viz.: that every man can do as he pleases with what is his own so long only as his conduct does not injuriously affect others, has no application here.

4. That while the State must bear the burden of suppressing crime and of supporting paupers, yet it derives from this duty no corresponding right or power to arrest or to remove those conditions which are certain to breed both criminals and paupers.

5. That an individual or corporation may interfere with the natural distribution of population, and cause several thousand laborers with their families to settle in a location where they would otherwise not have settled, and where there are no opportunities of earning a living except what are furnished by such individual or corporation as employer, and that the State has no right to see that these people shall not become a burden to the State by thus being made either paupers or criminals, but that when they are, as it were, in the hands of the employer, and have it not in their power to go and make a living elsewhere, the employer may, in case of a disagreement, lock them all out, and may bring on several thousand more (who otherwise would not have come there), and put these in place of the former, and in case of a second disagreement, may bring on a third lot, and so on, each time leaving his former workmen and their families without the means of subsistence, and in a condition in which they are certain to become a burden on the State,

part as criminals, and part as paupers. And yet the State has no right or power to interfere, notwithstanding the fact that but for the action of such employer these people would not have settled in that locality, but would have distributed themselves over the country more nearly in proportion to the natural means of subsistence offered, and would not have become a burden on the State.

6. Or that several hundred employes may impose terms upon an employer with which he can not comply without actual loss; and if he declines to accede they can prevent him from employing other men, and thus force him to shut down, although by so doing a whole series of other manufacturing establishments are obliged to stop work and their men to be idle because they need the goods made by the first; so that in the end all industries will become paralyzed, the public generally put to great inconvenience, thousands of men everywhere, who have no trouble with their employers, will be thrown out of work, and those conditions which breed crime and pauperism are created in a most aggravated form. Yet the State must stand idly by, simply because the parties that originated the quarrel are too stubborn to compromise or to agree to arbitrate.

The bare statement of these propositions is all the refutation they need. Every duty imposed upon the State implies a corresponding right. The duty of the State is not simply to protect life and property, but, also, to enable all those agencies that are necessary to the existence of modern society, to perform their functions properly. Besides, every government possesses the inherent right of self-preservation, at least so far as that it may, by all means within its power, resist those antagonistic or disintegrating forces which tend to its destruction. It can resist foreign invasion, can suppress internal rebellion, and can suppress and punish crime. It can do things without number which are designed for the benefit of the entire public, although in doing them it may in a measure modify or curtail what have been supposed to be the natural rights of man. To hold, therefore, that it can not inquire into or remove those conditions which not only breed crime and pauperism, but which, if left alone, must in time bring about the ruin of society and the overthrow of the government, would be an absurdity. It is the duty of the government to conserve and protect all interests, and, being its duty, there can be no question about its power.

The objections so commonly urged against paternal government have here no application. For in all cases where it is found to exist, as in the countries of the old world, or in the imposition of protective duties in this country, the State steps in at the beginning and regulates affairs without first giving individuals an opportunity to get along without State interference, while here the State allows employer and employe to manage their own affairs, and claims the right to interpose only after they have failed; and then only in cases where the interests of the public are being injuriously affected in consequence of such failure.

The question is, can there lawfully be *any* government or public agency to regulate or to control this condition of affairs. As to nearly all other conditions or disturbances which injuriously affect society, no one questions the right of the State to interfere. Now, why should it not interfere in this instance?

That the machinery or form of government adopted, to meet troubles of this character, must be "of the people, for the people and by the people," in order to be successful, is unquestionably true. But that it is as much the duty of the State to prevent injuries to the public at large from strikes as it is its duty to prevent injuries from any other cause, is equally true.

BUT, ADMITTING THE RIGHT, IS IT PRACTICABLE TO ENFORCE IT?

This is a serious question. The first inquiry one hears is: "Well, what can," or "what shall the State do?" And the answer frequently heard is: "Create boards of arbitration to settle all these disputes between employer and employe." Yes, that is all right, so far, but, having got the board created, let us see what, from the nature of things, it can and can not do.

At the threshold it meets some natural limitations which no legislation can overcome.

1. The board can not compel the employer to run his mill, for he may not be able to do it, or may think that it can not be run without loss, or for a number of reasons he may not desire to run it. And, I repeat, the board can not run it for him.

2. The board can not impose terms which would make it impossible for the employer to continue his business without actual loss, for to do this would be to render his property employed in his business worthless;

would practically destroy it without making compensation for it, which, according to the settled principles of American jurisprudence, can not be done.

3. The board can not force a man or a large number of men to enter a factory and to go to work and to continue to work against their will.

With these limitations in view, let us set the board in motion. A strike, with its usual accompaniments, exists in the neighborhood. The board takes cognizance of it, inquires into the trouble according to rules of procedure which it has established, and it finds that the employer is in the wrong, and it so decides. It fixes a price which he shall pay, or determines in other respects what he shall do. Now, if he elects not to run his mill, that is the end of the matter. But if he desires, either then or in the future, to go on, then the board can require him to do so on the terms it laid down, and can further provide that he shall not employ any new men until he has given his old employes an opportunity to go to work on the terms fixed by the board. If he objects that he should not be interfered with in his business, it may be replied that there was no interference until there was such a condition of affairs about his premises as was injuriously affecting the good order or well-being of society. And if he objects that he should be permitted to employ whom he pleases, it may be answered that he had interfered with the natural distribution of population, and had led a large number of people, *i. e.*, his former employes, to settle around him, who otherwise might not have settled there, and that it would be against the well-being of society that these should all at once be thrown out of employment and their places filled with others, as they would thus be in danger of becoming a burden on the public; that if he desires to make a change it must be done gradually, so that there will be no danger of the public peace being disturbed or of the public burdens being increased. It is clear that in this case it is feasible to carry out the decree or the award of the board.

But we now accompany the board to another strike. Here, after careful inquiry, the board decides that the employes are in the wrong, and it fixes the terms upon which they shall return to work. Now, if they all decline to go, then, as already stated, the board can not compel them.

But it is scarcely necessary to consider such a contingency, for it is not likely to happen. All experience points the other way. As a rule the employes have no alternative—they have no other means of getting bread for themselves or their children. It is true that at present they sometimes hold out to the point of starvation, but this is because they have got themselves into a situation where they can not gracefully or with self-respect back down, whereas a decision of a properly constituted tribunal would help them out of this dilemma.

It must also be borne in mind that, at present, public sentiment is frequently with the strikers, and it is the force of this in many cases which prevents them from going to work; whereas, in a case where they refused to abide by the decision of a properly constituted tribunal, public sentiment would be against the strikers, and this alone would operate powerfully to dissolve the strike.

Again, in nearly all cases, many of the men who first stop work are opposed to a strike, and are only deterred from resuming by the fear of being expelled from their union, in which they are interested in insurance funds, benevolent funds, etc.; and if the law were to protect them against expulsion, where no other ground existed than their compliance with the award of the board, they would go to work at once.

Further, it is worthy of note that in nearly all labor troubles in the past, it was the laboring men who were the most willing to submit to arbitration, and I believe there is not a case of this kind on record in which an arbitration was fairly entered into that the award was not promptly accepted by the men. It may, therefore, be safely assumed that if this board were so constituted as to command the confidence of employes in regard to its integrity and fairness, there would never be any trouble about enforcing its awards against them. Should experience, however, demonstrate that something more was necessary to insure compliance with the award of the board, by either employer or employes, it might be provided that if an employer refused to carry out the award, he should forfeit say six days' wages to each of his employes; or if the employes refuse to abide by an award, they shall forfeit, say six days' wages to the employer. Of course, to make this provision enforceable against the men, it would be necessary for the employer always to be six days in arrears in paying them. But this is the case now with most large employers, especially railroad corporations, and in the case supposed it would further have to be provided that during a strike no judgment should be rendered in favor of an employe for such specified arrearage.

The board should further have power to inquire into a case where the employer has discharged all the striking employes and is filling their places with others; for it is the bringing on of others, and thus increasing the population of that locality beyond the means there provided for earning a living, that vitally interests the public. It is at present a matter of common occurrence that men are hired and taken from one end of the country to another, to fill the places of striking employes, when, but for such bringing, they would never have thought of going to the points where they thus swell the population.

But it is safe to say that if a law for compulsatory arbitration were passed there would not only be very few arbitrations under it, but there would be very few strikes. For the consciousness that arbitration can be forced upon them would induce both employer and employe to get together and to try to adjust their own differences, and this nearly always results in a settle-ment, the difficulty at present being that many employ-ers will not talk with or meet their men.

Consequently, the employer does not understand the men nor the men the employer, and thus trifles fre-quently lead to trouble, when, with a better understand-ing, they would be unnoticed; so that any measure which will make the relations between employer and employe more familiar will be productive of much good.

Even a board which had full power to make a thor-ough investigation without the consent of the parties, but had no power at all to enforce its award, would prevent a great deal of trouble; for the consciousness that a full investigation can be made and the result published to the world, showing who is in the wrong, will alone lead to an effort at adjustment.

BOARD—HOW CREATED.

It is apparent that the method of creating this board is of the greatest importance, and that both employers and employes must be given a voice, if they desire, in selecting the board in each case. For, if the board were to be constituted by the usual political agencies, or if there were to be one permanent board, it would not command the absolute confidence of the parties, and would soon be regarded as many of our courts, whether rightfully or wrongfully, are now regarded, *i. e.*, with more or less distrust. Therefore, in each case where there is dissatisfaction, or a dispute liable to result in a strike, a separate board should be created by the employes selecting one member, the employer one member, and the two thus selected agreeing upon the third. This is the practice now in vogue in nearly all cases of this character wherein arbitration is now resorted to.

There should be a provision authorizing some court, on application of either employer or a fixed proportion of the whole number of employes, or in case of an actual strike, where neither employer nor employes apply, on application of a specified number of citizens, to select such member of the board for any party to the dispute that declines to select his own. But this should not be done until after notice is given to either the employer or a named proportion of the employes, as the case may be. This would place it within the power of either party, as well as the public, to secure a prompt settle-ment of all disputes in reference to the rate of wages, etc. As the authority of the State to interfere is based chiefly on its duty to prevent public inconvenience and social disturbances, as well as to prevent increase of public burdens, this board could not take cognizance of cases where there are but few employes. The line hav-ing to be drawn somewhere, the minimum might be 'fixed at, say ten. The rules of procedure by the board are matters of detail which present no insurmountable difficulties.

BOARD OF APPEALS.

As a board of appeals would necessarily be distant from the scene of the trouble in most cases, and a hear-ing before it accompanied with much expense and cause much delay, which delay alone would tend to destroy all the benefits to be derived from arbitration, and per-haps bring the whole system into disrepute, I believe it would be a mistake to create such a board; for one of the strongest arguments in favor of arbitration is, that there can be a speedy adjustment of difficulties. Besides, only the strong could avail themselves of the services of a board of appeals. Should such a board, however, be created, then there should be a provision requiring the decision of the local board to be accepted and carried out, until it is reversed or modified by the board of appeals; otherwise, every party dissatisfied with the find-ing of the local board would appeal merely to get delay, and it would not be long until the whole system would not only be rendered abortive, but be brought into disrepute.

COSTS.

The costs of an arbitration should be taxed very much as they are now in law-suits. At present the public pays the judge, the jurors, and furnishes a court-house, and requires the parties to pay the witnesses, the sheriff and the clerk. As the public is just as much interested in the settlement of disputes between employer and employed as it is in the average law-suit, it should bear at least the same proportion of costs. The arbitrators, in particular, should be paid by the public, so that they may never be suspected of considering the certainty of getting their fees in rendering a decision. Provision might be made requiring a bond for costs to be given by the party applying for an arbitration, and the board should have power to apportion costs in proper cases.

Upon the question of arbitration there has until recently been a wide divergence of opinion between employer and employes. The public, it may be noted, nearly always favors arbitration without stopping to inquire carefully into the matter. As a rule, employes favor arbitration, but until recently employers have generally been opposed to any outside interference. But a great change has already taken place in this regard in the minds of employers, and many of them are now advocating compulsory arbitration. Not that they like to have the State step in between them and their men, but because this is the only way in which they can be protected from the consequences of strikes on the part of their neighbor's employes. At present, many strikes force the shutting down on the part of employers who have no trouble with their men, and cause thousands of men to quit work who have no complaint against their employers; the only way in which these troubles can be limited to the original parties to the quarrel is to provide for creating in each case a board of arbitration, with full power to inquire into the trouble, whether the parties consent or not.

As already stated, the public, which is always interested and frequently a direct sufferer, favors arbitration. As a rule employes favor it, and employers are beginning to see that it is to the interest of every employer who has no trouble with his men to have such a board, for he can then seldom be made to suffer because of the wrong-doing of some other employers, or of the folly of other employes. We may, therefore, reasonably expect soon to see laws enacted creating boards of arbitration similar in character to those that we have been considering.

JOHN P. ALTGELD.

Chicago, April 26, 1886.

PENSIONS FOR SOLDIERS.

[*Published in the Comrade, at Chicago.*]

A Review of the Relationship Existing Between the Ex-Union Soldier and the Government.— How Pensions Are Earned and the Way They Should Be Adjusted and Paid.

Editor of The Comrade:

Sir: Your note asking: "What does the Government owe its soldiers of the late war, and have they any claims that should be settled in dollars and cents? If so, how?" is at hand. As you wish me to give reasons for any opinion I may express, I submit the following as the result of such reflection as I have been able, amid the press of other business, to give the subject.

In considering this question we must regard the Government as being the American People, so that the question is: "What do the American People owe the Union soldiers of the late war, and have the soldiers a claim against the people that can, or should be settled in dollars and cents?" And it is only the latter half of this question, viz., whether there is a claim that should be settled in dollars and cents — about which there can be any controversy or great difference of opinion. All admit that the brave men who imperiled (if they did not all actually sacrifice) their lives to save our institutions, are entitled to the affectionate regard and the everlasting gratitude and homage of a free people. But, can the people discharge the whole claim merely with gratitude and homage? Or, has this claim a dual character, being in part for the debt due to lofty patriotism and heroic devotion — a debt which is above money, and can not be estimated in dollars—and being in part for actual loss of money and material sacrifices made, which can be estimated and liquidated in dollars and cents?

One of the bravest and most patriotic men who fought through the late war, in speaking on this subject, said: "We stand on higher ground. There are debts that can not be settled across the counter. The most sacred obligations are those that can never be paid, and the only partial compensation possible is a return in kind. Of this nature is the debt which a saved nation owes to its defenders." I have no doubt that these views are held by many of the soldiers, and, so far as it relates to compensation or pay for lofty patriotism, devotion to country, or sturdy discharge of duty, they are clearly right. Money can not pay for those. And, it may be added, that the willingness to leave family and friends and rush to the defense of your country when danger threatens, without waiting to see whether there can ever be any compensation — the readiness to imperil and even sacrifice your life for a cause—the unflinching discharge of duty however hard — all come within the list of deeds that are above money. And it is upon these that the safety and perpetuity of a nation depend. Whenever these virtues have to be purchased in advance with money, then the end is near.

To quote again from the soldier referred to: "If future citizens of this republic will not come freely to their country's defense in the hour of need except for such (moneyed) inducements, then efface from your banners the honored colors and emblems and let the dollar of your daddies on a golden ground be their flag to lead them to battle and to deserved defeat. Then will this Republic go the way of all republics, and fall, from sheer inability to stand up longer in its own rottenness."

This is strong language, and every syllable of it is true when applied to the purchase of patriotism. But it does not cover the whole case. A patriot may make material sacrifices which can be, should be, and are paid for in dollars and cents. If the Government takes a man's property, nobody questions for a moment his right to compensation. Can not a man's time be placed on the same footing with property? Some rely on property for their support — others rely on their time — if then the latter is taken, why should there not be compensation? Suppose the man enters the army and serves through the war without receiving any compensation, would he not be entitled to pay in dollars and cents for his time? And if the Government paid him for this, could it be claimed that it was paying him for his patriotism? Clearly not. It would only be settling the money part of the claim. The debt properly chargeable to patriotism would remain unpaid. So if he had been paid half what his time was reasonably worth, there could be no question but in equity he should be paid the other half, and if he were, it would not be paying for patriotism.

Therefore it seems to me that the question is: Has the soldier made any material sacrifices of time, property or health, for which he has not been compensated, and if he has, does common justice require that he should be compensated?

Before considering this in detail, I will simply notice:

Public Policy.— It is claimed, and with reason, that in a country like ours, wherein no standing army is maintained, and no burden imposed for a permanent military establishment, and where the government has to rely absolutely on the patriotism of its citizens to repel foreign invasions or suppress domestic insurrections, public policy alone would require a very liberal and comprehensive spirit in dealing with the soldier. That if the government were even to be lavish, and go beyond the strict requirements of justice, it would be, from a politic standpoint, a good investment, because it would tend to insure a ready response to any call the government may make when in distress hereafter, and would tend to stimulate the men while serving. It would be a sort of premium paid to insure the safety of our homes and our institutions in the future. So that it would be in accord with a wise public policy for the government not only to do simple justice to the soldier — that is, to pay him what it morally owes him — but to go beyond this, and even do more than it is in strict justice bound to do.

WHAT, THEN, DOES COMMON JUSTICE DEMAND?

Other Governments.— It is urged by some that our government has already dealt more liberally with its soldiers than any other government on earth, and, therefore, nothing further should be asked. Now, it is not necessary to inquire whether this is true or not, for it makes no difference what other governments have done. Most of the governments of the world are founded on despotic principles, and treat both the lives and the property of the common people as if they existed only to serve the pleasure or the ambition of the rulers. And the soldiers are treated as so many fighting cattle, that are left by the roadside or in a poorhouse to die when they are no longer of use. But that is not the case here. Our government is said to be of the people, for them, and by them; and all the people are supposed to have an equal interest in maintaining it, and when it is threatened with danger, it is the common duty of all to march to its defense. The burden rests on all, and when, therefore, some go and some do not, some make sacrifices and some do not, common justice requires that those that make the sacrifice, and thus save the government, should be in some way recompensed or made whole for what they have done over and above what their neighbors did, for inasmuch as the duty rested equally on all, the burden should be borne equally by all.

To illustrate: It is admitted that when our institutions are threatened, it is the duty of all to assist in protecting them; that all should pay taxes in proportion to the property they own, and all should give their time and personal services to the common cause. The man with property having a double interest in preserving the government — *i. e.*, to protect his property and also his person and family — must therefore both pay taxes and give his time and personal service to the government, while the man without property, being interested only in the protection of himself and family, must give his time and personal service only. Now, if all citizens had an equal amount of property, and all entered the service of the government, and after a victorious war all were fortunate enough to return alive and in good health, it is clear none would in common justice be entitled to a pension or extra pay because all had contributed equally and all had derived an equal benefit from the result. But if in the case just stated one-tenth are slain or die from exposure, and one-tenth more are maimed or rendered unable to make a living or carry on their business as before, then inequalities arise; the dead and also the maimed have given more than their neighbors to the common cause. The family of the dead have given up their support. Whether that support consisted of brains and muscle or of a farm can make no difference in the scale of justice. It has been given to save the country, and they have, therefore, given more than their neighbors, and justice demands that they be compensated for the excess they have given. Likewise the maimed or disabled. They have been deprived of their ability to carry on business or use their limbs as before, and to this extent have given more than their neighbors, and justice requires that they should be compensated.

The government could in each of the cases given above, institute an inquiry as it does when it seeks to take a farm—ascertain the amount of damage the individual has sustained in excess of his neighbors, and pay this in a lump, or it can provide for paying it in install-

ments during the life of the party injured and call it a .
pension. But in either case it will be simply making
compensation ; it will not be giving away anything ; it
will be simply doing justice—for let it be clearly understood that a pension is not a charity ; it is a payment
made in consideration of services which the government
acknowledges having received.

Let us now go farther. If, instead of every man
entering the service, as we have supposed above, only
a part go (as is always the case), then if they all return
in as good condition as they went, and if while away
they were paid wages equal to what they could have
earned in their respective callings had they remained at
home, and they do not have to commence anew when
they come back, then they have contributed no more
than their neighbors, and are not entitled to any compensation except perhaps for the exposure and hardships endured. On the other hand, if the wages paid them
are not equal to what they could have earned in their
respective callings had they remained at home—if they
had to give up business, and when they returned had to
commence anew ; in short, if they are in any way worse
off after returning than they would have been had they
remained, or if they endured inconveniences which their
neighbors did not, then they have given just that much
in what has money value, over and above what their
neighbors, who did not go, have given, and common justice demands that to that extent they should receive
compensation ; and when they do, it is not payment
for their patriotic deeds, but simply compensation for
what can and should be adjusted in money,

What are the Facts? It is true that all men of the North did not go into the army—some did stay at home. Therefore, if those that did go earned less money while away than they would have earned had they remained at home, or endured hardships which they otherwise would not have endured, or if after their return they were in any way worse off than they would have been had they remained at home, then, to say nothing about patriotism in so promptly responding to their country's call, to that extent they have contributed more than their neighbors, and in justice and good conscience are entitled to compensation.

I think it will have to be admitted in all quarters that those that entered the army (I speak of the privates) were not paid, as a rule, what they could have earned at home—that they endured hardships which they would not have had at home—and that they returned far worse off than they would have been had they remained at home. I am speaking now only from a financial standpoint, assuming that they all returned healthy and sound.

Thirteen and sixteen dollars per month and finding were the wages paid to the privates in the late war. This was, if anything, less than was paid to common farm-hands at the same time, so that those that could perform only the commonest kind of labor could earn more by staying at home than by serving their country, to say nothing of the privations and hardships which the soldiers had to endure. Even if the wages paid had been equal to that paid for common labor at the time, then. to the extent that the soldier suffered privations and endured hardships, has he contributed more to his country's defense than the man who stayed at home? If this is true of the common laborer who served, it follows that every mechanic or skilled man of any kind who entered the army as a private could have earned from two to four times as much by staying at home, and the difference between what he was actually paid and what he would have earned had he stayed— added to the privations, exposure and hardships of a soldier's life—constitute what he has contributed of that which can be estimated in money to defend the country over and above what those gave that stayed at home. So the man who gave up a business or the opportunity of making money and served in the army has—if the business or the opportunity was worth more than the wages actually paid him—contributed the difference to save his country. That is, he has contributed that much more from a money standpoint, than the man who stayed at home.

Taxes paid.—It is no answer to say that the man who stayed at home paid taxes, because the soldier, if he had any property, had to pay taxes just the same. Besides, as heretofore stated, the man with property had a double interest in saving the country—one on account of himself and family, and the other to save the value of his property. In fact, the latter may in some cases have been the greater, because, while the destruction of the government might not effect him personally, it might destroy the value of his property.

Therefore, taxes paid by those not entering the army must be considered as being simply the contributions which property makes to save the government, and thus to save itself. And as long as taxes are paid only on property, they are in no sense a substitute for personal service in the army, and their payment can not in any way discharge the obligation that the man who pays them is under to serve personally in the army the same as every other citizen.

It may be said that it was necessary that some should stay at home and carry on the industries of the country, and that when doing so they were serving their country just as effectually as if they were in the field. This is only in part true. True if he who stayed at home could make no more at home than in the field, and if the danger and hardship were equal in both cases, then it is clear that the man who served in the field contributed no more to save the country than the man who stayed at home. If, on the other hand, by staying at home he can make more money than by taking the field—if, in fact, he sells his products, whatever they are, to the very government which is in danger at the highest price he can possibly obtain, so that in fact he gives the government nothing directly; and if the danger and the hardship at home are not equal to those in the field, then it is clear that the man in the field contributes more than the man at home, and it is equally clear that whatever the excess may be, common justice requires that he should be compensated for it.

The question is not whether it is necessary that some shall remain at home. The question is, has one contributed more to save the country than the other; and if yea, then, inasmuch as it is admitted that all should contribute equally, does justice demand that compensation be made to him who contributed the excess; that is, the excess of what can be estimated in money. Patriotism, courage, devotion to duty, prompt response to the call of one's country, and the willingness to take the risk of losing life should be regarded as being above money value and to be compensated for only by the gratitude of one's country.

Health.—I have thus far assumed that all that returned from the war were as sound physically as they would have been had they stayed at home, and we have found that even if this were so the soldier contributed more than the man who did not go into the army, and that this excess had an actual moneyed value. But it is a well-established fact that comparatively few returned from the army sound men. In most cases where they were apparently well, exposure had sown the seeds of disease which sometimes did not develop for years, but which did finally develop, and not only cause them suffering, but also greatly cripple their ability to do business or make a living, and consequently they have to be regarded very much as if they had actually been maimed on the field. Yet they can not now furnish sufficient evidence to get a pension under our laws. So that no matter from what standpoint the subject is considered, it soon becomes apparent that the soldier contributed more to save the country than the citizen, and is entitled to compensation. How then shall this be paid? In a lump or in installments by way of pensions? Here practical difficulties arise. To determine the exact amount due each soldier is impracticable; even if it were not, the total would be so large, that the treasury could not meet it, so that whatever is paid must be paid in installments in the shape of pensions. But how? On what basis? These are difficult questions. No plan that will do exact justice can be devised. All that is possible is to approximate. Several systems are advocated which I will consider.

Service Pensions.—By this term I understand to be meant a pension for service rendered, as distinguished from simple enlistment, the idea being to pay for services performed or sacrifices made, and to pay nothing where no service was rendered or no sacrifice made.

Of course there will be difficulty in drawing the line, but this has nothing to do with the principle involved. Bear in mind that a pension is not a charity nor a gift; it is simply a payment in discharge of a debt which, instead of being paid in a lump, is paid in installments. And the principle involved here is simply one of making compensation.

We have seen that, in common justice the soldier is entitled to compensation for what he contributed over and above what his neighbor contributed. Now, how shall this be ascertained and paid? If it had been practicable to do so, and if it had been insisted on, justice might have required the government to institute a separate inquiry in each case, and if anything was found to be equitably due, to pay it. But owing to the great number this was not practicable. Whatever the cause, it has not been insisted on. Now, one way of adjusting a claim is to confer with the claimant, and, if possible, arrive at an agreement. The claimants in this case are the men who served in the war, and if they are willing to accept compensation in installments instead of in a lump, and the government recognizes the justice of their claims, that is certainly the easiest way of arranging it. But a pension made uniform for a certain length of service would not do justice, because it would hardly ever be the case that any two men had made precisely equal sacrifices in order to serve in the army. To meet this objection the advocates of a service pension propose a graduated scale, giving to the man who served only three months a small sum, to the man who served a year a larger amount, and to the man who served three years or more a still larger sum—payment to begin when the soldier reaches the age of say fifty-five years. This plan, it is claimed, would lighten the burden on the treasury, as only about one-fourth of the living soldiers would begin to draw pensions at once, and then these would begin to die off as new ones are added. This plan recognizes the impossibility of devising any way to do exact justice; it does not even try to approximate it, but seems primarily to aim at *making provisions for the old age of the soldier*, and in this view strikes me favorably. It is free from the objection urged against indigent pensions, for to obtain the latter the soldier must almost proclaim himself a pauper, and, as the brave are usually sensitive, they should not be subjected to this humiliation. Upon the whole, this plan, as thus limited, seems reasonable and moderate, and if the soldiers are satisfied therewith the government should be. The government has at different times placed all the survivors of former wars on the pension list; it is true it usually waited until they were nearly all dead. But still it recognized the principle that the government should care for the old soldiers, and, if the principle is right, then I say the government should not wait until most are dead, but should extend its hand the moment they arrive at a specified age.

Objections.—It is objected in some quarters that to allow a service pension would make enormous demands on the treasury, and to that extent would increase the burdens of the people. But this has nothing to do with the question. If these men have just claims against the government, and that government is able to pay them, then justice demands that they be paid, whether it take a large or a small sum out of the treasury.

Who are the Objectors?—It is a curious fact that this objection is urged most strongly by men many of whom have made fortunes out of the government. It is urged by what are commonly called "Wall street influences" —by men who, when the government was in the greatest distress, would not enter the service themselves or render patriotic assistance, but bought the government bonds at sixty cents on the dollar and then were paid interest on the full face of the bonds, and at their maturity insisted on having the face of the bonds paid in gold, which at that time was worth a premium, so that they were paid nearly two dollars (besides interest) for every dollar they advanced the government. They gave their country very much the same kind of assistance that a pawnbroker gives a poor man that has met with an accident—cautiously makes some advances, takes the best security he can get, and then tries to get two dollars for every one he advanced.

One might suppose that after having reaped their harvest they would be satisfied. But not so. For now, when it is proposed that the government shall do simple justice to those that left their business and their homes, and risked their lives to save the government, and prevent even the very bonds of which we have spoken from becoming worthless, these Wall street influences are exerted against the ex-soldiers.

There are people who imagine that brains and muscle and human life should at least be placed on as high a plane as money; that if the man who loaned the government money to carry on the war is paid nearly two dollars for every dollar loaned, then the man who gives up his business and his home, and risks his life and endures the hardships of war, should be recompensed in the same liberal manner for the sacrifices he has made.

But the ex-soldiers do not go this far in their demands. They do not ask for double compensation; they ask only that the government which was saved through their efforts, and which is now great and powerful, shall make them whole—simply recompense them for the sacrifice they have made—and will feel grateful if they are but made whole.

The People.—The masses of the people are not adverse to dealing justly and even liberally with the ex-Union soldiers. They can always be relied on to support an honorable and a liberal policy. When after the war it was urged by many that some of the bonds of the government should not be paid in gold because they did not call for it on their face, and had not been paid

for in gold, the masses sustained the government in
paying gold, not only because it was thought that the
honor of the government was in some way involved, but
because a wise and far-seeing public policy required
that the government should deal liberally with its cred-
itors, and this same public can be relied on to favor not
only a just but a liberal policy toward the ex-soldiers.

Frauds.—No doubt it is true that great frauds have
been perpetrated on the pension department, and that
many are getting pensions that should not, but will anybody claim that therefore those that in justice are entitled to a pension should be kept out of it?

Private Pensions.—I must admit that I favor general
rather than special or private pensions, I believe in put-
ting all belonging to the same class on an equal footing.
Private pensions are invidious and undemocratic.   They
are only for a fortunate or a favored few.   Only those
that have influence with some Congressman or "have
a friend at court" can hope to get a private pension,
and these are not always the most worthy.   A very
large number of special or private pension acts has been
passed at every session of Congress for a great many
years on the ground that the general laws were so
framed and construed that many worthy and invalid
soldiers who deserved a pension could not prove
their claims under them so as to have a pension allowed.
Now this, should be otherwise.   The pension laws
should be so framed, construed and executed that
every soldier who has any just claim to a pension can
readily get it under a general law, and not be required
to secure a special act of Congress before he can get
what he is justly entitled to.

Gen. Oliver Edwards, of Warsaw, Ill., hit the mark when he said: "I believe private pension bills, as a rule, are an injustice to most of us, on the ground that very few old soldiers have sufficient political influence to secure a private pension."

Indigent Soldier's Pension. — Careful inquiry has recently brought out the fact that there are at present upwards of ten thousand ex-Union soldiers in the various alms or poor-houses of the United States; at times their number has reached nearly twenty thousand. How many soldiers have already died there and been buried in the potters' field, is not known, but as the average death-rate in alms-houses is from ten to fifteen per cent. a year, it is safe to say that every year for a number of years over one thousand of the old Union soldiers have died amid the squalor of the poor-house, away from friend and family, and been buried in the field set apart for strangers. But the ten thousand represents but a small portion of the indigents, because only a small portion of the poor of any class actually enter the alms-house. Usually friends intervene and support them. So that it is, perhaps, within bounds to say that for every soldier in the poor-house there are at least five who are being supported as objects of charity by friends. If this is correct, then we have the humiliating spectacle of the most powerful, most wealthy and most enlightened government on earth, after a victorious war, in which its very existence was at stake, allowing upwards of fifty thousand of the men who rescued it from destruction to be supported by private charity; upwards of ten thousand, besides many thousands soldiers' orphans, to be confined in the public poor-houses of the land, and over one thousand to be buried every year as paupers. There may be people who can view this spectacle with composure, but there are those who feel that it is a shame and a disgrace.

It matters not whether they are in the poor-house because the pension actually paid is so small that it will not half support them, which is the case with some, or whether they have not been able, under existing laws, to secure any pension, which is true of most of them. In either case the great patriotic masses of the American people do not want to see the soldiers who fought to save the Union, thus, as it were, left by the roadside to die.

We have seen that those who actually served in the army have a just claim against the government, which has not yet been paid. Then there are thousands of men who left the army apparently well, but in whose systems exposure had planted the seeds of disease, which afterward slowly developed, so that they could not make a living, and yet, under the strict proof required by our existing laws, which practically require the applicant to prove his claim beyond a doubt, they are unable to satisfy the pension office, and so get nothing. In fact, so eager do some pension officials seem to be to defeat a pension when they can, that in cases where the proof satisfied the law and showed the applicant to be entitled to a pension, they have written to some postmaster in the locality where the applicant resided, to see if they could not get some information that would defeat the pension.

We can form some idea of the large number of men who in justice are entitled to pensions, and who have been unable to secure one, by considering the number of private pension bills annually passed by Congress, bearing in mind that there is not one private soldier in a hundred who has sufficient influence to get Congress to pass a special bill in his favor. And yet during the first two years of Cleveland's administration, not only did Congress pass, but President Cleveland actually approved eight hundred and sixty-three bills. In addition to these there were a number passed by Congress which were vetoed by the President.

That these eight hundred and sixty-three bills were founded on justice is shown by the fact that they received the approval of the President, who is not charged with being partial to private bills.

If we consider how much time and effort it requires to get any measure passed by Congress — how very few of the bills introduced ever are passed — and that not one private soldier in a hundred has sufficient influence to enable him to get Congress to pass any measure, and then reflect that during two years Congress actually passed and the President approved eight hundred and sixty-three private pension bills, we can see that there are many thousands of poor soldiers who in justice are entitled to a pension but are unable to get it, and who, if they have no other means of support, must depend on private charity or else make their bed in the poorhouse.

But if this were not so — if the men who served in the army had no just claim to compensation, and the indigent soldier, of whom we have been speaking, had no just claim to a pension—would not an enlightened and a wise public policy require that the government see to it that those that imperiled their lives in order to save it from destruction should not, in their old age, have to eat the bread of charity, draw their last breath in an alms-house, or be buried in a pauper's graveyard?

On March 18, 1818, just thirty-five years after the close of the Revolutionary War, and only four years after the close of a second exhaustive war with Great Britain, at a time when the country was poor and had not yet fully recovered from the effects of the last war, Congress passed a law granting pensions to all that had served in the army of the Revolution "for a period of nine months or longer at any period of the war, and who, by reason of reduced circumstances, shall stand in need of assistance from their country for support."

Here the principle that the government should assist those that imperiled their lives for its preservation, and that are in need of assistance for support, is distinctly recognized and acted on. Can any good reason be given why the powerful government of 1887 should pursue a less liberal policy toward the soldiers than the exhausted government of 1818?

Invalid and Disabled.—I have thus far noticed only those that do not receive any pension, and will add a few words in regard to those to whom pensions have been granted. According to the reports of the pension office the whole number of people in the United States in 1886 drawing pensions was 265,855, since that time the number has been slightly increased.

The following table shows the sums paid per month for the different kinds of injury:

Total deafness	$13 00
Inability to perform manual labor	30 00
Loss of a hand or foot	30 00
Total disability in one hand and one foot	36 00
Loss of one hand and one foot	36 00
Amputation at or above elbow or knee	40 00
Amputation at hip or shoulder joint	45 00
Loss of both hands	72 00
Loss of both feet	72 00
Loss of both eyes	72 00
Need of regular aid and attendance	72 00
Widow and dependent relatives	12 00
Child	2 00
Anchylosis of elbow or knee joint	10 00
Anchylosis of ankle or wrist	8 00
Loss of the sight of one eye	8 00
Total deafness of one ear	2 00
Slight deafness in both ears	4 00
Severe deafness in both ears	8 00
Loss of hand except thumb	17 00
Loss of thumb	8 00
Loss of index finger	4 00
Loss of any other finger, without complication	2 00
Loss of all the toes of one foot	10 00

Etc., the table being long.

The following table shows the number drawing the different sums:

29,247	$ 1 00 to $ 2 00 per month.
66,421	2 00 to 4 00 "

39,578	$ 4 00	to	$ 6 00	per month.
51,722	6 00	to	8 00	"
12,992	8 00	to	10 00	"
19,383	10 00	to	12 00	"
4,804	12 00	to	14 00	"
8,878	14 00	to	16 00	"
3,557	16 00	to	18 00	"
1,626	18 00	to	20 00	"
15,963	20 00	to	24 00	"
9,007	24 00	to	30 00	"
647	30 00	to	40 00	"
1,046	40 00	to	50 00	"
983	59 00	to	75 00	"
1			100 00	"

By glancing at these tables it will be seen that the amount paid each pensioner is very small. Over one-third of all get from one to four dollars per month. Comparatively few get as high as twelve dollars per month.

Anyone can see that the pensions paid to disabled soldiers are in most cases not only inadequate to their support, but inadequate to make compensation for the sacrifice they made over and above that made by their neighbors to save the government. Take the man who through exposure has become totally deaf. Will anybody claim that to pay him thirteen dollars per month will be a just compensation?

Take the man who, when he entered the service, was robust. He was then able not only to make a living and support a family, but get something ahead, now he is totally unable to perform manual labor. Can it be claimed that thirty dollars a month is a just compensation to him? So of many of the other sums, without reviewing them in detail. They are inadequate to make compensation, and inadequate in many cases to support the pensioner or his children, so that it is no wonder our poor-houses are filling up with the old soldiers and their children. As already pointed out, it makes no difference what other governments do. We must proceed on a different principle. With us all should contribute equally to the protection and support of our institutions, and when some have to give more than others they are justly entitled to compensation for the excess.

JOHN P. ALTGELD.

Chicago, January 3, 1888.

JUSTICE TO THE DEAF SOLDIER.

[*Published in the American Tribune, at Indianapolis, Dec. 27, 1889.*]

NOVEMBER 14, 1889.

My Dear Mr. Foster:—Your favor of the 25th ult., stating that "A deaf soldier has no show to enter the civil service, while the amputation cases are found in every department at Washington," reached me some days ago, and confirms what my own observation had already led me to believe.

It is remarkable that the government of this great republic should discriminate against the deaf soldier. But there has always been against him a discrimination invidious and unjust, tending to create a feeling of bitterness. Until about a year ago, the pension paid to a totally deaf soldier was only $13 per month. Think of $13 per month for a man totally deaf, while at the same time those that were disabled by reason of a loss or disability of limb or limbs, were paid from two to three times this amount, and more. Under the law of August 27, 1888, the totally deaf soldier is paid $30 per month, while soldiers suffering from other disabilities may receive as high as $72 per month, the loss of only one arm or of one leg entitling the pensioner to receive $36 per month, and yet experience has long shown that such a man can get employment where a totally deaf man can not, and certainly in point of suffering that of the latter is infinitely greater than that of the former.

The rules of the civil service and the practice thereunder to which you refer, simply show that the same condition of things exists in the Federal service that is found in the world outside. The deaf soldier has little show of getting a job in either. It is fair to assume that the men who framed the rules, and the men who from time to time controlled the appointments, were honest, intelligent and humane, and certainly as ready to assist the deaf soldier as any private employer would be. And the fact that the former has had little show in securing or holding positions in the Federal service simply demonstrates how unreasonable it is to expect him to get work from private employers, and how unjust it is to discriminate against him in fixing the pension to be paid him. No private employer will from choice select a deaf man. If he employs him at all it is as a matter of charity, and he will keep him only as long as he feels that charity requires him to. So, that even while doing the little work which may be given him, he must feel himself an object of charity; instead of receiving a cold potato at the kitchen door, a pittance is doled out to him in the shop. This is all wrong. Our country should not force such a humiliation on those of its defenders that were unfortunate. The American people are liberal, and, above all things, want to see justice done. The difficulty grows out of the fact that the full extent of the disability and suffering resulting from total deafness is not at once perceived. When a man has lost a leg, or an arm, or his eyesight, the character of the affliction can be seen, and while not fully, it is still more nearly appreciated. But the deaf man can walk and see, so that at first view he does not seem to be so badly off as the other. It is not till afterwards that we discover that it is almost impossible for him to get anything to do. Particularly is this true now, when thousands of men who are in possession of all their faculties, find it very difficult to earn a living, and nobody but himself and his God can fully understand how severe is the suffering that comes from the utter isolation from all mankind into which he is forced. No voice of wife or child can gladden him; no spoken word of friend can cheer him; as a rule he must forever sit down alone, and can commune only with his own sad thoughts, and it it seems to me that the government should see to it that these thoughts are not embittered by the feeling that the country which he helped to rescue when it was in peril, and in whose service he was disabled, now neglects him in the days of its greatness and of his misery.

What is necessary is to make the public once understand the full meaning of your affliction. This once accomplished you will be fairly dealt with. You and your comrades have already done very much in this direction, and I hope soon to see full justice done you. With kind regards, I am   Very truly yours,

JOHN P. ALTGELD.

CAPT. WALLACE FOSTER,
        Indianapolis.

THE ADMINISTRATION OF JUSTICE IN CHICAGO.

[Published in the Chicago Papers.]

CHICAGO, February 12, 1889.

HON. SHERWOOD DIXON,

House of Representatives, Springfield.

Dear Sir:—In answer to your letter asking my views upon you bill, which provides that the judges of the trial courts may, under certain conditions, give an oral charge to a jury, permit me to say that I am not satisfied with your bill, because it does not go far enough; still it is a step in the right direction, and I hope the General Assembly will take up the matter of regulating the practice in our courts and treat it with that thoroughness which its importance demands.

The main objections to our system of practice in the common law courts, referring particularly to Cook county, are:

First. The uncertainty as to result without regard to the justice of a cause brought about in part by legislation, which experience has shown to have been unwise, in part by requiring a unanimous verdict, and in part by the fact that the higher courts have embarrassed and complicated the administration of justice by what have been called "frivolous technicalities," applied not to the merits of a cause but to some question of procedure, so that hundreds of cases are reversed and kept hanging in the courts for years, until the subject matter of litigation is lost and the parties are worn out with expense and worry—not because the case had been wrongly decided in the trial court upon the merits, but solely because there was a difference of opinion concerning some question of procedure. Consequently, dishonest men, with no meritorious defense, are encouraged to litigate, and, as a matter of fact, have almost as good a chance of success—at least for several years—as those that have an honest case, and many honest men with meritorious cases are afraid to go into the courts because they feel that they have only a little better chance there than a scoundrel.

Second. Another objection is that at present a lawsuit costs him who loses but little, if any more, than he who wins; so, a man without a just cause of action or meritorious defense can keep a case in the courts for years and subject his opponent to great expense and annoyance without taking any chances. As a result, many suits are brought which ought not to be, and many others, in which there is no defense, are fought for years, simply because an unscrupulous defendant finds it to his advantage to fight rather than to settle. So that many meritorious cases are kept out of the courts, while our dockets are crowded with cases, many of which ought not to be there, and many others of which should be speedily disposed of.

Third. Another objection is unreasonable delay. This grows out of the conditions I have just mentioned, and at the same time augments them. As a rule, it now takes from two to four years to dispose of a suit in our common law courts, whereas it should not take over forty days. At present, when a man begins a suit, he generally has to wait nearly two years before it comes up; in the meantime, the situation of the parties may have changed, or the subject matter of the suit become worthless. Then he is notified by his lawyer that his case is about to be reached and that he must prepare for trial. Thereupon he partially neglects his business, has consultations with his lawyer and looks around for his witnesses. In the course of a few days—or a few weeks—the case is actually placed on the call for the following day. Then he attends court with his witnesses for from two to ten days at great expense until the case is reached on the call, when it is discovered that on account of the engagement of counsel on one side or the other in some other court the case has to be passed for a short time. Then in the course of a week—or sometimes of three or four weeks—he gets his witnesses together again and goes to the court-house where he finds some other case on trial, and he is told to wait. In the course of a day or two his case is again reached, when the chances are about two to one that it will again have to be passed. And very frequently, after having neglected his business for weeks, and having been to great expense and trouble in getting his witnesses and attending court, it is found that on account of absent witnesses or some other cause the case must be continued, and that it will not be reached again for upward of a year, when he will have all his work and trouble of preparation, etc., to do over again. If, however, the trial is begun, then he is astonished to find that it is apparently not the justice of his cause which is the main subject of inquiry, but that, instead,

it is the rules of procedure about which great solicitude
is shown. When the evidence is all heard and the lawyers have made their arguments, then he learns that we
have had legislation in this State which changed the
practice as it existed at common law and still prevails in
the Federal courts, by which the judge was to point out
to the jury just what the issues are and state to them the
law governing the case; but that, instead, the judge can
not give the jury any other than written instructions.
As a consequence, the jury is often left with very con-
fused notions as to what the issues of fact are; and, as
there is usually not time for a judge to write out a clear
and concise charge covering the whole case after the
evidence is closed, he is frequently obliged to give a
number of instructions prepared by counsel for the
respective parties, and which frequently fail to give to
the jury much light or guidance; so that the jury is liable to either bring in a verdict which is entirely wrong
and must be set aside, or else to disagree and thus compel
the parties to wait until the case is again reached in its
order, and then do all this work over again. As the law
requires a unanimous verdict, the suitor finds that if
there should be a corrupt man on the panel—or a crank,
or a man who felt offended at something said by another
juror, he has it in his power to produce a miscarriage of
justice without giving any reason. If, however, the
suitor safely runs all these gauntlets and secures a verdict which, after a motion for a new trial has been
argued, is left to stand, then a judgment is entered,
and the defendant appeals to the appellate court. This
takes about one year more, and occasions considerable

expense for lawyers' fees, printing, etc. Then it is found that the appellate court reverses about forty per cent. of all cases brought to it, and sends them back to be tried over again; and they are reversed, as a rule, not on the merits—not because an actual injustice has been done, but a great majority of cases are reversed because of what has been styled "some frivolous error" in the procedure. Frequently some point which neither side thought of or urged in the court below is made a ground for reversal because, to quote the language of the higher courts, "it may have influenced the jury;" not that it probably did influence the jury, or that the result should have been different on the evidence. So that our suitor finds that two chances out of five are against him in the higher court. If his case is reversed and sent back, then he finds himself just where he was when he started, and he has had upward of three years of expense, trouble and worry for nothing. He must do all his work over again, and it will require from two to four more years to get through with it. If, on the other hand, his case is affirmed by the appellate court, then, if the amount involved exceeds one thousand dollars, an appeal is again taken to the supreme court. This involves another delay of about a year and the paying of lawyers' fees, printers' fees, etc. Here again his case may be reversed and sent back, and if it is, the suitor finds himself just where he started, and all his outlays and his worry have been for nothing. But, as the supreme court at present can not review the facts, but considers only questions of law, the chances of a reversal here are not so great. If the judgment is affirmed so that the lawsuit is finally ended, then he learns that the other—that is, the losing—side need pay him nothing for all the expense, delay and trouble to which he has been subjected. Even though his suit was founded on a promissory note. That is, a man with ever so honest a claim may be kept in the courts for years, kept out of the use of his money and put to great expense and trouble, and the other side need not pay his lawyer's fees—need not pay his printer's bills—need not pay for the delay—nor for the trouble and annoyance to which he has been subjected.

Is it any wonder that many of our business men would rather lose a claim entirely than to go into court with it? Is it any wonder that many conscientious lawyers advise their clients to accept any kind of a settlement rather than attempt to litigate? Is it not reasonably certain that if the law were to provide that every time a case is decided on its merits in any court of record the court shall fix a reasonable attorney fee to be paid by the losing party to the winning party, it would weed out much of the litigation we now have, and bring about a condition in which a man having an honest claim would not feel that he might as well lose it all as to go into a court of justice with it?

4th. Still another objection urged with much force is that, our present system entails a heavy expense on the public—on the non-litigating people—which they ought not to pay.

Leaving out of consideration the probate and the county courts, which to a certain extent are administrative, there are in Cook county eighteen judges, including the superior and the circuit court judges. Two of these are constantly at the criminal court, leaving sixteen attending to civil business. It is true three of these are in the appellate court, but their salaries have to be charged to the public.

The salaries of these sixteen amount to......	$112,000
The expense of the clerks' offices of the superior and circuit courts for a year is.....	69,468
The expense of sheriff's office, chargeable to these two courts, over and above its earnings, is	75,000
The expense of keeping up court-house, and chargeable to these two courts, is........	20,000
The jurors' fees for these two courts amount to....................................	62,756
Total.................................	$339,124
The total earnings of the superior and of the circuit court clerks' offices amount to....	107,487
Leaving........................	$231,737

as the sum which the people of Cook county pay annually for the benefit of its litigants. The present fee to be paid on commencing a suit is $6 ; and by a defendant on entering an appearance is $1.50.

The total number of suits brought, including appeals from justices, in the superior and the circuit courts during the year 1888, was 12,380, as follows: 3,460 suits in chancery ; 7,960 suits at law ; and 2,325 appeals from justices.

They were disposed of as follows: Judgment entered by default or confessions, 2,759: 3,039 were dismissed for want of prosecution, and 3,407 were tried. So that there were about 3,000 more cases brought during the year than were disposed of.

If we take $339,224, the total expense to the public, and divide it by 12,380, the total number of suits brought, we have $27.40, the amount which each suit should contribute in order to defray the expense; or if we divide by 9,205, the number of cases disposed of, we have $38.59 which each case should contribute.

But as it would be unjust to require a small case, which consumes but a few hours, to contribute as much as one taking up several days, it would perhaps be better to repeal the statute which provides that in Cook county $6 advanced by the plaintiff and $1.50 by the defendant shall be in full of all costs to be paid to the clerk of the court. In that case the clerk would collect fees for everything that is done and turn them over to the county treasurer, as is now the practice throughout the State; and it is believed that this would give ample funds to cover the whole expense. It may be added that the law limiting the fees to be paid in Cook county was passed at a time when the clerks pocketed all the fees paid and amassed vast fortunes. It was intended to limit their income. But since clerks are paid a salary and are required to pay all fees into the county treasury, the reason for the law has ceased to exist. If, however, the statute can not be repealed, then I would leave the fees as they are, and suggest that the clerk be required to tax a fee of twenty-five dollars per day to be paid to the county for each day or fraction of a day consumed at the trial—this to be paid by the losing side, unless otherwise ordered by the court,

Referring again to the expense of keeping up our system of jurisprudence in proportion to results attained, I will add that the total amount of monied judgments rendered in the circuit and superior courts of Cook county during the year 1888 was $7,831,174, the greater part of which was in cases in which there was default or a confession, and a very large per cent. of which is worthless because of the insolvency of the defendants. To this work must be added judgments in cases seeking other than monied relief, such as ejectment suits, injunction suits, etc., and suits in which it was sought to recover money but in which the court found for defendant.

If we thus take the expense to the public, as already shown, and add to this the expense to the litigants in the 12,380 cases, in the way of lawyers' fees on both sides, witnesses' fees or time on both sides, incidental expenses on both sides, loss of time and neglect of business on both sides in preparing for trial, attending court, etc., to say nothing of the worry and anxiety—it is a question whether the cost will not exceed the total results attained—that is, whether it does not on the average cost us more to secure for a man his rights than they are worth to him. Just what this expense and loss to litigants and witnesses would average, it is of course impossible to say. It has been variously estimated at from $150 to $250 to each side, or from $300 to $500 in each case. If this estimate is nearly correct, then there is little doubt that the expense and loss amount to more than can be realized on all the judgments rendered, or than would have been required to settle all matters in dispute.

There can be no doubt that, if we had encouraged arbitration, instead of discouraging it, a great saving would have been effected to both public and litigants. But instead of encouraging a speedy adjustment of disputes, by having parties submit their claims to arbitrators selected by themselves, the courts have almost invited the party defeated in an arbitration to come into court and tie the whole matter up for several years and then have often set the award aside on purely technical grounds.

What I would respectfully urge upon the consideration of the General Assembly is an amendment of the law so as to provide:

First. That in all courts of record in this State the judge shall orally state the law governing the case, as was the practice at common law, and is now the practice in the Federal courts.

Upon this point I will simply add that, the statute requiring the instructions to be in writing was passed in order that there should be no dispute as to what the charge was; and inasmuch as the law at present provides for a stenographer to attend the sittings of every circuit court to report the proceedings, the reason for requiring that the instructions be in writing no longer exists; and, as there generally is not time to write a comprehensive charge, and, consequently, cases are frequently submitted in an unsatisfactory manner to a jury, the law should be changed. What we need is to restore trial by jury more nearly to the condition and form in which it existed at the common law and still exists in the Federal courts, taking away, however, the power of one man to thwart justice; and when this is done, this system of trial will remain the best that has yet been devised. On the last point I will add that, in all other important, and even vital, matters, we accept the decision of the majority. A majority settles all questions of taxation and expenditure, all questions of peace and of war. A majority decides who shall make the laws. A majority decides what shall be law, and, finally, a majority decides who shall interpret and administer the law. In short, questions which reach to the very hearthstone of the citizen, and involve the existence of our institutions are settled by the majority, and if, concerning any of these matters, a man were to urge absolute unanimity, we would question his sanity. But, in determining a dispute over property, we put it into the power of one man—be he rogue, or crank, or sullen fool—without any risk to make a miscarriage of justice, or a farce out of a proceeding which may have consumed days and have cost both the public and the litigants large sums of money. And when asked why we permit such an anomoly our only answer is, that they did things in this way more than a hundred years ago; when in truth, trial by jury then was a very different thing from what it is to-day, for then the judge practically tried the case. If we were now to accept a verdict of three-fourths of a panel, we would preserve all that is conservative and useful in our jury system, and would put an end to the "funny verdicts," that we hear about, and which are generally due to one man; and, particularly, would we put an end to the tampering with justice, which in large cities is a serious evil.

I am in favor of trial by jury, and am opposed to its abolition; but the system is now so hampered as to make it a kind of absurdity. Let us make it a rational institution, and it will command the respect of everybody.

Second. That when rendering judgment on the merits in any case in a court of record, the court shall fix a reasonable attorney-fee, to be paid by the losing party to the winning party: Provided, that if it appears that an offer to compromise had been made and kept good by the losing party, and no more is recovered than had been offered, then no attorney-fee shall be allowed for what was done thereafter; and provided, that an attorney-fee shall only be allowed for trying a case on the merits.

Third. Either let the clerk of the court collect fees for everything that is done, and turn them into the county treasury, or else tax as costs, to go to the county, a reasonable sum for every day, or fraction thereof, which a case consumes at the trial; so that the non-litigating public may at least partially be relieved of the burden of expense created solely by litigants.

Fourth. That before any appellate court or the supreme court shall reverse a case and send it back to be tried over, the judges of such court, or a majority thereof, shall state, in writing, that an injustice has been done the appellant in the judgment on the merits by the trial court; and shall also specify wherein such injustice consists.

As to this fourth suggestion, I will simply say that if the framers of the Constitution, and the people in adopting it, intended, in creating a system of jurisprudence, that courts should be places for lawyers to fence, and judges to theorize, and that cases should be treated simply as a corpse in a dissecting-room — that is, used to illustrate a principle — then no change should be made, for in many cases the present system produces everything that could then be desired. But if the object in creating and maintaining courts was to do justice between man and man, and if rules of procedure were to be used simply as means to this end, then no reasonable objection can be urged against this provision. The trouble now is that we lift cases into the domain of opinion where there always is a diversity of views, and then, on points which settle nothing, and do not decide the merits, we keep cases bounding backward and forward like a foot-ball, to the ruin of litigants — the appellate court reversing the trial court, and the supreme court reversing the appellate court.

Fifth. That if a matter is submitted to arbitration, the award shall be final, and shall be set aside only for fraud; and that when set aside, the arbitrators shall make a new award; and that in cases of mistake, or where the award is uncertain, the arbitrators may amend it or correct it.

In conclusion, let me remark that in the mercantile world, in the manufacturing world, in agriculture, in medicine, in fact, in nearly every field of knowledge or human activity, there has been an advance, a steady improvement, a movement in the line of common sense, an honest effort to keep abreast of the spirit of the nineteenth century; while in our methods of administering justice we seem rather to have retrograded. What changes we have made in this State have tended rather to complicate than to simplify. A century ago trial by jury in civil causes was simple, expeditious, and, upon the whole, satisfactory. We have hampered and crippled it in its workings until many good people are seriously advocating its abolition. A century ago the courts of appeal wrote opinions that were short and to the point, and generally decisive of the case; now, courts of appeal, not only in this State, write long essays — learned disquisitions which frequently evade the main question and settle nothing. On behalf of our great profession, I ask, "Can not we, also, go forward?"

Very truly yours,

JOHN P. ALTGELD.

THE ABOLITION OF CONSTABLES, JUSTICES AND THE FEE SYSTEM.

CHICAGO, July 19, 1889.

HON. DAVID BARTLETT,

Member of the Constitutional Convention,

Bismark, North Dakota.

Dear Sir:—In answer to your letter inquiring about the jurisdiction, usefulness and popularity of County Courts in this State, and whether they could not be made to take the place of Justices of the Peace, so as to do away with the latter, permit me to say that, in this State, County Courts have jurisdiction in all tax matters, insane cases, all probate matters, election matters, and in civil cases where the amount involved is less than one thousand dollars. In this county, owing to the press of business, the legislature created a Probate Court several years ago to relieve the County Court. I may say that the County Courts have jurisdiction in those matters which come nearest to the people, and most directly affect them, and, all things considered, I believe they are the most useful and the most popular tribunals in this State. So far as I can observe, business is usually done by them not only in a legal, but also in a business-like and common-sense method, and without unnecessary delay, the latter being something which can not always be said of our higher courts. While I have a high re-gard for some men who now hold the office of Justice of

the Peace, yet I would recommend the abolishing of this
office, and that of Constable, and, instead, the giving to
the County Court jurisdiction in all matters now heard
by justices; but care should be taken at the same time
to provide that the County Judge, as well as Clerk and
Sheriff, should be paid a fixed salary, and that these
should, under no circumstances, have any fees, but that
all fees, where any are collected, should be paid into the
county treasury. If you have Justices of the Peace you
can not pay all a salary, because of their number. And
while there will be here and there one to whom the
office will be incidental, there will be a great many who
will depend largely on the fees for a living, and this
leads everywhere to the same results, viz., injustice,
oppression, extortion and frivolous law-suits, ruinous in
the expense and in the loss of time which they entail.
The courts become clogged with business, while the poor
and the ignorant suffer. Do away with both Justices
and Constables, for they must depend on fees, and, as a
rule, are always on the lookout, eager to "drum up"
business; and it is difficult to conceive of a worse demoralization and rottenness than usually grows out of this
system. Provide for sufficient deputy-sheriffs to do the
court work and all the work required to keep peace, and
pay each a salary, and under no circumstances let any
keep the fees. To permit any officer, whether judicial
or executive, connected in any manner with the administration of justice, to collect and keep fees, is to offer a
standing temptation, if not a bribe, to do wrong in very
many matters. And it is asking too much of human
nature to expect a hungry man to be very scrupulous

about the means or methods which will secure him bread.

Have the courts easily accessible and always open for business. There is no sense in having *terms* of court, and these held only a few times a year, so that there must be delay in getting a trial, whether there is much business or not. If the same judge is to hold the court in several counties, or if there is but little business, he can easily arrange matters by having the clerk give notice of the time at which a case will be heard. There is no reason why the average case should not be tried in the Circuit Court in fifteen days after service, just as it would before a Justice of the Peace.

Although this has been hurriedly written, I wish to assure you of my interest in the prosperity and happiness of your new State, and of my hope that you will be able to avoid errors and abuses which, once rooted, will be difficult to cure.

Very respectfully your obedient servant,

JOHN P. ALTGELD.

PROTECTING THE BALLOT BOX — THE AUSTRALIAN PLAN.

CHICAGO, ILL., January 22, 1889.

HON. RICHARD BURKE, Senate Chamber, Springfield.

My Dear Senator:—Your esteemed favor in relation to the Australian system of voting came to hand.

I have considered the question of engrafting this system upon the laws of Illinois, and am strongly in favor of so doing. I would have written you sooner, but as we already have an elaborate election machinery in Illinois, particularly in Chicago, it required much time to examine details in order to learn whether we could adopt the Australian system, and at the same time keep what is called our new election law substantially intact. This law, as you are aware, was adopted by a popular vote, and while it is in some respects defective, it is still a very great improvement upon the old lax system, particularly is this true of that part which provides for a careful registration of voters. Because it is an improvement upon the old system the new law is popular with our people, and unless its salient features will remain undisturbed by the adoption of the Australian system it will be useless to give the latter subject any attention. But I am convinced not only that this can be done, but that it would be approved by every lover of

(65)

an honest election, and a fair and entirely free ballot, and I believe that the enclosed bill will accomplish the desired result. If adopted, this system will secure us not only an honest and free expression of the popular will upon any question from both rich and poor, high and low—which alone would be enough to warrant its adoption—but it would do more, it would put an end to the small political boss, with his retainers; it would wipe out the partisan ticket-peddlers, and the entire crowd of half ruffians who sometimes are found at the polls, and who make themselves so offensive by importuning the voter, that many modest men hesitate to go there.

Further, it would enable a poor man to run for office, for he would need no ticket peddlers, nor any of the machinery that is now necessary to get his tickets into the voter's hands, and it would make him absolutely independent of the party boss. In short, it would place every candidate upon his own personal merits before the people; and by enabling the elector to vote for the best men without scratching his ticket, it would destroy that partisan tyranny which, by thorough organization, is at present enabled to foist on the public bad men and bad measures, simply because it is embarrassing for a man to scratch his ticket in the presence of his party associates.

Again, it would stop the practice that prevails among some employers of forcing their men to vote as directed, and it would, also, stop to some extent the use of money at the polls, for under this system it would be impossible for the purchaser of a vote to make sure of its delivery.

In regard to the importance of protecting the ballot, so as to make it what the spirit of our institutions contemplate that it should be, there can be among thoughtful men no difference of opinion. It is the vital organ of our whole system; destroy its functions and we perish. It is true that, like other republican institutions, it possesses great vitality, and can stand some abuse. We have seen one great political party, with apparent justification, charge its adversary with having thwarted the expressed will of the American people in seating a chief magistrate of the nation, and with having thereafter, in various States, repeatedly outraged a free ballot by bribery and corruption.

While the other great political party, with equal justification, accuses its opponent with systematically defeating the will of the majority in certain localities by fraud and intimidation. But while these things show that our system has great powers of endurance, and great recuperative force, we must bear in mind that we are dealing with the heart, and, although it may do its work for a time, yet a continuation of abuses must not only weaken it, but eventually stop its action, and with its expiring beat will come the end of our free institutions. We read that when the children of Israel were marching through the wilderness, by Divine instruction they deposited those things which were most sacred in the ark, near which only those especially commissioned by Jehovah were permitted to come. Every stranger attempting to approach it was smitten dead upon the spot.

The American people have likewise been given an

ark, in which to deposit the most sacred things known to man, namely, the ballots of free men, and we should see to it that only those authorized to do so by law be permitted to approach this ark, and that every person attempting to lay unclean hands upon it be overtaken by the wrath of a free people, which should be as destructive as the lightnings of Jehovah.

Very truly yours,

John P. Altgeld.

IS THE WORLD WORSE?—DIVORCES—MORAL TRAINING.

CHICAGO, ILL., September 30, 1887.

GEORGE R. STETSON, Boston, Mass.

My Dear Sir:—Your favor of the 7th inst. came to hand, and I thank you for the kindly reference to my little book.

I fully agree with you in regard to the importance of "proper home influences in childhood and of thorough and well-disciplined education in early life." In fact, upon these hangs the hope of the future. You have placed me under obligations by sending me a copy of your articles on "Illiteracy and Crime" and "The Necessity of Moral and Industrial Training." I have read them with great interest, and hope they may have a wide circulation.

While I am in hearty accord with you in your aims, and admit the necessity of more thorough moral as well as industrial training of the young, yet, if you will pardon me for saying so, I do not believe that the world is any worse now than it was fifty years, or more, ago, as you seem to infer, from the fact that arrests and convictions for crime, as well as the number of divorces in proportion to population, are increasing. On the contrary, I believe that, all things considered, the world is a little better now than it has been in the past. But we have devised and adopted new agencies for detect-

ing and recording the foibles and transgressions of not
only men, but even of children, and, in order to convince us that they are doing something, these agencies
bring to our attention thousands of cases which before
went unnoticed.   Just as the microscope reveals a
whole world which existed, but was almost unknown
before, so our modern police systems, detective agencies,
municipal governments, with their multifarious ordinances, etc., bring to light and record acts, the greater
part of which used to pass unnoticed.   I can remember
the time when the magistrate took notice of only the
more serious offenses, and when, if a man was found
drunk on the streets, he was simply taken home; if a
boy got into mischief, his father would whip him, and
that was the end of it; if two men quarreled, they would
fight it out, and then go home; even many dangerous
criminals went undetected, but now all this is changed.
Not only are the grave offenders more generally
detected, but all the parties guilty of trivial offenses
must now be *arrested, tried, put in jail*, etc., so that the
record will, of course, show a greater number of arrests
and convictions than formerly.   But this, it seems to
me, does not necessarily prove that men are any more
depraved or vicious now than they were in the past.

Further, the effect of numerous arrests, incarceration, prison associations, etc., is to break the self-respect
and weaken the moral character of many of the young,
and thus to prepare them for the commission of crimes
of which they would never have been guilty except for
their degrading experiences.   Therefore, while prison
statistics may assist us in forming a correct opinion

concerning the present moral condition of society, it seems to me they are of little value for purpose of comparison between different periods.

In regard to the increase in the number of divorces in proportion to the population, allow me to ask, Would this not almost necessarily follow an era of great educational activity, an era in which there were a thousand agencies at work, not only among men but among women, all tending to place the latter on an equality with men, and tending, in many cases, to create dissatisfaction with existing conditions? Would there not almost necessarily follow a period of transition or re-adjustment, and when the re-adjustment has taken place, will the organization of society not rest on a more intelligent basis than before, and therefore the world be a little better than before, although it may appear worse while the re-adjustment is in process? Besides, is it not true that the number of divorces is in proportion to the progress made in the emancipation of women? In those countries where women are merely beasts of burden there are no divorces. Further, is separation, with all its ills, not better for society than union and the rearing of a family amid depraving and brutal conditions? It seems to me that children who have frequently to see their mother thrashed by a brutal or drunken father, can not get a very exalted idea of life, and that any system which will keep a man and woman together under these circumstances, is barbarous, and can not possibly be productive of any good to the world.

" The degeneracy of the times " has always been a favorite theme, but one which is liable to mislead, and

ever must be so, for the imperfections, weaknesses
and follies of "the present" are not only seen, but are
felt, whereas the imperfections, weaknesses and follies
of "the past" are not only unfelt, but are mostly unseen,
because the mists of oblivion hide all but the more conspicuous objects and events from our view. While,
therefore, different periods of history may be compared,
it is very difficult to compare "the present" with any
other time.

However, while claiming that the world is better now
than formerly, I admit that it is still bad, and that
there is a crying necessity for more thorough moral
and industrial training, and I hope you may be able to
arouse the interest of the American public in this question, and thus pave the way for improved methods of
instruction.

I like your idea of moral text-books for use in schools.
If properly prepared, I believe they will serve an excellent purpose. The trouble now is with much of the
moral teaching that it holds up the punishment for
wrong doing as a remote event, before the happening of
which there will be abundant opportunity to reform, to
be forgiven, etc., so that the child gets no proper compre-
hension of the instantaneous, degrading and weakening
effect upon its nature of doing a mean or a wrong act.
The child gets an abstract or theoretic notion of right
and wrong, and thinks it can go and do the wrong and
yet be precisely the same person afterward that it was
before, simply having taken the chance of, at some time,
being punished. In other words, our youth, as a rule,
are not made to understand that every time they tell a

lie or steal or do any wrong act, their nature undergoes a change and they are no longer quite the same persons that they were before; or, on the other hand, that every time they do a noble act, they expand and instantly become stronger and greater than they were before. Their idea of punishment is that it is an arbitrary decree of religion, they get no idea of the degrading and weakening effect of sin on both mind and body. We tell a child to avoid fire, and it obeys; not because it may be damned for disobedience, but because it knows that there will be instant suffering. Make the child once thoroughly understand that if it does any wrong act there will follow instant suffering, and it will heed where now it does not.

In many cases morals can be successfully taught from a purely religious standpoint, but in very many others this can only be done from a practical point of view, and the needs of these cases could be met by moral text-books such as you recommend.

Asking your pardon for thus obtruding my views on your attention, and hoping you will favor me with a copy of any article you may publish in the future, I am,

Very respectfully yours,

JOHN P. ALTGELD.

THE RICH MAN'S BREAD AND THE POOR— CARDINAL MANNING'S POSITION.

[*From the Chicago Times, January 15, 1888.*]

To the Editor:—I have received from you the following in regard to the utterances of Cardinal Manning:

"LONDON, Jan. 2.—The cable dispatch which Dr. McGlynn read at the anti-poverty meeting in New York last night, surprising as it may seem, did correctly report Cardinal Manning's words. They occur in a little article at the end of *The Fortnightly*, sent in answer to some recent strictures by *The London Times* on recent utterances of his eminence. The cardinal devotes his three pages to a demonstration that the recognition of the right to property involves and rests on the admission of the right to live. The exact words of the passage are: 'I answer that the obligation to feed the hungry springs from the natural right of every man to life and to the food necessary to the sustenance of life. So strict is this natural right that it prevails over all positive laws of property. Necessity has no law, and a starving man has a right to his neighbor's bread.' The cardinal then goes into a disquisition on the historic poor-laws of England, and shows that in the reign of Queen Elizabeth this natural right was over and over again recognized and enforced by statute."

You ask whether the recognition by statute of the right referred to by the cardinal would be wholesome.

Now it seems to me that an unwarrantable effort is being made to create a sensation out of what his eminence said, for while some of his sentences, when standing alone, sound strange, yet when considered together in connection with the occasion which provoked them and with the people to whom they were addressed—that is, when taken in the sense in which he evidently meant to be understood—they are neither radical nor revolutionary, but simply announce a principle which society has long recognized, and, to some extent, acted on, viz., that it is the duty of society to take care of its indigent. The laws of Illinois, which annually take several million dollars in the way of taxes from one class of citizens against their will to support the helpless of various kinds, all rest on this principle, and the statute in relation to paupers expressly recognizes the right of the recipient. They all take one man's bread and give it to another. Now, when Cardinal Manning said, " Necessity knows no law, and a starving man has a right to his neighbor's bread," he was not addressing the poor, but he had been laboring to arouse the English public to discharge its duty toward the poor, and used the words referred to in answer to some criticisms on his course. They were addressed to the rich, not to the poor. It was an indirect argument as well as warning. Had he held the views attributed to him he would have talked not to the rich, but to the poor, and told them to go and supply their necessities from their neighbor's property. But, instead of this, he tried to convince the rich that a starving man has rights, but did not say how these rights should be enforced. He never has said that, as society is now organized, the starving may lawfully seize their neighbor's property, and until he does we must presume that he meant that this right, like all other rights, should be enforced according to law.   That this was his meaning is further shown by his reference to the Elizabethan poor-laws, and his approval of them, for these laws did not authorize the starving to take by force other people's property, but made liberal provisions for feeding the poor, while they imposed severe restrictions. And I will say here that no statute can or ever will be passed authorizing every man to judge of his own necessities and then go and help himself to his neighbor's property.   Such a law would in one jump carry us back to barbarism.   The mistake lies in confounding the *right* of which the cardinal did speak, with the *method of enforcing it*, of which he did not speak.

Take the right of a creditor to be paid out of his debtor's property.   No right is more clearly recognized by law—yet he can not go and seize his debtor's property and sell it himself to pay his claim, but must proceed through agencies prescribed by law.   So the right of the hungry to bread—it can only be enforced through agencies created by law.   The law can make no distinction between stealing bread and stealing gold with which to buy bread, nor can it recognize necessity as an exonerating excuse for larceny, although in fixing the penalty all extenuating circumstances are considered.

However, law is only potent when backed by public sentiment, and there is no doubt that if a starving man were caught stealing bread, the public, with the possible exception of a part of the clergy, would hold that not much should be done about it; and, if he were prosecuted, while the law would have to pronounce him guilty, the penalty would be light.

We read that both Christ and his apostles satisfied their hunger—and they were not yet starving—by eating another man's corn, without his consent, as they passed through his field; and they did this even on the Sabbath. When one thinks of this and then reads some of the letters of the clergy of this city published in the Sunday *Times* holding that a starving man should die rather than touch his neighbor's bread, one can not doubt that it is a long time since Christ was on earth, for we are evidently much more advanced in morals than He was.

Taken in the sense in which I believe the cardinal meant to be understood, I approve his utterances, and will add that it is a hopeful sign of the times that a man of so great learning and influence should interest himself in a practical manner in the condition of the poorer classes, for out of investigation will come a more healthy and happy condition of affairs—not in the way of alms-giving, but in the way of making it possible for the poor to take care of themselves.

There was a time when the adage "He who will not work neither shall he eat," seemed to cover almost the whole question, because there was, especially in this country, plenty of work to be had at living wages, and nearly all who would could keep themselves out of the reach of hunger. But times have changed, so that now there are tens of thousands of men in our large cities and a good sprinkling all over the country who are ready and

willing to work, but can get nothing to do a large portion of the time, and get very low wages when they do
work, so that they and their families are frequently
reduced to absolute destitution with the accompanying sickness and suffering. In all of our large cities there
are thousands of women who try to support themselves
and their families by sewing. They work for large
establishments and are paid wages so shamefully low
that even when well and at work they can not supply
their wants. They get forty cents a dozen for making
shirts, and in the same proportion for making other gar-
ments, and by working twelve to sixteen hours a day
can earn only from $3 to $5 per week; and sometimes
even this amount is reduced by means of fines, so that the
moment they are sick or out of work they are at starvation's door. Now, it is an insult to both of these great
classes to talk to them about laziness or shiftlessness—
expressions which are constantly on the tongues of people who started in life with good brains, good training
and excellent advantages, and who are now well-housed,
well-clothed, and well-fed, who believe "everything is
for the best in the best of worlds;" who move only
among the comfortable and self-satisfied, and who know
nothing about the actual condition or the wants of the
poor; who never entered a really poor man's hovel,
where there was but little fire, or saw him sit down with
a large family to a table upon which there was nothing
but a little black bread.

Honest investigation into the condition of the poor
will produce beneficial results, and if this agitation shall
serve to enlighten the public at large in regard to the

real character and condition of our poorer classes, then remedies will soon be found which will without violence and without revolution greatly improve this condition and serve to increase the greatness, the prosperity, and the happiness of our country.

JOHN P. ALTGELD.

SLAVE GIRLS OF CHICAGO.

VIEWS ON THE CONDITION OF THE POOR DRUDGES IN OUR
FACTORIES. — FACTS TO SHOW THAT LEGISLATION CAN
DO AN ENORMOUS AMOUNT OF GOOD IN THE MATTER.—
HOW PAUPER LABOR AFFECTS WAGES AND TENDS TO
PRODUCE THIS DEPLORABLE STATE OF THINGS.

NOTE.—During the Summer of 1888 *The Chicago Times* published a series of articles exposing in a graphic manner the appalling conditions of the great multitude of children and women that
are working in our factories and in other industrial establishments
of Chicago. The articles called attention, particularly, to the fact
that there are many thousands of children of tender years who for a
pittance are doing the work of adults and becoming stunted in both
body and mind when they should be at school, and to the further
fact that many thousands of women work ten hours, and more,
per day, and get only from $3 to $4 per week, and board themselves and frequently lose a part of this because of fines, which in
some cases seem to be imposed with a view of still further reducing
their wages, while the sanitary and moral surroundings of both the
children and the women in the shops are often of a revolting character. In answer to a letter from the editor, concerning these subjects, the following article was written and published in *The
Chicago Times*, September 9, 1888.

To the Editor:—In answer to your letter relating to
the "slave girls" of Chicago: I have read all the articles published in *The Times* with great interest, and
while the reporter, owing to the short time spent in each
establishment, almost necessarily got wrong impres-
sions in some cases and perhaps has done some firms an
injustice, yet I know from experience and personal
observation that upon the whole the picture is not

overdrawn, and I will add that in making this exposure so general and so thorough *The Times* has rendered to the toiling poor, and in the long run to society, inestimable service.

The first and all-important step toward improvement always is to get light into dark places. Ingersoll says that the sun is the only God that ever protected women. Whether this is so or not, it is true that sunlight is the great purifier, reformer and elevator of the universe. Wrong thrives in bad light and fowl air. Turn the sunlight of intelligence on an evil long enough, and it will dissolve it. *The Times* has turned the light on the condition of the toiling girls and women of Chicago at least long enough to give a view of the situation, and the remedy will gradually appear.

No complete remedy can be made to order in advance. What is needed is a change of condition, and this can only come by degrees. As to these people themselves, it is necessary to raise their standard of intelligence; until this is done they can do but little to help themselves, for ignorance and helplessness go together. Society can do this and it can furnish them protection — nothing more — nor will much more be required, for this once done they will be able to take care of themselves. The trouble is that the light can not be turned upon the case long enough and it will probably be a long time before such powerful rays will again be thrown on it. Meanwhile society, with its ten thousand other affairs, must move on, and the majority will soon cease to take an active interest in this matter; in fact, will forget about it.

But enough interest has been aroused to set in motion some of the forces which will bring about a change, and there will be found to be some men and women who have this matter at heart, and who will keep the fire slowly burning and keep up an agitation through weary years, sometimes getting a little disheartened, but in the end triumphing. All great movements require time, labor and sacrifice.

You ask, "Can anything be done for these girls by legislation?" Emphatically yes. It has already done much for them, both here and in Europe, and will do more. Understand me; legislation can not fix prices, but it can, and to a certain extent does, reach almost every other feature of the case, and indirectly may even affect prices. For example: Legislation can prevent children of tender years from being stunted in factories when they should be at school, and thus it can not only reduce the number of competitors, but wipe out the practice of hiring children to do the work of adults, one of the worst of existing abuses. Legislation can secure to every shop girl good light, good ventilation, reasonably comfortable quarters while at work, healthy sanitary conditions, such as sufficient wash-bowls (not dirty sinks), ample closet-rooms, etc.

In countries that do not boast as much of their enlightenment as we do, legislation has for years given to every child, no matter how poor, a certain number of months' schooling and incidental training every year and it will eventually do so here, and as general ignorance is perhaps the main cause of the helplessness of the poorer classes, when we once give all children at

least half a chance to develop into intelligent men and
women, instead of growing up on the streets to become
criminals or in shops .to become stunted for life, we
shall have made considerable headway in furnishing a
remedy.

Again, legislation can and in time will put an end to
the wholesale importation by mine-owners, large employers, and other interested parties of European paupers
who do not come as independent immigrants—of the latter this country does not complain, in fact it owes much
of its greatness to them, but these paupers are brought
over like so many cattle and necessarily glut the labor
market and drag down the American laborer (whether
native-born or naturalized) with his family. I know it
is said, "Oh, legislation amounts to nothing unless
there is public sentiment to back it," and this is true.
But this agitation will create public sentiment, in fact it
is never brought into existence in any other way, and it
generally takes time, much hard work, and much tribu-
lation to create it, and has it occurred to you that public sentiment usually accomplishes little in matters of
this kind until it crystallizes into legislation? In fact,
society gives expression to its sentiment on a public
question by means of legislation. While legislation not
backed by public sentiment may be a dead letter, public
sentiment produces definite and lasting results only
through legislation. Moral suasion and the benign
influence of religion are beautiful, but unfortunately in
all ages there have been men who went straight from the
sanctuary into the world and plundered and trampled
on the weak, and, what is more, they lost neither their

seats nor their influence in the temple. So that after all it is legislation which protects the lowly. And legislation itself is a matter of growth; it is scarcely ever efficient at first, and only after experience has suggested the necessary alterations and amendments does it become potent.

If anyone doubts the efficacy of legislation in this direction let him study the history and results of the factory and mining legislation in England and some of the continental countries, and he will find that while we are great politicians and make a great noise, yet in practical and enlightened statesmanship some of the European countries are a full half-century in advance of us. Early in this century there existed in the English factories and mines a condition of things which reduced women and children almost below the brutes, a condition compared with which the Chicago slave-girls are lolling in luxury. To quote an eminent author: " A whole generation were growing up under conditions of physical degeneracy, of mental ignorance, and of moral corruption."

In 1802, after much agitation, an act, very narrow in its scope, was passed to protect apprentices in certain factories. In 1815 Sir Robert Peel endeavored to secure similar protection for children in certain factories, but he was not able to secure the passage of such an act till in 1819, for it met with the most bitter opposition, as did every one of the many measures thereafter passed to protect women and children. Not only did the employers do everything within their power in opposition, but so-called statesmen, political economists, philosophers, and many of the clergy united to oppose them. Every argument and every sophistry that the mind can conceive was exhausted by these eminent people, and they predicted the industrial and financial ruin of the British empire as the result of such legislation. It is a curious and sad fact that in the long, weary upward march of the human race there was scarcely ever an act proposed for the protection, emancipation, or elevation of the poor but met with the most violent opposition from the so-called better classes, as well as from statesmen and philosophers and from many of the clergy.

After the act of 1819 the agitation was kept up by a few humanitarians. In 1825 another act was passed broader in its scope, and owing to continued agitation thereafter, at intervals of from two to six years down to 1878, acts broader and more stringent in their character were passed, resulting in the most advanced system of factory and mining legislation in the world—a system which has been adopted by almost every civilized country in Europe. Although the earlier acts were evaded in every way and were practically dead letters, yet in the end they accomplished more than their friends had expected of them.

In 1867 the great duke of Argyle, in writing of this legislation, said: "Some of the old opponents have admitted that their fear of the results in an economical point of view has proved erroneous. But there is no clear and well-grounded intellectual perception of the deep foundations of principle on which it rests. Nor is there among a large section of politicians any adequate appreciation of the powerful influence it has had in improving the physical condition of the people and securing their contentment with the laws under which they live. When, however, we think for a moment of the frightful nature of the evils which this legislation has checked and which to a large extent it has remedied, when we recollect the connection between suffering and political disaffection, when we consider the great moral laws which were being trodden under foot from mere thoughtlessness and greed, we shall be convinced that if, during the last fifty years, it has been given to this country to make any progress in political science, that progress has been in nothing happier than in the factory legislation. No government and no minister has ever done greater—perhaps all things considered, none has ever done so great a service. It was altogether a new era in legislation — the adoption of a new principle — the establishment of a new idea."

I will only add on this point that we have already recognized the principle and adopted some of this factory legislation, and have already derived some benefits from it. It is, perhaps, true that it is not properly enforced, and it will probably require much more legislation to make it efficacious, but if only a few zealous and determined people will continue this agitation, they will, in time, secure not only the needed legislation, but a proper enforcement of it.

The same is true of the compulsory education act. It may be a dead letter now, but it will not always be so; by and by some earnest persons will come along and stir the matter up, and men will be made to under-

stand that if they want to enjoy the honors or emolu-
ments of office, they must discharge all the duties of
that office, whether they be agreeable or not. There
are few questions that more vitally affect the State, for
children growing up on the street are almost certain to
become criminals, and thus a menace and expense to
society. Likewise, the toiling of women and children
in shops amid conditions which dwarf, stupefy and
destroy, must produce pauperism and crime, and it is
as much the duty of the State to prevent these as it is
its duty to repel a hostile invasion.

You ask whether woman should be paid the same
wages as man when she does the same work? To this
there can be but one answer. If she does the same
quantity and quality of work under the same conditions
as a man, simple justice requires that she should be
paid the same wages. To deny her this is to deny her
justice.

In answer to your question: "Are not the wages in
many lines of protected manufacturing and mining
industries out of all proportion to the profits of the employers?" I will simply say that I do not wish to discuss the tariff here, but the exposure just made by *The
Times*, as well as the facts now being brought out before
the congressional committee in New York, added to
what was already known in regard to the importation
of Italians, Belgians, Poles, Hungarians, etc., in the
manufacturing and mining districts of the East, all show
conclusively that the American laborer has for many
years had to compete with the cheapest kind of European labor. The wages in the shops and in the factories

of Chicago, as shown by *The Times*, were in many cases not fixed with reference to the amount of protection, but by the lowest European standard. They are at starvation's edge, and they never get below that in Europe. For example, $2, $3, and $4 per week and board oneself for ten hours' toil a day. So the wages paid in the cigar manufactories and other establishments of the East, as shown by the congressional investigation now in progress, are below what it is possible for an American to live on. They are fixed, not with reference to the tariff, but by the people that are brought over here from Europe. It is almost the lowest European standard. Establishments that used to pay $10 a week to American laborers now pay $3 and $4 to imported Europeans for doing the same work. It is true that all establishments do not employ imported laborers, but enough do to fix the standard of wages. If only a few establishments in the same line get their work done for $4 a week by foreigners, this will become the standard all along the line, even in houses employing Americans, for the latter can not pay $10 and compete with the former, and as it has been shown that there is scarcely a line of industry in which these imported laborers have not been introduced, it follows that the standard of wages has been largely fixed by what these imported people will work for.

For years we have heard of the Italians, Poles, Hungarians, etc., who were imported constantly into Pennsylvania, and in many cases when these people refused to submit to further reductions of wages they were simply discharged and their places filled with fresh importations. So that now Mr. Powderly claims that almost all American citizens, both native-born and naturalized, have been driven out of the mines and the great manufacturing establishments of that great State. The proprietors have been protected, but the laborers have had to *move on*, and that, too, in many cases by the assistance of policemen's clubs and Pinkerton rifles.

I see that the investigation in New York disclosed the fact that our estimable protectionist townsmen who built the Texas state-house, sent to Scotland for most of their skilled labor and employed Texas convicts to do the unskilled labor. And so it goes all along the line. There seems to be protection for everybody but the laborer, and he is gradually getting between two millstones—above him the protective tariff makes him pay high prices for the necessaries of life, while below him the imported laborer is steadily and surely pulling away the foundations on which he stands. If this process is not arrested, then, like the Indian, the American laborer must wither from the land, as he is already doing in Pennsylvania and in some sections of the East. Legislation, and only legislation, can arrest this process. It is easy and pleasant to talk sympathetically about these matters and to advance beautiful theories, but if we want to do practical work we must face cold facts.

JOHN P. ALTGELD.

ANONYMOUS JOURNALISM AND ITS EFFECTS.

[*Published in Belford's Magazine for October, 1889.*]

In the evolution of the newspaper from the occasional news-letter of the seventeenth century to the great journal of to-day, the press has changed from a passive instrument, dependent upon and voicing only the sentiments of an individual, to a kind of self-conscious entity which is bigger than any individual; an entity which Frederick Knight Hunt, nearly forty years ago in England, called the Fourth Estate of the Realm.

The successive stages in this development may be generalized as, first, personal organs; second, party organs; and lastly, independent journals.

In the first two stages it was still an instrument depending upon the editor. But in the third it is an institution upon which the editor depends. When the paper was small the author of almost every article was known to the public. The editor had an interest in the paper, if he did not own it entirely. His name appeared at the head of its columns as its editor; and he wrote most, if not everything, that appeared in it. In fact, he held himself individually responsible for everything, and was personally known to nearly all who read the paper. There were exceptions, but I speak of the rule.

Thus when, near the close of the last century, the *National Gazette* persistently attacked Hamilton and the Federal party, the country turned to the editor, Philip

Freneau. When Horace Greeley wrote most of the matter that went into the *Morning Post* and the *Log Cabin*, and when he subsequently founded and edited the *New York Tribune*, the public looked to Greeley. When Thurlow Weed published the *Albany Evening Journal*, its articles were accepted or rejected according to the confidence had in Weed.

So of the country newspapers of to-day; the personnel of the editors, who are generally also publishers and men-of-all-work, is known almost co-extensively with the circulation of their papers, and they are more influential in the community, as citizens, than are the writers on great city journals.

This consciousness of the editor, that his identity is fully known to the public, creates a sense of responsibility which, in time, strengthens and develops the man. If, in moving among his fellow-men, he feels that they know exactly what he has said and done, he will be more candid; he will learn to look men in the face; he will be more apt to stick to the truth and hold to what is right; he will be more ready to acknowledge his error when wrong; he will be more apt to keep within the range of the sympathy and good opinion of his fellow-men. Instead of being simply an editor, he will continue to be a man among men. The man will grow as well as the editor, and both will become greater than is possible where there is only a one-sided development.

Consequently we find that the earlier newspaper writers were prominent public characters. In fact, in the end, they became greater in the public eye as men than as editors. The man outgrew the editor. Instead of his being lost in the newspaper, as is now the case, the newspaper was merged in the man. Being thus greater than the newspaper, he survived connection with it.

Horace Greeley was known to the whole American people as a great character. Even if the paper he founded were to go out of existence, the memory of Greeley could not.

Thurlow Weed became one of the most conspicuous and influential politicians in the United States—not as an editor, but as a man. The paper was only the medium through which he expressed his thoughts. The giant could not hide behind his sword. How many newspaper editors are there to-day who hide—and successfully too—behind their papers?

In 1860 the majority of the men who were prominent in national affairs had been connected with newspapers. There are not so many now; and, as a rule, the newspaper editor who is in public life to-day is connected, not with the large city papers, except where he is a proprietor, but with some smaller paper which is known to voice only his sentiments.

What is said above applies equally to the great public men of the old world who were newspaper editors. For whether fomenting a revolution in France, or defending libel prosecutions in England, they did not hide behind their papers, but, as a rule, stood erect "before all Israel and the sun;" and while their papers are forgotten, the men are not. But now every large newspaper is an institution which, in some instances, has more than fifty different persons who contribute regularly to its columns. All these write anonymously. The paper, the institution only, is seen and known. The name of the man claiming to be the legal owner or publisher, may also be known; but the editors—the authors of the various articles, comments, criticisms, and statements—are not known, not even collectively; much less is it known who is the author of any particular article, statement, or comment. So far as the public and the persons directly affected by anything contained in the paper are concerned, it is all anonymous. Now, there is a universal contempt felt for the man who writes an anonymous letter and sends it through the mail; and, paradoxical as it may seem, no one expresses more contempt and indignation at the cowardice and want of manhood of the anonymous letter-writer than the average newspaper editor, who not only makes his living by anonymous writing, but who would not be willing to sign his name to one-half of the articles he publishes. The moral, or rather the immoral, effect of anonymous writing on the writer himself must be the same in all cases where he conceals his identity because of an unwillingness to be known as the author of the sentiments expressed, whether he publishes them in a newspaper or sends them through the mail. In each case there is a hiding—a st nding behind a hedge, and throwing missiles at people who may be traveling along the king's highway; in neither case will the act tend to develop strength of character, although he may write ably and say smart things.

When, therefore, the editor was, so to say, relieved of the moral responsibility which comes from having to look people in the face, feeling that they knew what you have said; when an inducement was almost held out to him to be careless, or reckless, or to give play to his prejudices and vent to his spleen; when, in short, he was put in the position of hiding while throwing missiles, and kept in that attitude from one year's end to the other, then the period in which great characters were developed in the newspaper offices came to an end. At present we see only a great paper. The men—that is, the editorial writers—are neither seen nor known. They may be changed with almost the same facility as the type-setters, and, like the type-setters, they acquire no individuality by which they are known to the public. They are not even forgotten, because they are never known, although the proprietor may wield even greater influence than formerly.

The newspaper men of to-day have as much natural ability, as high aspirations, as much common honesty, and as strong an inclination to do right as had those of three-quarters of a century ago. In fact, it must be said of the rank and file of newspaper men, that it is doubtful whether any other calling contains so large a percentage of young men who possess, in the highest degree, the attributes necessary to achieve success and eminence in the world. As a rule they are intelligent, industrious, tireless, plucky, practical and ambitious, and, in moral character, will compare favorably with the devotees of any other profession; and, if the conditions of newspaper work were the same now as they were earlier in the century, the newspaper fraternity would develop more great men and furnish more great public characters than are furnished by any other class. But the blight—the weakening influence—of anonymous writing settles upon all, especially those connected with the large city papers; and, as a rule, they move along comparatively unknown, and die unhonored by the public, never establishing a reputation commensurate with their ability or with the great amount of work they do—an amount of work which, under more favorable conditions, would win them immortality.

It is true, there are a few newspaper writers in the United States who have become widely known, but they did not accomplish this by anonymous writing; on the contrary, their fame is in exact proportion to the extent to which they signed their names to their articles.

The effect of this anonymous writing is to give us what is practically an irresponsible press. To be sure, theoretically, the owner or publisher of the paper is responsible for everything that appears in it; but practically, as all the world knows, this amounts to but little. If the facts in a particular matter are carelessly or incorrectly stated, whereby a common citizen is injured, or if some one connected with the paper maliciously makes insinuations which set people to talking about, and thus ruin, the character of a private person, the owner of the paper is theoretically liable. But practically this amounts to nothing; for all the injured party can do is to commence a libel suit. After a year elapses this suit is brought to trial, when the tables are turned, as it were. and in order to see what damages, if any, should be given, the whole life of the complainant is overhauled; the worst construction possible is sought to be put upon everything he has done. Money and power, with all the agencies they control, combine to break him down; and if, after going through this ordeal, a verdict is rendered for the plaintiff, the case is carried to the higher courts and, as a rule, is reversed and sent back to be tried over. In most cases, after years of vexation and expense, the injured party gets nothing. If, however, in the end a judgment should be obtained, it will not pay for the vexation, the loss of time, and the expense occasioned by the suit. So that, as a rule, a libel suit is worse than a farce for the injured person. It is a remedy which kills the party using it and inflicts comparatively little injury on the defendant. The malicious, the mendacious, and the reckless have practically nothing to restrain them.

Roscoe Conkling once said: "A thief breaks into your house, steals your watch, and goes to Sing Sing. The newspaper man breaks into the casket which contains your most precious treasure,—your reputation,—and goes unscathed before the law."

It may be said that publishing a newspaper is a business enterprise, and that self-interest will induce its owners to see to it that nothing but the truth is told. This looks plausible, but experience has shown that it is not true. There is scarcely an issue of a great city newspaper that does not contain an article which, either through an imperfect statement of facts, or an insinuation or false accusation, injures some private citizen, who practically has no remedy.

A writer in the *North American Review* recently said: "The newspaper usurps the functions of judge, jury, and executioner, and often adds to these the office of the police detective and prosecuting attorney. . . . The glass through which he (the newspaper man) peers is anything but a transparent medium. It becomes a lens that distorts and perverts the things behind it. The best men in journalism are not proof against the taint of its bad tendencies. The system is the criminal, and moulds its members. All that can be generalized is that honorable journalists, on the whole, try to practice the better side of the profession, and that the unprincipled avail themselves to the full of its dangerous powers."

Possibly, when all things are considered, it is best that libel suits should in many cases be abortive; otherwise a newspaper might be overwhelmed with libel suits based on trivial errors; or might be harassed by people who want to extort money. And it should be added that no measure calculated to harass or cripple the press can be tolerated. The press must not only remain free but have all reasonable latitude. But the public is entitled to fair play, as well as the press; and it does not follow because one remedy does not seem well suited to protect the public that therefore the public is not entitled to any protection. Would it be asking too much to require a signature to everything that appears in a newspaper, so that the public may always have some guaranty of good faith, and know who it is that is talking, and that when anything is said against a man it will not seem as if an irresponsible institution were attacking him in the dark?

In short, while discouraging any attempt to get money out of the newspaper man's pockets, is it asking too much to require him to do what all other men, except criminals, have to do, and that is, work in the light of day?—to stand up and be known and seen?

Of course some of the newspaper people will object—will pronounce it impossible—and, as usual, predict all sorts of calamities as the result of such a requirement. Especially will this be true of those that "avail themselves to the full of its dangerous powers." No class exercising a dangerous power or accustomed to an unrestricted license ever looked with favor on a proposition to restrict that license or power.

One of the leading dailies of Chicago, in discussing the proposition to require a signature to every article in a paper, said: " The power of the press is not a dangerous and unrestrained power; the freedom of the press, like the freedom of the winds, corrects and purifies, because it is free. A newspaper pays for its errors and blunders, and is subject to the great law of compensation as an individual is. It has created here in this country a higher law, to which it is itself subject and whose penalties it can not escape. In this free land of ours it comes to pass that there is a public opinion—that sober, slow verdict of the people—that is over all of us; parties and syndicates, great statesmen and great newspapers as well, we all must bow to it, and because of its freedom, we all do bow to it."

Here are the old arguments that have been repeated for centuries, every time that it was proposed to have the State interfere for the protection of the weak against the assaults of the strong.

1st. "There is a higher law to punish wrong-doing, therefore leave hands off."

Now suppose a man with a club habitually secretes himself in a dark place and batters out the brains of every unsuspecting editor who may come that way. There is a higher law which will punish this man, but will the living editor be content with this assurance, or will he insist that at least an effort ought to be made to discover the identity of the man with the club?

2d. "It is not necessary to do anything; for an enlightened self-interest, open competition, a healthy public sentiment, and the knowledge of the fact that wrong-doing must be paid for and will sooner or later be punished are alone sufficient to regulate the whole matter."

Look at this a moment. Is there an instance in all human experience where it was found satisfactory to have the strong alone—whether good or bad—say how far they should go in dealing with the weak? If human selfishness always has gone to unreasonable lengths when it had a chance, why expect it to restrain itself in this case? As to public sentiment, in cases of attacks on or insinuations against individuals, the newspaper creates all the sentiment there is; hence this will not be restraining.

Further, is it not known now that wrong-doing must be paid for and will be punished? And if this knowledge has not been and is not now sufficient to protect private individuals, how can we expect it to do so in the future?

The fifth maxim for journalists, recently laid down by Mr. Dana, is: "Never attack the weak or the defenseless, either by argument, by invective, or by ridicule, unless there is some absolute public necessity for so doing."

Without inquiring why the absolutely defenseless should ever be attacked, and admitting that some journalists do not do so, I will ask: How long will it take an unprincipled newspaper man—and there will be such till the millennium—who wanted a sensation to sell his paper, or who had a grudge against some individual —how long would it take him to make up his mind that the public necessity existed?

The trouble with all these arguments is that they rest on a wrong principle. One of the parties affected is not represented or given a hearing; whereas rules to regulate the conduct between individuals should be fixed with reference to the interests, and by the voice of both, and not by the whim, caprice, or arbitrary dictation of the stronger.

Years ago, when it was first proposed to subject the railroads to reasonable regulation, the railroad people and their friends scoffed at the idea. The most considerate of them argued: " Railroads are private enterprises, supported by private capital, with which the public has no right to interfere. Besides, they are subject to the laws of competition, which alone will give all the regulation necessary. Further, they are dependent on the public for support, and an intelligent self-interest will insure fair dealing with the public; any interference by the State must be disastrous," etc. And they asked: " Can you run the railroads better than the experienced men who are now running them?"

But notwithstanding these arguments the public felt that, while railroads were a necessity and must be protected, and while they ought not to be harassed by unreasonable interference, yet some measure of protection for the public was necessary; and the answer in regard to running a road was: "No, we don't claim to be able to run a road; we concede that you can do that better than we can, and we want you to do it; we simply insist on some measure of protection against the abuse of the power in your hands." As a result, measure after measure was passed, ending finally in the Interstate Law. At first these acts produced little effect, as is nearly always the case with new legislation; but at present they are beginning to be respected, and, what is more, the railroads now favor reasonable regulation.

There is no doubt that, if every person writing even a squib for a newspaper had to sign his name to it, there would be greater care taken to learn the facts and to state them correctly. Every writer would become more careful and read his articles over a second time before printing them, thus greatly improving the character of newspapers by making them more reliable, while, at the same time, it would be a protection to the private individual.

Certain it is that it would make all newspaper writers stand on their own merit with the public, and would enable those that have superior abilities to get credit for their work, which they do not get with the public under the present system of anonymous writing.

It is true that in 1850 a law was passed in France requiring a signature to every article in a newspaper, and that it did not produce any great results. But this signifies little under the circumstances, for it was enacted not as an independent measure conceived in a spirit of fairness, but as a part of an arbitrary system intended to harass and, so far as possible, crush the press. It went almost hand in hand with a heavy stamp tax, a government censor and the dungeon. Requiring a signature only made it easier for the Government to find the writer and put him into jail. Therefore, it was natural that the whole newspaper fraternity should labor to defeat the law by the use of fictitious names, and in every other manner possible. In addition, it should be remembered that many of the most beneficial measures in the world's history were failures when first tried.

But here the conditions are different. Many newspaper men already admit the evil effects of impersonal journalism and urge a change in that regard. The *Journalist* of October 6, 1888, had a strong editorial, advocating a signature to every article. Among other things it said: "Few men would be willing to send out statements over their own signatures which they knew to be untrue, a temptation which is very strong when the writer is hiding behind the cloak of anonymity. It would encourage better work. If a man is certain that a story is to be known as his work, he will take more care in the writing. Again, if a writer succeeds in making a reputation, the paper gains the additional *éclat* of having such a man in its employ. The best work is almost always done by men who sign. Sporadic cases of anonymous excellence are seen in every paper, but the men who sign are the men whose work is read, and who make an impression on the public mind. This is not altogether due to the fact that it is the work of men who are strong enough to force signature. It is partly because a man who signs feels that he is bound in duty to himself to keep up a certain average of excellence in his work. He is the proprietor of a 'brand,' and his goods must be kept up to sample, or the future value of his 'brand' is gone. The question of signature lies largely with the writers themselves. If there were a general insistence upon the matter, the papers would give in, and once the custom was adopted it would never be abandoned."

I will simply add that, as the better class of journalists are already in sympathy with the idea, we may safely assume that if a signature be required by law to every article—not for the purpose of enabling the Government to imprison the writer, as in France—but simply to ensure care and good faith on the part of the writer and fair play to the public, there will be but little opposition, and, instead of being crippled, the press will command more confidence and wield more influence for good than now; and editorial writers, instead of being unknown operatives, will establish a reputation equal to their labor and ability, while the private individual will feel that if he is to be attacked, it must be done in the light of day.

JOHN P. ALTGELD.

THE IMMIGRANT'S ANSWER.

(Published in the Forum for February, 1890.)

The questions whether immigration shall be encouraged or restricted, and whether naturalization shall be made more difficult or not, must be considered, both from a political and from an industrial point of view; and in each case it is necessary to glance back and see what have been the character, the conduct, and the political leaning of the immigrant, and what he has done to develop and enrich our country. Has he been law-abiding, industrious and patriotic, and is the government indebted to him for anything; or is it a case of a spoilt pauper child housed, fed and clothed in a fine Christian uniform, all at the expense of native Americans, and to no purpose?

We will look at the political side first, and, as our space is limited, we will go back only to 1860, calling attention, however, to the fact that up to that time, no matter from what cause, the immigration had been almost entirely to the Northern and free States, and not to the slave States, as will be seen by the figures about to be given. These, when carefully examined in connection with election returns, will show that but for the assistance of the immigrant the election of Abraham Lincoln as president of the United States would have been an impossibility, and that had the cry, "America for the Americans," prevailed at an earlier period of our history, the nineteenth century would never have seen the great free republic we see, and the shadow of millions of slaves would to-day darken and curse the continent.

I will cite no doubtful authority, but will take as a basis the United States census of 1860. The total population of the States was 31,183,744, of whom 4,099,152 were foreign-born, and of the latter only 216,730 were to be found in all the eleven States which seceded. The remaining States had a total population of 22,313,997, of whom 3,882,422, or a little over one-sixth were actually foreign-born. To these we must add their children, who, though native-born, yet, as a rule, held the same views, were controlled by the same motives and influences, spoke the same language, and generally acted with their elders; who, in short, for all practical purposes, and especially for our purpose, must be treated as a part of the immigrant population. If we add two children for each foreign-born person, we find that fully one-half of the population in the States that remained true to the Union, consisted of the foreign-born and their children, and was made up chiefly of Germans, Scandinavians and Irish.

The Scandinavians have always, nearly to a man, voted the Republican ticket. The Germans, likewise, were nearly all Republicans. In fact, the States having either a large Scandinavian or a large German population have been distinguished as the banner Republican States. Notably is this true of Iowa, Wisconsin, Minnesota and Michigan, which have a large Scandinavian population; and of Illinois, Ohio, and Pennsylvania, which have a very large German population. The Irish more generally voted the Democratic ticket, but were not united; and in New York, where they were most numerous, they have repeatedly given the Republican ticket substantial aid. Taking the States in detail, Iowa had a total population of 674,913. Of these, 106,077, or about one-sixth, were foreign-born, and nearly all were Germans and Scandinavians, who to a man voted the Republican ticket. The total vote cast for president in Iowa in 1860, was 128,331, of which Lincoln received 70,409, giving him a plurality over Douglas of 15,298. Now, if simply the actual foreign-born vote had been left out, it would have amounted to one-sixth of the whole, or 21,388. These would nearly all have been taken from Lincoln's vote, which would thus be reduced to less than 50,000, leaving to Douglas a plurality of over 5,000; and if, instead of substracting only the foreign-born vote, we were to subtract the vote which for our purpose must be regarded as immigrant, Lincoln's vote would be reduced to less than 40,000.

Wisconsin had a total population of 775,881. Of these, 276,967, or a little over 35 per cent., were foreign-born, nearly all Germans and Scandinavians, and they supported the Republican ticket. The total vote of Wisconsin in that year was 152,180, of which Lincoln received 86,110, giving him a plurality over Douglas of 21,089. Now, if the foreign-born vote were omitted, the total vote would be reduced by about 35 per cent., or 52,263; and nearly the whole of this would have to be deducted from Lincoln's vote, thus not only wiping out his plurality, but giving Douglas a plurality of nearly 30,000—this by deducting only the actual foreign-born vote, and not the additional vote which, as we have seen should be included.

Michigan had in that year a total population of 749,-113. Of these, 149,093, or about one-fifth, were foreign-born, nearly all Scandinavians, Hollanders and Germans, and almost solidly Republican. The total vote of Michigan was 154,747, of which Lincoln received 88,480, giving him a plurality over Douglas of 23,423. If the foreign-born vote, amounting to about one-fifth, or 31,000, be left out, nearly all the loss must fall upon Lincoln's vote, giving Douglas a plurality.

Illinois had a population of 1,711,951, of whom 324,-643, or almost one-fifth, were foreign-born. Of these, 87,573 were Irish, the remainder nearly all Germans and Scandinavians, adherents of the Republican party. Of the total vote of Illinois, 338,693, Lincoln received 172,-161, giving him a plurality over Douglas of 11,946. If the actual foreign-born vote is to be eliminated, that reduces the total nearly one-fifth, or upward of 66,000. Supposing the Irish foreign-born vote to have been solidly Democratic, which it was not, about 40,000 would still have to be deducted from Lincoln's vote; this would not only wipe out his plurality, but would give a very large plurality to Douglas.

Ohio's population was 2,339,500. Of these, 328,249, or about one-seventh, were foreign-born; 76,826 being Irish, and the remainder mostly Germans, who, as a rule, were Republicans. The total vote of Ohio was 442,441, of which Lincoln received 221,610—a plurality over

Douglas of 34,378. If the foreign-born vote had been omitted, the total would have been reduced by nearly one-seventh, or about 63,200. Assuming that most of the Irish were Democrats and voted for Douglas, nearly 50,000 votes would still have to be deducted from Mr. Lincoln's total, which would give the State to Douglas.

These five States alone are sufficient to demonstrate the situation; for if Lincoln had lost them and carried the other States in the Republican column, he would have had only 129 electoral votes, while he needed 151. But the facts are that in every State carried by Lincoln there was a large foreign population, which was mostly, and in some States entirely, Republican, and which continued to be Republican down to a very recent date; and if the vote of this class had been omitted in 1860, it would have reduced Lincoln's vote to such an extent as to defeat him in most of the States that he carried. I am speaking only of the foreign-born voters; but, as already shown, to these should be added a large percentage of the people who, although native-born, are of foreign-born parentage, and must be considered with them in viewing the general political course of immigrants. It is an indisputable fact that the vote of the naturalized citizen and of his son, has been a most powerful and indispensable factor in giving the Republican party the control of the government; and even to-day its power and popularity are greatest in those States in which there is a large naturalized vote.

The eleven States that in 1861 hoisted the flag of secession had a population of 8,726,644. Of these, only 216,730, or about 2½ per cent., were foreign-born, and

they were, subsequently, found to be Unionists. The
men who sought to destroy our institutions, who proclaimed the principle of inequality, who insisted that
the strong have a divine right to the fruit of the poor
man's labor, and who finally fired upon the flag of the
Republic, were not only Americans, but they were the
sons of Americans; while, on the other hand, the heavy
German population of northern Kentucky and of Missouri, by their adherence to the Union, turned the scale
and prevented two great States from giving their powerful aid to the Confederacy. The great majority of
those that were Americans and sons of Americans in
these two States were in favor of secession. Then,
when the war began, those Northern States that had
the largest foreign-born population furnished the largest quota of soldiers to the Union armies. Even Missouri contributed nearly 200,000 men, although it was
the scene of repeated raids, during which a portion of
its population, called by the Southern leaders "damned
Dutch Unionists," was made to pay dearly for its patriotism. The records of the War Department show that,
of the 2,678,967 men that from first to last were enlisted
in the Union armies, 494,900 were entered on the records as of foreign nationality. No doubt some of these
were native-born, but not very many, for, as a rule, the
native-born recruits spoke the English language and
were booked as Americans. How many of these there
were we can not tell exactly, but, considering the fact
that nearly half of the population was of foreign
nationality, and that recruits generally came from the
common people, there is no question but that one-half

of the men who enlisted in the Union armies were either foreign-born or of foreign-born parentage. These would not have been here to enter our armies but for immigration, and better soldiers never marched to the music of war. There is not a swamp or field or dark ravine where treason made a stand, but is covered with the graves of Germans and of Scandinavians who died for the principle of equal rights. Though the Irish more generally voted the Democratic ticket, yet their patriotism was prompt to respond to the call of their adopted country, and there is not a battle-field where blood was shed for the Union that has not the bones of Irishmen rotting upon it.

Again, material resources are as necessary for the prosecution of a great war as are men, for the latter can do nothing without equipment, food, arms and munitions of war. When the Rebellion collapsed, the South had yet large armies of men, but its resources were exhausted. It had no shoes, no food, no arms for its soldiers. It had not, within all its boundaries, sufficient ammunition to fight a great battle. The North, on the contrary, had yet inexhaustible resources, for which it was largely indebted to the sober, steady, intelligent industry and frugality of its immigrant population; for those States in which this population was the largest were found to possess the best agriculture, the finest cities, the most shops, the largest factories and the fullest warehouses. Further, the labor of building the great railway systems of our land, which are so necessary for the development of a country, and for the rapid concentration of men and material in time of war, was almost entirely done by these people.

Now, if Kentucky and Missouri had joined the Confederacy, and if the Northern States had not possessed the incalculable strength in both men and material resources that they got through the naturalized citizen and his children, they would not only have been unable to subdue the South, but they would have been unable successfully to resist Southern aggression; and some Southern colonel would to-day be calling the roll of his slaves in the shadow of Bunker Hill monument, for the country could not permanently have remained part slave and part free.

I do not claim that the foreigner gave to the country new ideas, nor do I wish in any manner to belittle the great achievements of the native Americans of the North; I am simply directing attention to the fact that, standing alone, they could not have elected Lincoln, could not have successfully resisted Southern aggression, and could not have put down the Rebellion; and that it was the naturalized citizen and his children who, by joining hands with them, turned the scale in favor of the ideas and the institutions of the North, and thus directly helped to shape the destiny of our country.

In this connection, I wish to call attention to the remarkable historical fact that the great political party of the country that held out a friendly hand to the immigrant, and that favored and secured liberal naturalization laws, so that the new-comer could, in a reasonable time, become a citizen and voter, has been all along opposed and repeatedly defeated by these very naturalized voters; while, on the other hand, the great political party—first Federal, then Whig, and lastly Republican

—from whose ranks has always come the opposition to a liberal naturalization law and to make the new-comer a voter, and from whose ranks to-day comes, with increasing frequency, the cry of "America for the Americans," is the very party which has all along received by far the greater portion of this naturalized vote, was enabled by the aid of this very vote to keep control of the government for over a quarter of a century, and to-day is in power by the aid of this vote.

The one political party can truthfully say to the great majority of the naturalized voters: "I did what I could to give you the franchise, and you have constantly used that franchise to defeat me;" while the other political party might truthfully say to the same people: "From my ranks has come all the opposition to you, and it is from my ranks that to-day comes the demand for restrictive naturalization laws; and in return for this treatment you have stood faithfully by me, have kept me in power, and have given office and honors to some of the very men who opposed and slandered you." It is incomprehensible why opposition to making a voter of the immigrant should come from members of the Republican party.

If we look at the question in still another light, it will be found that in those States which have the largest naturalized vote, and in which this has been a potent factor, there are more churches, more libraries, more schools, better schools, and more general intelligence than are to be found in those States where the people are not only American-born, but are the children of American-born parents. As a rule, the poor among the immigrants are more frugal, are more industrious, and are more used to continuous hard work than are the poor among native Americans, and consequently they generally succeed in making a living, while the latter frequently fail.

It has been charged against the naturalized citizen that he has at different times, engaged in riots and disturbed social order; but in most of these cases it will be found that as many American-born as foreign-born have participated, the fact being that nationality had nothing to do with the matter, but that the disturbance grew out of industrial or political excitement. But even if this were not so, it does not lie in the mouth of an American to make this charge, for the most disgraceful acts of riot and mob violence that stain our annals were committed, not by the foreign-born in their rags, but by Americans dressed in broadcloth; and that not in a Dutch or an Irish settlement, but in the streets of Boston. This mob, known in history as the broadcloth mob, was diabolical in its fury, and sought to tear William Lloyd Garrison to pieces, not over a question of starvation wages, not to avenge an act of injustice and oppression, but simply because he had dared to proclaim that no man can have a right of property in another human being. If there have been mobs and riots among the foreign-born in our country, they were nothing but impotent protests, by ignorant though honest people, against that rapacious greed which took the bread they toiled for away from their children's mouths, while the broadcloth American Boston mob shrieked for the life of the man who dared to advocate human freedom.

I have been speaking, be it noted, of the immigrant who came of his own accord to our shores, with the purpose of renouncing forever his foreign allegiance, and swearing fealty to the Republic. I do not include assisted paupers, habitual criminals, or laborers, whether yellow or white, brought over under contract to supplant and drive out American workmen, both native-born and naturalized. Against these classes our gates should be closed.

Coming now to the question, Shall naturalization be made more difficult? I ask: Why should it be? Does the history of the past furnish any reason for such legislation? If yea, what is it? If nay, then why begin now? If these people are to live here, they should be a part of us, and should be made to feel that they have an interest in public affairs. To have a large foreign population among us and to deprive it of the right of citizenship, with all its privileges, would be to create jealousies, discontent, and, in short, the conditions which, in time, must produce disturbances, and in a critical juncture might endanger our political existence. We have seen that but for the vote and the influence of the naturalized citizen, Lincoln could not have been elected, and that the destiny of our country must have been different.

But suppose this were not so; if the laws had prohibited a foreigner who had made his home among us, from becoming a citizen, and if the millions of foreigners in this country that had accumulated property and acquired local influence, had found themselves compelled to obey the laws and to pay taxes to support our institutions, while they had no voice in making those laws, in levying the taxes, or in managing those institutions, would they not have been discontented and secretly hostile to the government which thus treated them; and is it at all probable that when that government was attacked, either they or their sons would have rushed to its defense?

The idea of limiting the franchise is not new. Wherever and whenever there have been men who thanked God that they were not like their fellows, it has been advocated, and wherever it has been tried, it has been a failure. It is simply the dying echo of aristocracy, and is inimical to the spirit of our institutions. Van Buren earned the gratitude of all true Republicans by striking it out of the constitution of New York. There are yet a few States in which a vestige of it remains; but it will be found that these States march not in the van, but with the lumber wagons of civilization.

It is frequently said that the people who come here are, as a rule, ignorant, and know nothing about our institutions, and, therefore, should not be permitted to vote after a residence of only five years; that they can not act intelligently, and will simply be tools for crafty politicians to use at the expense of good government. Now, if the premises were true, the conclusions might seem plausible; and were it a matter of speculation only, they would, perhaps, be accepted. But the premises are false. Besides, this is no longer a matter of argument. We have had a century's experience, and this must decide the question. If the vote of these people, has, in the main, been marked by ignorance and been cast against beneficial measures and good government, then the charge must be accepted as true; on the other hand, if their vote has, in the main, been on the side of right, and justice and good government, then the charge must be treated as being not only groundless, but a slander. We have already seen that the great majority of these votes has steadfastly been cast for the men and the measures which, for a quarter of a century, have shaped the destiny of this nation; surely, no voice from the Republican party will declare that they were wrong. This being so, no Republican should be permitted to make the charge of ignorance against a class of voters who helped to support these men and these measures, and without whose support the success of the latter would have been impossible.

In this connection it should be borne in mind that the so-called scholar is not the most intelligent, the most reliable, or the safest guide in public affairs. The great Selden was not joking when he affirmed that " No man is wiser for his learning, and no fool is a perfect fool until he learns Latin;" and Wendell Phillips was in dead earnest when he said:

" Book learning does not make five per cent. of that mass of common sense that runs the world, transacts its business, secures its progress, trebles its power over nature, works out in the long run a rough average justice, wears away the world's restraints, and lifts off its burdens. Two-thirds of the inventions that enable France to double the world's sunshine, and make old and New England the workshops of the world, did not come from colleges or from minds trained in the schools of science, but struggled up from the irrepressible instinct of untrained natural power. Her workshops, not her colleges, made England for a while the mistress of the world, and the hardest job her workmen had was to make Oxford willing he should work his wonders. . . . Liberty and civilization are only fragments of rights wrung from the strong hands of wealth and book learning; almost all the great truths relating to society were not the result of scholarly meditation, but have been first heard in the solemn protests of martyred patriotism and the loud cries of crushed and starving labor. When common sense and the common people had stereotyped a principle into a statute, then book men came to explain how it was discovered."*

I will add only that years ago, when the book men both North and South were learnedly demonstrating that slavery was a divine institution, these common people from foreign shores simply said, "It is wrong for one man to get another man's labor for nothing," and then took sides, not with the powerful and wealthy, but with the party that was then the object of ridicule, because it dared say that slavery was wrong. The history of this country demonstrates that the common people are swayed by a patriotic instinct or impulse in favor of the right—something which can not be said of the wealthy or of the book men.

I know that occasionally the local government of a large city is cited to prove the ignorance of the naturalized voter; but only a superficial observer will make this assertion. This question has been examined by some of the ablest men of America and of Europe, and they all agree that the cause of bad government at times in cities is partisanship and the saloon. And the saloon owes its power to the fact that it is courted by the local leaders of both political parties; each political party is ready and eager to make any combination which will enable it to defeat its opponent.

---

* Wendell Phillips on "The Scholar in the Republic."

When the rich and the educated divide themselves up almost equally between the two great parties, and one-half vote the Democratic ticket and the other half vote the Republican ticket; if then the naturalized voters, or, if you please, the common people, come along, and part vote the Republican ticket, the remainder the Democratic ticket, it is both nonsensical and dishonest to say that the result, no matter what it is, is due to the ignorance of the voters. Such a charge could be truthfully made only if substantially all the well-informed and the property-holding classes were to range themselves on one side, and the ignorant people on the other, and the latter were to carry the day and run things badly. But so long as the rich and the educated partisan in the Republican party will resort to any means to carry an election, and will stand in line with all classes of voters on that side, while the Democratic partisan does the same thing on the other side, the result must be attributed to a party and not to a class. There never was a dishonest government in any city in this country that did not come into power by the assistance of a large class of voters who not only were intelligent, but who boasted of American ancestry. And it is safe to say that there never will be one; for partisan feeling seems to blind men who are otherwise intelligent, fair and honest, so that four out of five of the prominent and intelligent men in each political party will rather see their party win with men who are dishonest and unfit than see the opposite party win with honest and competent men. And, strange as it may seem, the man who comes to the polls in his carriage is, as a rule, more narrow and more bigoted than the poor man who has to lose half a day's wages in order to vote.

There is an objection to further immigration that at first blush seems plausible, namely, that it increases the competition among the unskilled laborers, who already find it impossible to maintain their families in a manner becoming even the humblest American citizen. Ocean travel has become cheap, safe and speedy, and many European countries are over-populated. These people are aware that in from two to three weeks they can go from the place of their birth to almost any part of the United States. They have heard of this country and have an exaggerated idea of its advantages; and the question naturally suggests itself: If these people are permitted to come, will not that reduce the unskilled laborer to the condition of the European laborer; and, to avoid this, would it not be better to prevent any more people from landing upon our shores? To a man who sympathizes with the American unskilled laborer, whether native-born or naturalized, in his hopeless condition, this argument, I repeat, at first seems plausible; but aside from the impossibility of enforcing such an exclusive policy along our sea-costs and 4,000 miles of border crossed everywhere by railroads, there are insurmountable objections to it. First, it is contrary to the spirit of the age, and to the law of human development and the highest civilization, which require the freest intercourse possible, not only between men, but between nations; and no people ever yet profited, in the long run, by pursuing a policy at variance with this law. Secondly, it could be but a temporary expedient of such doubtful character that any great nation must hesitate to adopt it. Thirdly, it would be so decidedly narrow and provincial that, aside from its effect upon ourselves, we can not take such a position in the face of the world. The truth is that the labor question is becoming more urgent, and the condition of the laborer is improving as fast in Europe as in this country; and the laborer's only hope for the future lies in united action, not alone in one country, but throughout the civilized world. This united action will be brought about much more quickly by unity of interest, free intercourse and friendly co-operation, than would be possible if we were to isolate ourselves. In fact, it is only by this intercourse that the laboring masses can be so educated as to enable them to stand together, and by united action secure justice for themselves and their children; while isolation would prevent the spread of intelligence, make united action impossible, and thus put any great achievement out of the question.

Besides, the American laborer does not suffer very much from competition with the immigrant who comes of his own volition. The latter, coming here to improve his condition and that of his family, soon joins his American brother, and asks wages which will at least enable him to do this. But the condition of the laborer has been made deplorable by the importation of ship-loads of men under contract. These do not come with the motives or with the ambition of the class we have been considering; they have no thought of becoming citizens, but are practically slaves, who will work for wages upon which the American laborer can not exist

Agents for large corporations are constantly importing them. Steamship companies, to get the passage money paid by American employers, bring them over by the thousands, so that many great centers of industry in the East have been filled with them, and the American laborer is being crowded out. Both the native-born and the naturalized laborer have been almost driven out of the great State of Pennsylvania by these importations. True, there is a law against such contracts, but it is a dead letter; so that we have in this country the strange spectacle of the government keeping up the price of a great many articles by shutting out foreign competition, and at the same time permitting the manufacturers of these articles to import the pauper laborers of Europe to produce them.

But this is not natural immigration; and whether the people thus brought be Chinese, Hungarian, Polish, or British paupers, they should be excluded; but natural immigration should not be interfered with. Free circulation of the blood is necessary to a healthy growth, whether of an individual or of a nation, and any restriction of the natural processes arrests development and enfeebles both body and mind. Thousands of years ago the cry, "China for the Chinese," prevailed and became a law in one of the richest quarters of the globe, among a people that had already a high civilization. From that time their faces have been turned backward, and they have simply been worshiping the shades of their father; and yet there are in this age and in this country men who would have us practice Chinese statesmanship. JOHN P. ALTGELD.

THE EIGHT-HOUR MOVEMENT.

(An address delivered before the Brotherhood of United Labor, at the Armory in Chicago, February 22, 1890.)

Mr. President and Ladies and Gentlemen:

On March 5, 1867, there was enacted in Illinois a statute of which Section 1 read, as follows: "On and after the first day of May, 1867, eight hours of labor between the rising and the setting of the sun in all mechanical trades, arts and employments, and other cases of labor and service by the day, except in farm employments, shall constitute and be a legal day's work, where there is no special contract or agreement to the contrary." A number of other States about that time enacted similar laws. In 1868 a like act was passed by Congress, which was to apply to all works carried on by the federal government, and soon thereafter General Grant, then President, gave the measure the influence of his great name by directing that the same wages should be paid for eight hours' work that had been paid for ten. Since that time there has been more or less continuous agitation upon this subject; we have had many widespread and serious industrial and social disturbances as well as destructive, if not ruinous strikes growing out of an attempt to introduce the eight-hour system.

And now, after twenty-two years of legislation, after many years of agitation, and long after the movement has had the sanction of some of the ablest and best men of the land, we have met to consider the feasibility of extending this system, acknowledging by our very presence here that the difficulties in the way have thus far refused to succumb to legislation, to agitation or to the personal influence of great men. And I will say here that I come not as a prophet or a leader; I bring you neither a new religion, a new light, nor a new remedy; I propose to talk to you as I would to a brother, and to view the situation, with the difficulties it presents, in the light we now have.

We will first see what has been done toward shortening the hours of labor. About 1820, there began in England an agitation in favor of reducing the number of hours, especially in factories, from twelve and even fourteen to ten, and it was not until 1847 that this resulted in a ten-hour law. The basis for this class of legislation, or rather the ground for State interference, is that the State is interested in the physical well-being of its citizens and has a right to prohibit whatever weakens their vitality. After the passage of that law, reducing the hours to ten, the agitation was continued until, in many lines of industry, they have been reduced to nine, and in a few cases to eight.

After the reduction in England, the agitation proceeded in this country, and in 1853 the managers of the manufactories in Lowell and Lawrence and Fall River voluntarily reduced the hours of labor, first to eleven and then to ten hours per day. And in 1874 Massachusetts passed a law making ten hours the limit for females and males under eighteen years. And it made this law compulsory — treating it as a police regulation for the protection of the health and the lives of the operatives named.

About thirty years ago the eight-hour system was introduced into Victoria, or South Australia, and has prevailed there ever since in the trades, factories and mines. It was introduced there not by legislation nor by any violent measures, but by mutual concessions between the employer and employe. In 1886 the large establishments at the Stock Yards tried the eight-hour day for five months; at the end of which time the strong public sentiment in its favor having somewhat abated, the employers, by a concert of action, succeeded in re-introducing the ten-hour day, but it is to be said for them that, as the large competing establishments in other cities did not adopt the eight-hour system, the Chicago packers were placed at a disadvantage, and they are, therefore, not to be greatly blamed. The eight-hour system has also prevailed for a number of years in most of the large cities of this country in what are called the building trades — among masons, carpenters, painters, plasterers, etc. The arguments offered, pro and con, on this question are familiar to most of you. They are not new, excepting the results of experience — nobody can to-day lay claim to much originality in connection with them. They all were made in England early in this century, when it was proposed to reduce the working day to ten hours, and later, when the working day, in many cases, was successfully again reduced to nine hours, and they all were repeated, with more or less vehemence, in the New England States of this country between 1840 and

1870 during the agitation for a reduction in the hours of labor from twelve and even fourteen to ten, which resulted successfully, and they have again been frequently repeated in late years in connection with the eight-hour movement. In brief, it is urged in favor of shorter hours,

First. That, labor-saving machinery has so greatly increased production that the same amount of labor is no longer required to supply the world with the necessaries, the comforts and the luxuries of life, and that the laborer should share with the rest of the world the benefit which this machinery has conferred upon mankind; that while it is true that it has also increased the wants of men so that all the work performed by machinery can not be considered as clear gain in point of saving manual labor; it yet has, to a much greater extent increased production, and has, to a much greater extent, supplanted human labor; and that as the total quantity of labor to be performed by hand is reduced, the hours of labor should be proportionately shortened and the laborer given time for healthful recreations and mental and social improvement.

Second. That this labor-saving machinery has so far supplanted human labor that there are now more than a million of men in this broad land in enforced idleness, it being claimed by seemingly competent judges that there are in Chicago alone from 50,000 to 60,000 men, to say nothing of many women who work for a living, who can get nothing to do; that if the hours of labor were reduced from ten to eight, the labor of all these people would again be required, they could again be employed

and thus be saved from the fearful consequences, morally and physically, that follow absolute destitution.
That unless this is done, labor-saving machinery will be
a curse.instead of a blessing to mankind.

Third.   That at present, as a rule, the workmen, and
especially women and boys, are kept in a state of physical and nervous exhaustion so that great intellectual,
social, or even moral improvement is retarded, and in
many cases made impossible; that this exhausted and
worn condition not only stupefies, but that it creates a
demand in the system for stimulants and therefore
naturally produces drunkenness with its accompanying
evils.

Fourth.   That while the foregoing is true of adults,
the effects are still more marked upon their children,
that in time, under our present system, the children of
the laborers not only become incapable of doing the
best kind of work, but they make a low grade of citizens, become inferior men and women physically, mentally and morally, and that society at large, that is the
State, and in the end the employer, suffers from this condition; that at present, as a rule, the boyhood and girl-
hood among the laboring classes terminates at fifteen,
that at thirty-five to forty they break down with rheu-
matism and the ailments that follow in the wake of
exhausting toil and exposure, and at fifty too many of
them are in their graves. In 1874 Governor Washburne,
of Massachusetts, who had previously opposed the
movement for shorter hours — declared in his official
address that, "It can not be denied that the strength of
mill operators is becoming exhausted and they are

becoming prematurely old and losing the vitality requisite to the healthy enjoyment of social opportunity."

Fifth. That when one class of people is confined to, and is exhausted by manual labor, and another has the advantages of intellectual training, the former class will soon be absolutely in the power of the latter. A man who returns to his home exhausted is in no condition to engage in intellectual exercise. The mind sympathizes with the body, and when the physical faculties are prostrated with fatigue, it is impossible for him to employ his mind so as to win for himself a fair position in the social scale. He has no opportunity to circulate among his fellow citizens and take part in current events, and thus in time a feeling of antagonism and discontent is engendered—he becomes narrow and selfish, and a social friction is created, which in the end is injurious to all.

Sixth. That before the division of labor and the extensive introduction of machinery, each laborer, as a rule, made an entire thing, so that his mind was occupied and the work was not so fatiguing. Now all is changed, he works on a single process, frequently on a very minute object, the effect of which on the mind is most unfavorable when long continued; the constant concentration of the mind upon one thing in time narrows it to that thing, the laborer becomes like the machine, his nervous system is weakened, his mind dwarfed and his body stunted. That when the laborer worked by hand he could rest when he was tired—quit an hour earlier if he were not well—but now he must work while the machine works and that this constant and regular draft on the nervous system causes him to wear out with the machine and in many cases sooner—for human muscle and nerve can not compete with steel unless given plenty of time to rest and recuperate.

Seventh. It is urged that if the hours were reduced, the laborer and his children would be in a better condition physically, mentally, socially and morally, and therefore not only would become better citizens, but would do better work, and, in the long run, much more work; that it would add from fifteen to twenty years to the average life of the laborer. In short, that it would place the whole laboring class upon a higher plane, and thus benefit the State and the employer; that long hours mean comparatively low wages, low wages mean cheap men, and cheap men mean low civilization. ON THE OTHER HAND IT IS URGED,

First. That shorter hours mean reduced production; that the world needs all the production we are now capable of, and that if there is a reduction in the product of the world, there must be consequent suffering, and that the poor will suffer most, and the world will retrograde instead of advancing.

To this it is replied that it can not be shown that there will, in the end, be less production. On the contrary, that under shorter hours the laborers will have increased vigor and higher intelligence, feel more interest in their work —and will, in the end, accomplish not only as much work, but a higher grade of work; that, in fact, this is no longer an open question, it having been settled by experience; that when in England the reduction was made from twelve and fourteen hours to ten, as soon as things had adjusted themselves to the new conditions, it was found that there was not only as much work done in the ten hours as had been in the longer hours, but that it was a higher grade of work, and that, when, subsequently, a further change was made from ten to nine, while there was some falling off at first, yet, owing to the introduction of better machin- . ery and the improved condition of workmen, the product soon increased to what it had been, and that when in the New England States, about the middle of this century, the manufacturers voluntarily reduced the hours of labor to ten, there was scarcely any falling off in the production after the new system was in full operation, while the condition of the laborers and their families greatly improved in every respect. When the eight-hour day was tried at the stock yards, there was a slight falling off in the production, but not in proportion to the reduction in hours. One of the large employers who opposed the movement stated that had the hours been nine instead of eight the men would have accomplished as much as they formerly did in ten. But if this were not so, the objection would not be valid, because at present there are multitudes for whom there is no work, and if as many hours of actual labor are required as are now devoted to it, then, by reducing the number of hours which each shall work, all could be employed; and that, if this were done, the production would be greater than at present. Further, that there would then be from fifteen to twenty years added to the life of the laborer, and that, consequently, the total production would, in the end, be very much greater than at present.

Second. That if the laborer were to accept eight hours' pay for eight hours' work then he would have less money to spend than he has now, and consequently be worse off, and that if he were to be paid ten hours' pay for eight hours' work there would necessarily be a great increase in the cost of production, and that, as the laboring classes themselves consume the greater part of what is produced, they must suffer from the increased cost of production, that the things which they need will be made dearer, while they will have no more money than they have now, and that, consequently, they would still be sufferers.

To this it is answered that the question of wages must be left to regulate itself; it being in a measure, at least, independent; that it is true if they got only eight hours' pay for eight hours' work some of them would get less money than they get now, but all would then be employed, the laboring class would get as much as they get now, and none of them would be driven to the point where they must either beg or steal. But the assumption that if there were to be ten hours' wages paid for eight hours' work, and a consequent increase in the cost of production, the laborers would be worse off than they are now, is at variance with all experience. Plausible as the reasoning may at first blush seem, it is not correct. I will simply direct attention to the fact that everywhere, and in all times, in this country and in Europe, when wages were high, the working classes prospered, when wages were low they suffered. In fact, high prices and good times have gone hand in hand, while low prices and hard times have always been twin brothers, and the people who always suffer most when prices are low are the laboring people. Low wages and low prices, as a rule, mean black bread and no meat for the man who toils with his hands, and, in many cases, it means the poor house, the police station, and the bridewell, for his children.

Third. That while the time will come when eight hours will constitute a day's work, yet we are not ready for it now; that the laboring classes are not yet sufficiently advanced, that they haven't sufficient strength of character, that they were yet too ignorant, and too unruly, and too much inclined to dissipate to make the change, and that we must wait until they have reached a higher development.

Now, to this I answer that once it was urged in England that people should not be given their political freedom until they had become fitted for it, until there was no danger of their abusing it, and Lord Macaulay replied that, "If men are to wait for freedom until they have become good and wise in slavery, they will wait forever." That observation answers this objection.

Fourth. That there ought to be no unity of action among the laborers, for if there was, the liberty of each laborer to work as many hours as he pleased would be taken away, and that the dearest thing that the laborer could cherish is his liberty to work as long as he wishes.

Now, it is a remarkable and a sad fact, that when we find a class of people in a condition where they are absolutely helpless, where they are absolutely in the power of a stronger class, where they are the slaves of adverse circumstances, and where individual action can accomplish absolutely nothing, that there should always be found persons who try to keep them in that condition, and who will resort to any sophistry which may serve this purpose. And I will say that, as a rule, these persons are not the employers themselves, employers usually are men of brains; generally, too, they have hearts, and while they may allow what they consider to be their interests to carry them too far, still they are rarely heard advancing such an argument. Arguments of this character are made by a class of men who can be designated as "hangers on," men who want to bask in the smiles of the rich and of the employers; men who, in some capacity, either socially or financially, are dependent upon the patronage of the rich. This class of men will resort to methods and measures to hinder reform and to defend abuses, which would make employers blush. By way of contrast, I wish here to quote a few words from Governor Washburne, of Massachusetts, in his message to the legislature; he said: " The fact that there is unrest and dissatisfaction when man is confined to unremitting toil, is one of the brightest and most healthy omens of the times. It is an indication that his better nature is struggling for emancipation; it is a hopeful sign of finer and nobler manhood in the future. Such efforts for improvement should never be discouraged, but always encouraged."

Fifth. Again, it is urged that shortening the hours of labor simply means increased idleness, increased drunkenness, increased vice; that the extra time given the men will not be put to a good purpose, and that, therefore, the existing condition should continue.

Now I will say, in answer to this, that if it were true it would apply alike to all mankind. Human nature is pretty much the same, and if it is true that you should not give men the opportunity to improve because it might be abused, then there is no hope of improvement. Besides, it is a question of justice and right; eternal justice requires that every man should do his share of the work required to be done to supply the world with what is necessary, and if some are now doing more than their share, they have a right to a change, and if the men have a right to a reduction as a matter of justice, they are entitled to it even if they should abuse their leisure. One set of men have no right to set themselves up as judges of their fellows, and deprive the latter of rights which they enjoy in common with all. We all abuse, to a greater or less extent, the privileges and blessings conferred upon us, yet this is no reason why we should be deprived of them by our fellow-men. Take the rich and the sons of the rich; they enjoy privileges and advantages which were never enjoyed before. All art, all literature and all science are open to them, and a field for doing good such as was never before seen; yet nobody will say that they are making a fair use of these privileges. Will it, therefore, be claimed that they should be deprived of them? It is no doubt true that if a large class were suddenly given more leisure time, in the first reaction after the long strain there would be some dissipation, but it would be only the effect of a sudden relaxation, and it would not last long. It may be true that, for a short time after the four million slaves in the South had been granted their freedom, they were, if anything, worse off than they were while they were slaves, but will any intelligent man to-day claim that, therefore, they ought to have been kept in slavery? However, we are not left merely to surmise or to speculation. At every reduction of hours in England there followed an improvement in the physical, mental, moral and social condition of the laborers. In Victoria, or South Aus⁻ tralia, the eight-hour system has been in operation for over thirty years, in all lines of industry, including mining and manufacturing, and instead of producing demoralization, it is not only prosperous, but is called the happy home of working men, and the American con- sul reports that "the moral and physical condition of the people is sound and healthy." In 1871 Mr. William Gray, in writing on the effects of the reduction from twelve to ten hours in the New England factories, said: "The testimony of all impartial persons, including orig- inal opponents of the ten-hour act, goes to show that the manufacturing masses have proved themselves worthy of the boon conferred on them. They have not abused the gift. Their intelligence has increased, their habits have improved, their social happiness has advanced; they have gained all, and more than all, they expected from the legislation. The intelligence, the general tone, the bearing of the operatives have kept pace with the advancement of the age. It would be scarce too much to say that the humble factory worker, in securing just legislation, has been the civilizer and moralizer of his employer." One of the largest employers in Chicago, who opposed this movement in 1886, stated to me that after the system was once started, he could not notice any increased drunkenness or disorder of any kind; that, on the contrary, the men seemed well behaved, and attended faithfully to business. It is also a fact that the condition of the artisans in the building trades, and of their families, has greatly improved since the adoption of the eight-hour system by them.

I quote from another author, whose words should be seriously pondered: "There is nothing, perhaps, more to be regretted than the fact that extraordinary commercial prosperity and an unprecedented accumulation of wealth have hitherto done so little to shorten the workman's hours of labor. It is unreasonable to expect that the moral qualities in man's nature can be duly developed if life is passed in one unvarying round of monotonous work. We are constantly being reminded of the ennobling and elevating influence produced by contemplating the beauties of nature, by reflecting upon the marvels which science unfolds, and by studying the triumphs of art and literature. Yet no inconsiderable portion of the toiling masses are reared in such ignorance, and surrounded from early childhood to old age by so much squalor and misery that life could be to them scarcely more dreary or depressing if there were on literature, no science and no art, and if nature had no beauties to unfold. The undue length of time which men have been accustomed to work, represents, so far as many branches of industry are concerned, a thoroughly mistaken policy. In many instances it is undeniable that men would not only get through more work, but would do it more efficiently if they had more opportunity for mental cultivation and for healthful recreation. No small part of the intemperance which is laid to the charge of laborers is directly to be traced to excessive toil. When strength becomes exhausted, and the body is over-fatigued, there often arises an almost uncontrollable desire to resort to stimulants." I call your attention especially to the last few lines in which he says that over-fatigue and physical exhaustion create an almost uncontrollable desire for stimulants, and that much of the intemperance laid to the charge of laborers is due to excessive toil. This is not the language of a cheap agitator, it is not the language of a sentimentalist, but it is the language of Henry Fawcett, who for many years has occupied the chair of political economy in the University of Cambridge, England. A man who has for many years been a member of the English Parliament, a man who has been a member of the English Cabinet, having been for some time postmaster general of the British Empire, a man who is regarded as one of the most intelligent and accurate writers on social and industrial conditions now living.

EVOLUTION OF THE LABOR CAUSE.

Before considering the practical difficulties immediately in the way of a more general introduction of the eight-hour system, it is important that we should understand the history and the nature of the development of labor. It is important to know whether the conditions of labor can be suddenly and arbitrarily made, or whether they are a matter of growth, a matter of development requiring time. If we will but glance back for a moment, we very soon see that the labor problem, like all other problems and conditions of existence, is governed by the law of evolution, has grown up from a condition of wild disorder to, at least, comparative order.

Scientists tell us that in the physical world, even after the earth had assumed its present form, it required long ages of change before there was such a thing possible as a peaceful valley or a green meadow. In religion it took thousands of ·years of development, from a period of demons and supernatural monstrosities, from bloody sacrifices and horrible torture, to the pure and simple doctrines of Christ, proclaiming peace upon earth and good will toward men.

In politics mankind struggled along through various forms and conditions of brute force to near the beginning of the nineteenth century before there could be proclaimed to the world that all men were created equal, and even this had to be done in the woods of America — an out-of-the-way place, a new continent outside of the limits of what was then called civilization.

In the industrial world we first perceive the struggle for liberty and for justice by what are called the captains of industry, the employers, for, mark you, they are only a little ahead of the wage-workers in their struggle for justice.

In ancient times, particularly in the Roman and the mediæval world, a manufacturer or a merchant, though his ships might cover the inland seas, though thousands of men might be doing his bidding, yet he had no voice in the government, was not considered fit for a gentleman and patrician to associate with, had no voice in making the laws that should govern him nor in determining what taxes he should pay; he was plundered indirectly by means of taxation, and when this did not suit the purpose of dissipated and rapacious officialism, he was plundered directly. To be born a patrician, to be a member of the priesthood, or a successful military chieftain, entitled a man to rule. The man who supplied the world with necessaries had no social or political standing, and this continued to be so throughout the middle ages — continued to be so in most all Europe till toward the end of the last century, and is to a great extent still the case in Russia and in the Turkish provinces of Europe. It is true that in a few Italian cities the conditions were different; a few rays of the coming dawn having struck them first, but, as compared with the rest of the world, they were so small as to be unworthy of notice. In England the employer acquired his rights earlier, and has for some time had a voice in the government. But even in England the much-praised Magna Charta was not for the benefit of either employer or workman, but simply of the nobility — the idle, who, by reason of the accident of birth, were enabled to appropriate the labor of others.

But, upon the whole, the employer in his struggles for justice is not a century in advance of the class we to-day call the wage-workers, and they, the laborers, were in ancient and later times practically all slaves. To be sure, we catch here and there in ancient literature a phrase about the laborer being worthy of his hire, but when we examine into the actual condition of the toiling masses, we are forced to treat such utterances as the emanations of fancy, for, not only was the labor of the masses at the absolute disposal of the master, but practically, and in every-day experience, their lives were also. True, there was in most countries a law providing that the master should not kill his slave, but if the master did so he generally went unwhipped of justice. This continued to be the condition, with slight exceptions, throughout all Europe down to near the beginning of this century. For unnumbered centuries they were absolute slaves, belonging to individuals; then they belonged, as it were, to the soil, and were known as serfs, and, in time, in England, they may be said to have belonged to the county or shire. In Russia the serfs were not freed until the middle of this century, and in the United States of America the slaves were not freed until after the middle of this century. It is true there were in some European cities organizations of skilled workmen, who enjoyed not only their freedom, but some advantages that may be said to have been ahead of their time, but, as compared with the great mass of the common people, they were so insignificant in number, and their situation was so exceptional, that we need not consider them further than to call attention to the fact that they developed the technical skill of their members, and enforced sobriety and honorable conduct, while by means of their meetings and discussions, they became, in a measure, educated, and thereby reached a much higher plane than was otherwise possible, and they thus wielded a powerful influence for good.

Thorold Rogers, in his great book on wages would have us believe that three or four centuries ago the condition of some workmen in England was better than it is to-day, and no doubt he found reference to isolated cases which indicated that this might be so. But we should get a very superficial knowledge of the condition of the common people of England if we were to take this as being in any sense indicative of their status.

In 1360, during the reign of Edward III., it was provided by law that if a laborer refused to work for the wages fixed by law, or by the justices of the county, or if he went outside of the county he was to be brought back by the sheriff, was to be imprisoned and was to have the letter "F" branded with a hot iron upon his forehead in token of his falsity. If he sought by any manner to increase the rate of wages he was to be imprisoned. Nay, at one time, if he accepted more he was to be imprisoned—and if an employer agreed to pay more than the fixed rate he was to forfeit three times the amount. From that time on, for four centuries, the legislation in England is of uniform kind, prohibiting by imprisonment all meetings of workmen and providing that the justices should fix the wages to be paid in their county; that if any laborer refused to work for the wages fixed by the justices, he was to be put in the stocks; if any laborer was found idle and did not apply himself to work, he was to have the letter "V" branded with a hot iron upon his cheek and was to be sold into slavery for two years, his children likewise to be sold, and if either he or they ran away they were to have the letter "S" branded on the cheek with a hot iron and were to be sold into slavery for life, and were to be fed on bread and water, and it was provided by law that they were to be made to work by beating, by chaining, etc., etc., and if they ran away again they were to suffer death. Children that had worked at husbandry till they were twelve years old, were forbidden ever to attempt to do anything else—other children were required to follow the occupation of their parents or be imprisoned. It is hard to conceive of a condition of the laboring classes that could be much worse than that of the English during these centuries.

In 1562, during the reign of Queen Elizabeth, the following statute was enacted: "All artificers and laborers being hired for wages by the day or week, shall betwixt the midst of the months of March and September be and continue at their work at or before five of the clock in the morning and continue at work and not depart until betwixt seven and eight of the clock at night, except it be in the time of breakfast, dinner or drinking; and all such artificers and laborers between the midst of September and the midst of March shall be and continue at their work from the spring of the day in the morning until the night of the same day, except in the time of breakfast and dinner."

I will simply add that under the laws of England during all these centuries if an employer violated an agreement with an employe he could simply be held in damages, but if an employe violated his agreement with an employer he could be fined and imprisoned, and it was not until 1875 that the law was changed in this regard so as to hold the employe only liable in damages for a breach of his contract the same as an employer, and Mr. Disraeli, who was then prime minister, remarked, that "for the first time in the history of the country the employer and employe sat under equal laws."

From this rapid glance at the history of the cause of labor we perceive that it is a plant that grows and that can not be arbitrarily made, and its growth is dependent upon the support of public sentiment; agitation has helped it along by educating and creating a public sentiment in its favor.

CAUSES OF FAILURE AND SUCCESS.

Coming now to the practical difficulties in the way, it seems to me that the main reason for the failure of the eight-hour movement in some cases is that the movement was not co-extensive with the employer's field of competition, while on the other hand, in those cases in which it was successful, the movement was co-extensive with the employer's field of competition. Let me illustrate: Houses and large buildings are not sold on board the cars at place of manufacture. Those engaged in erecting them in one city do not come directly in competition with those engaged in erecting them in another city. It is true that the workmen will go from one city to another, but they do not do this on a scale sufficiently large to bring the artisans in the building trades in one city so directly in competition with those in another. Most of the workmen have families, which they can not move without expense, and which they will not leave to seek work unless obliged to, so that in the building trades it is always a local question, and that is the reason why the short-hour system has been introduced successfully in this line, while it has failed in others. In Victoria there were only about a million of inhabitants, with the ocean surrounding them, and making speedy importation of laborers impossible. Now Chicago has over a million of inhabitants, yet if Chicago stood alone, and if its manufacturers did not have to come in competition with the rest of the country, it would be a very easy matter to have the system adopted here. In England the movement in favor of the reduction of hours was, in each instance, co-extensive with the field of competition among employers. It is true it embraced vast industries, but they were in a small territory, and all those carrying on the same business were affected alike, hence the movement was successful. In New England the movement for shorter hours was again co-extensive with what then constituted the manufacturer's field of competition, all of the leading mill-owners acceded to the movement, and they were all affected alike, and the movement was successful.

In 1886, when the eight-hour system was adopted at the Union Stock Yards at Chicago, it was not adopted by the large competing establishments in the East, that is, the movement in favor of shorter hours was not co-extensive with the field in which the packers had to compete, and consequently it failed. Manufactured goods are generally sold on board the cars at place of manufacture, and owing to the perfect facilities for transportation, a manufacturer in one city is brought into direct competition with another manufacturer in the same line a thousand miles away. Therefore, in my judgment, any attempt to introduce the eight-hour system into the manufacturing world must be general, and as you will readily see, this will require universal and thorough organization on the part of the laboring classes; without thorough organization, no movement of that kind can succeed, and the organization must not only be general, but it must embrace all lines of labor; it must be general in order that the movement may be general; it must embrace all lines in order: First, so that they can support each other, second, that there may be concert of action; third, that the million or more of men out of employment, and who are hungry, will not at once rush in and maintain the old system; and what is still more important, that the movement may be controlled by reason and moderation and kept free from violence. I do not believe that violence can accomplish any substantial results. On the contrary, it has repeatedly injured if not defeated the movement. I sincerely hope that the day of strikes is over, and that all differences in the future may be amicably adjusted on the basis of reason, justice and common sense, and I thoroughly believe that organization is one of the greatest educational agencies, and that the laborer is chiefly indebted to it for the improvement in his condition.

Organization by means of agitation helped to create the public sentiment that was necessary to effect reform, and it educated the laborer, by teaching him discussion, investigation, consideration, moderation and conservatism. The oldest labor organizations in the country are the most conservative. They have all taken high ground on the liquor question, they refuse to permit a saloon-keeper to belong to their order, and in times of violence they have, as a rule, been found on the side of

law and order, violence has in nearly all cases come
from the rabble and those outside of labor organizations.
It is clear that if the movement is not general, that
then, in order to maintain it in certain localities it will
be necessary to make some concession in wages, and it
is possible that if the movement should be general, that
in order to prevent too great a shock to business and a
loss to the employer, that there might have to be temporary concessions, for it must be borne in mind that
many manufacturers are under contracts to deliver their
products for some time in the future, at fixed prices and
as they are nearly all doing business on a very small
margin, even a slight increase in the cost of manufacture
would entail a loss upon them. Changes adopted by
mutual concession usually produce the best results.
Questions of this character can rarely be settled by
those who seek to get the highest possible wages for the
least possible work on the one hand, or those who seek
to get the greatest possible amount of work for the least
possible wages on the other hand. No system can be
permanently established unless in the end it shall prove
to be beneficial to the employer, hence it is important
to consider, from time to time, what the employer can
and can not do.

It frequently happens that a number of employés,
who consider themselves underpaid, see their employer's
carriage drive up to the office, and they look at it and
then at the large establishment, and conclude that he
could treble their wages if he only wanted to, when
the fact is that even the wealthiest men engaged in business are usually so spread out, that is, carrying on such

gigantic enterprises and doing business on so narrow a margin, that they are in a constant strain, and there are many who, with a capital of only a thousand dollars, expect to do a business of a hundred thousand dollars, and they are generally in such a situation that a slight disturbance seriously affects them. In railroading and in some other lines of industry the eight-hour system could not be adopted, but the day's work in these lines could be fixed with reference to the new standard, just as it is at present fixed with reference to the ten-hour standard. Now, in conclusion, I believe that by intelligent, united and well-directed action on the part of the laborers of this country, not only the eight-hour system, but any other, desirable reform can be successfully established, and it can not be in any other way.

Let me say that the nineteenth century is the only century that has lent a smile or a helping hand to the laborer. All the prior centuries struck him with their lash, beat him with their clubs, burned him with their hot irons, and let him rot in their jails. The means of advancement in this century has been the spread of intelligence, and, aside from the newspaper press, the two great agencies for the spread of intelligence among the laboring classes have been the common schools for the education of the children of the laborer, and organization for the education of the fathers of these children. Organization taught the laborer discussion, investigation, consideration, moderation, and it taught some employers that justice is the best policy.

AND

ITS VICTIMS.

BY

JOHN P. ALTGELD.

———

THIRD EDITION.

PREFACE TO FIRST EDITION.

In writing this work it has been my sole object briefly to call attention to the character of our penal machinery, and thereby, if possible, to lead others to examine it; for I am confident that when this machinery is once generally understood, improvements will be made in it which will benefit society, and will greatly lessen the sum of human misery.   J. P. A.

CHICAGO, August, 1884.

PREFACE TO SECOND EDITION.

The very flattering reception given the first edition has led me to believe that some good might be done by giving this work a wider circulation. I have therefore concluded to bring out a new edition.   J. P. A.

CHICAGO, April, 1886.

PREFACE TO THIS THE THIRD EDITION.

As the second edition of five thousand copies is exhausted, and as there is still a call for the book, I have decided to republish it in this volume.   J. P. A.

CHICAGO, April, 1890.

CONTENTS.

CHAPTER X.

CHAPTER XI.

CHAPTER XII.

CHAPTER XIII.

CHAPTER XIV.

CHAPTER XV.

PART SECOND.

CHAPTER I.

CHAPTER II.

CHAPTER III.

APPENDIX.

OUR PENAL MACHINERY

AND ITS VICTIMS.

PART FIRST.

CHAPTER I.

ARRESTS — NUMBER IN JAILS — NUMBER IN PENITEN-
TIARIES — DEPENDENTS AFFECTED.

According to the report of the superintendent of
police of the city of Chicago for the year 1882, there
were 32,800 arrests made by the police of this city during
that year, a number equal to about five per cent. of the
population.[1] This does not include the arrests made by
constables and other State officers, nor those made by
the local police in the adjoining suburbs of Chicago;
neither does it include the arrests made by the federal
officers.

Just how many of the above were actually incarcerated in prison, it is difficult to estimate; but it is safe to
say that the majority were actually locked up, even
though some of them were bailed out soon after. Supposing that fifty per cent. of the above, which, as will be
seen, is nearly right, were what are called "repeaters"
— that is, persons who had been arrested before — it

---

[1] The number of arrests by the police of Chicago for the year 1884 was 39,433, of
whom 30,887 were males, and 8,547 were females; and the general condition of these
as well as the proportion of each class, as it regards age, prior arrests, occupation,
etc., etc., was substantially the same as that of those arrested in 1882.

would still leave the number of new arrests, that is, the number of persons arrested for the first time, at 16,400. Then, assuming that the population will remain the same, and multiplying this number by 33, the number of years of the average lifetime, we find the astounding aggregate of 541,200 persons arrested during each generation by the police of Chicago alone.

The number of arrests in proportion to the population is not greater in Chicago than in the other large cities of America; in fact, it falls far below that of some cities. It is true that many of the above did not actually live in Chicago, and it is also true that the number arrested in proportion to population in small towns, and in the country, is much smaller than in large cities. Now, while we have no means of ascertaining the exact number of arrests made each year throughout the entire country, still, if we add the arrests made by constables, sheriffs and other officials, State and federal, it will be found that the above estimate of five per cent. will, when applied to the whole country, be not far out of the way. Assuming, then, that we have, in the United States, 50,000,000 population, it follows that there are in the neighborhood of 2,500,000 arrests every year (some writers estimate the number much higher); and, assuming further, that forty per cent. of these were repeaters (this is sufficiently large when the whole country is included, for outside of cities their number is much smaller), it will still leave 1,500,000 as the number of persons arrested each year for the first time. That is, one million and a half human beings are annually broken into what may be called a criminal experience.

If an average lifetime is thirty-three years, and the population should not increase, there will be, according to the above, in each generation, about 49,500,000 different human beings in this country arrested and subjected to a criminal experience.

NUMBER IN JAILS.

So much for arrests. It is impossible to tell how many persons are actually incarcerated in the police prisons, variously called station-houses, calabooses, etc.; but aside from these, there is a jail in nearly every county in the United States, making in all about 2,140. At the time of taking the census of 1880, there were actually confined in these jails 12,815 prisoners. The average length of confinement in jails is generally from thirty to forty days; so that, if the number of inmates is to remain the same, the above number must be renewed a little over ten times every year. This would make the total number of committals to the county jails in that year, 128,150. Allowing for increase of population, it would make the annual number now—(1883–4), 160,150.

If from the above, forty per cent. be deducted for repeaters, we shall have a result of 96,090, representing the number of persons that are annually put into jail for the first time.

NUMBER IN PENITENTIARIES OR STATE PRISONS.

In addition to the above, there are in the United States upward of fifty State prisons and work-houses generally called houses of correction, in which those

actually convicted are confined, and in which the prisoners are required to work, as the convict-labor system
has been introduced into, and now prevails in all the
State prisons and houses of correction in the United
States, except in Delaware. In the last State prisoners
do not work.

It should be explained that the so-called houses of
correction, or bridewells, are, in fact, miniature penitentiaries; the chief difference being that to the former are
committed those that are convicted of the minor offenses
and sentenced for a short term, as well as those that are
unable to pay a fine imposed by some police magistrate.
These houses are generally situated near large cities,
and frequently draw inmates from no other source.

According to the report of the Bureau of Labor
Statistics of Illinois, made to the legislature of that
State, about 50,000 convicts were confined in 1880 in the
various penitentiaries and houses of correction in the
United States in which prison labor was performed.
The average length of confinement in the penitentiaries
varies greatly from time to time, but is generally from
two and one-half to nearly four years, while in the houses
of correction it is generally from thirty to forty days. As
we do not know the precise average length of confinement in State prisons, we can not tell exactly how many
enter these institutions every year for the first time.

Allowance must here also be made for repeaters, who,
in some State prisons, make up twenty-five per cent.
of the inmates. But, after making all allowance, it
is apparent that the number of men — and a great
majority are young men—annually added to the misera-

ble throng, is very large; and if we multiply this number by the number of years constituting the average lifetime, we can form some idea of the number of victims which each generation contributes to this altar.

DEPENDENTS AFFECTED.

Pursuing the subject a little farther, we find we have only touched a small part of it. I will not here discuss the moral effect of arrest, imprisonment, etc., on the prisoner himself, but simply on those standing in close relationship to him, as father, mother, sister, brother, child, etc. The disgrace, the odium, the pain, reach out remorselessly to them, and to a greater or less extent they suffer on account of his fate. It is safe to say that there are, on an average, at least five persons that stand in this relation to every man who is wearing striped clothing and responding to a number in a State prison — to every one that is breathing the corroding air of the county jail, as well as to him who, for the first time, feels the ignominy of having rough hands laid on him and of being deprived of his liberty.

Multiply, now, the foregoing numbers by five, and then behold the multitude who are directly affected — who feel the shock, the quiver of every blow that is struck by our penal machinery.

Consider for a moment that for the 50,000 beings confined in the penitentiaries, there are at least 250,000 others that are suffering. Leave out the repeaters, if you like, as being past the pale of sympathy; take the annual 96,090 new cases of imprisonment in the county jails, and reflect that there are 480,450 others that are feeling the blow.   Then take the 1,500,000 persons arrested each year for the first time, and remember that there are annually 7,500,000 different human beings, and these of the poorer and weaker classes, who are shoved downward instead of being helped by our penal machinery.

CHAPTER II.

Again, look at the number of men employed by this system. There are the thousands of regular policemen in our cities — the thousands of special policemen — the thousands of so-called *detectives*, both public and private. Then there are in the neighborhood of 50,000 constables in this country, and about as many magistrates. Then there are nearly 2,200 sheriffs, and perhaps 10,000 deputy sheriffs. Then come grand juries — for most of the States still retain this system — meeting, on an average, three times a year, and composed, usually, of eighteen men each; then the petit juries for about 2,200 counties, meeting as often as the grand juries, and, including talesmen, composed of about the same number of men; then, lawyers for the State; next, judges for the trial, and appellate courts, clerks for these courts, keepers for police stations, keepers for about 2,200 jails, keepers for all the penitentiaries, to say nothing about witnesses for the State and defense. In all these you behold a vast multitude of men, numbering nearly a million, all forming a part of this machinery, many giving it all their time, some getting salaries and others relying on the fees they can collect from those arrested — actually getting their living, or trying to get it, out of the shortcomings and the transgressions of their fellow-men.

So much for a glance at the size of this machinery.

COST.

Turning for a moment from the size to the "cost of the thing," we find that the sums expended are more than any man can count. It is impossible to estimate the amount now actually invested in prison-buildings and equipments throughout the land. There are nearly fifty large penitentiaries supplied with work-shops, machinery, etc. Then there are nearly 2,200 jails, besides numerous police prisons. Perhaps $400,000,000 would be a low estimate of the cost of all these improvements. This is all dead capital. Nobody thinks of getting any return on it—even in those prisons that are said to be self-supporting, nobody thinks of paying interest on the investment. Placed at five per cent., the interest on this sum alone would be $20,000,000 per annum.

The above sinks into insignificance when compared with the yearly expenses. While a few of the penitentiaries have, for short intervals, been "self-supporting," the most of them must apply annually to the legislature for large appropriations. Then, the expense of keeping up the jails, the smaller prisons and the police force, may be called a dead loss.

In 1880 the average cost in Illinois of every prisoner in jail, including expense of arrest, etc., was about $27. Assuming this to be a fair average, it would make, on the present basis of population, a total yearly expense of $4,087,800, for jail prisoners.

For the year 1882, the expense of the police department of Chicago was a little over $800,000, making an average of about $24 for each of the 32,800 arrests. As the police department of Chicago is run as economically and the force is as effective and well-managed as any in the land, this is a low average, and yet if this sum were multiplied by the total arrests throughout the land, it would make $36,000,000 as the amount paid annually by the government simply for arrests; and to this amount most of the jail expenses—the costs of prosecution and of confinement in the larger prisons—must yet be added.

These sums are large; and yet they represent only a part of the expense. They approximate only the amounts paid directly in the shape of taxes; they do not include the large sums paid as costs by those convicted, nor do they include the large sums expended in various other ways in connection with our criminal procedure.

RESULTS.

Such is the size and the cost which a mere glance at our penal machinery reveals. *It is immense, it is costly, and its victims are counted by millions.* Surely one would suppose that in this country crime were repressed, that life and property were protected; and as the terrors of the law are scattered so profusely in the shape of numerous arrests, one would suppose that the hardened criminal were perfectly restrained, and the young deterred from the paths of crime.

But, strange to say, quite the opposite seems to be the case. The young are not deterred, nor are the vicious repressed. Revolting crimes are of most frequent occurrence in all parts of the land, and the feeling is spreading that from some cause our penal system does not protect society. In short, it does not seem to be a success.

It does not deter the young offender, and it seems not to reform nor to restrain the old offender.

This being so, one is naturally led to ask whether there is not something wrong with the system; whether it is not based on a mistaken principle; whether it is not a great mill which, in one way or another, supplies its own grist, a maelstrom which draws from the outside, and then keeps its victims moving in a circle until swallowed in the vortex.

For it seems, first, to make criminals out of many that are not naturally so; and, second, to render it difficult for those once convicted ever to be anything else than criminals; and, third, to fail to repress those that do not want to be anything but criminals.

CHAPTER III.

CRIME-PRODUCING CONDITIONS.

WHO ARE THOSE ARRESTED—OCCUPATIONS OF MALES—
OCCUPATIONS OF FEMALES — AGE — PARENTAGE —
HOME INFLUENCES—SCHOOL PRIVILEGES—HABITS, ETC.

Let us first see whence comes this multitude — from what strata of society is it drawn. Is it composed of the strong, the well-raised, well-trained, well-housed and well-fed class, and must it therefore be regarded as willfully criminal? or is it largely made up of the poor, the unfortunate, the squalid, and those that are the victims of their environment? We need not go far for an answer. Taking the report of the superintendent of the house of correction (bridewell) of Chicago, we find that of 7,566 persons imprisoned in that institution during the year 1882, all but 190 were incarcerated for non-payment of fines. That is, 7,376 had been fined for some small offense, and, being unable to pay the fine, had been sent to the house of correction to work it out. This shows that nearly all those there confined were of the very poor classes.

OCCUPATIONS OF MALES.

Glancing at the reports of their occupations, we find that 306 reported no occupations, 1,460 claimed to be common laborers, 214 sailors, 327 teamsters, 190 hostlers, 167 railroad employés, 96 waiters, 99 printers, 64

peddlers, 176 painters and glaziers, 111 shoemakers, 99
puddlers, 110 cooks, 77 firemen, 109 packers, 64 machin-
ists, 80 apprentices, 87 barbers, 61 blacksmiths, 150
carpenters, 149 butchers, 43 chair-makers, 44 cigar-
makers, 157 clerks, 48 brick-layers, 36 bar-tenders, 65
bootblacks, 23 boiler-makers, 59 farm-hands, 82 molders.

OCCUPATIONS OF FEMALES.

Of the 1,809 females committed to the same institution during the year mentioned, 359 were reported
prostitutes, 871 servants, 121 washwomen, 52 seam-
stresses, 26 scrubbers, 99 cooks, 24 dress-makers, 114
laundresses, etc., showing that the women likewise were
of the poorer classes, almost one-half being servants.

AGE.

Looking at their ages, we find they ran as follows:
eight years old, 1; nine years old, 5; ten years, 14; eleven
years, 25; twelve years, 47; thirteen years, 68; fourteen
years, 103; fifteen years, 95; sixteen years, 150; seven-
teen years, 185; eighteen years, 285; nineteen years, 231;
twenty years, 234; twenty-one years, 310; twenty-two
to twenty-five years, 1,184; twenty-six to thirty years,
1,343; thirty-one to thirty-five years, 960; thirty-six to
forty years, 978; forty-one to fifty years, 921; fifty-one
to sixty years, 358; sixty-one to seventy years, 74;
seventy-one to eighty years, 16; eighty-one to ninety
years, 9. Showing that 508 were under sixteen years of
age; 1,413 were under twenty-one; 2,907 were under
twenty-six, and 4,241 were under thirty years of age.

PERCENTAGE.

Again, *it appears from the same report that of the 7,566 incarcerated during said year, 3,460, or almost half, had no parents living; 1,105 had only mother living; 529 had only father living—making 5,094, or five-sevenths of all, whose home conditions were bad, while almost half of the whole number committed had no home at all.*

The same conditions are found in the larger prisons, as will be seen by examining the following table prepared by Fred. L. Thompson, chaplain of the Southern Illinois Penitentiary at Chester. It throws a flood of light on this subject.

TABLE SHOWING PRIME CAUSES OF CRIME, ON A BASIS OF FIVE HUNDRED MEN.

Home Influences.

Lost father at 5 years and under................................. 65

"   "   10 " " over 5........................... 20

"   "   15 " " over 10.................... 7

Lost mother at 5 years and under.................... 42

"   "   10 " " over 5.................... 29

"   "   15 " " over 10.................... 28

Lost both parents at 5 years and under............ 24

"   "   "   10 " " over 5 28

Never knew a home................................. 38

Left home at 10 years and under.................... 49

"   "   15 " " over 10....................167

"   "   18 " " " 15....................165

"   "   20 " " " 18.................... 47

"   "   21 " " upward................ 34

Without home influence at 18 years and under......419

School Privileges.

Never went to school...............................218
Went to school 2 years and less....................104
Went to school 5 years and over 2.................. 99
    "   "   10 "   "   "   5................. 79
Illiterate...153
Read and write very imperfectly...................189
    "   "   "   with higher attainments..........188
Learned to read and write in prison............... 32

Habits.

Frequented saloons................................406
Drunken habits....................................121
Drunk at time crime was committed............... 115
Gambled...246
Carried concealed weapons........................208

Age at First Penitentiary Crime.

20 years and under...............................150
25   "   "   over 20 140
30   "   "   "   25 90
40   "   "   "   30 70
50   "   "   "   40 24
60   "   "   "   50 21
70   "   "   "   60 5

In his report, accompanying this table, Mr. Thompsons says: "I have read every available thing on crime, its cause and cure; on prisons, their discipline, etc. I have talked freely with the convicts as to their early lives, their home influences, their early opportunities and their habits; and I have come to the conclusion that there are two prime causes of crime — *the want of proper home influence in childhood,* and *the lack of thorough, well-disciplined education in early life.* Of the first, there are at least five classes: Those who never knew a home; those who lost parents, one or both, while young; those who had vicious homes; those who ran away from home in the formative period of life; and those who were over-indulged in their homes. Of the second, there are those who never went to school; those who went but very little; and those who played truant, or were idle and refractory in school. The lack of this early influence and training at home, and of this discipline and learning at school, has left the individuals morally and mentally weak, the easy subjects of bad habits, vicious appetites, and designing men.

" These drift into the tide of bad associations, trashy, and then vicious, reading, to places of carnal amusements, to saloons, gaming houses, houses of ill-fame, to the society of the vulgar and criminal, to the committing of crimes—small at first, but bolder at last—and then into the penitentiary. The current of this steam is as traceable, and its sweep as powerful and merciless, as the channel of the Mississippi river. As the latter, un-molested, sweeps its drift into the Gulf of Mexico, so certainly the former sweeps its drift into the peniten-tiary or some other form of penal service, unless the strong arm of society is in some way put forth to the rescue. That you and others may see and feel this as I do, I have visited five hundred prisoners, taken in suc-cession, and put to them uniform questions, the answers to which I have carefully noted, tabulated, and present with this report. When you have studied this table, I am certain you will be convinced of the position I have taken as to the prime causes of crime. No one has a better opportunity to see the discipline of the prison, and study its effects upon the convicts, than the chaplain."

Looking a moment at Mr. Thompson's table, we see that *of the 500 convicts examined, 419, or upwards of four-fifths, were without home influence,* when at the age of 18 years, and under. This shows where the multitude comes from.

It also appears that *of the same five hundred, 218 never had attended school; and that only 188, or less than two-fifths, had what is usually called a good, fair education.* It also appears that more than half were under twenty-six years of age.

This showing is not exceptional to that penitentiary; on the contrary, these conditions are substantially the same in all the large prisons in the country. I have examined the reports of nearly all the large prisons in the United States, and find a remarkable similarity in them all, in so far as they treat of the question here under consideration.

The truth is, that the great multitudes annually arrested for the first time are of the poor, the unfortunate, the young and neglected; of those that are weak and, to a great extent, are the victims of unfavorable environments. In short, *our penal machinery seems to recruit its victims from among those that are fighting an unequal fight in the struggle for existence.*

The subject of *crime-producing conditions* has received but little attention in the past, and is only now beginning to be discussed. It has always been assumed, in our treatment of offenders, that all had the strength, regardless of prior training and surroundings, to go out into the world and do absolutely right if they wished, and that if any one did wrong it was because he chose to depart from good and to do evil. Only recently have we begun to recognize the fact that every man is to a great extent what his heredity and his early environment have made him, and that the law of cause and effect applies here as well as in nature.

CAN NOT SAY "NO."

Nor have we thus far sufficiently considered the fact that a large proportion of the human family can not say "no" at all times when they should. How common it is for people of education and character to do things which they know at the time to be injurious. Yet an influence which somehow they can not resist impels them, and they act, as it were, under protest—often doing things which at the very time fill them with dread.

This is true of many that have had excellent training, while among the less fortunate there are multitudes, with fair intelligence and industry, who want to do right, but who suddenly find themselves within the power of an evil influence, exerted by pretended friends, which they dread—which drags them down, often leads them, against their will, into crime, and from which, unaided, they can not free themselves. They are morally weak, not naturally bad. They are tools, not masters—mere instruments, not principals, and, so far as it concerns moral responsibility, might as well be inanimate and unconscious. Yet we treat them as if they were masters.

CHAPTER IV

REPEATERS.

In the Milwaukee House of Correction there were committed, during the year ending December 31, 1881, 1,420 prisoners; of these 58.52 per cent. were committed for the first time, while 41.48 per cent., or less than half, had been imprisoned before.

During the year 1882, there were committed in the Chicago House of Correction, or Bridewell, 7,566 prisoners; of these, 3.923, or a little over half, admitted that they had been imprisoned before.

These two institutions may be taken as showing the average of re-committals, in similar institutions, throughout the country, which may be set down as 50 per cent.; that is, one-half of all imprisoned admit that they have been in prison before.

But it must be remembered that all those imprisoned because of inability to pay a fine imposed by some police magistrate, as well as those convicted of the smaller offenses only, are sent to these institutions; hence the average of re-committals is much higher than in the other prisons.

For example, in the Illinois Penitentiary, at Joliet, there were committed, during the year ending September 30, 1882, 747 convicts. Of these, 121, or 16.20 per cent. admitted that they had been imprisoned in the penitentiary before. In some years the average is higher. It varies a little in all the penitentiaries, but in many it is

25 per cent.; and if we include the Southern States, where negroes are frequently re-committed for rather trivial offenses, it will average 30 per cent. No doubt a great many are re-committed without the knowledge of the prison officers, and consequently the number of re-committals really exceeds the above estimate.

Of the 121, mentioned above, 88 were committed for a second term, 29 for a third, 5 for a fourth, 3 for a fifth, and 1 for a sixth.

No doubt the average given above of 50 per cent. in houses of correction, and 30 per cent. for penitentiaries, would be much higher still, if it were not for the fact that the average life-time of the chronic criminal is short; exposure and misery carry him to an early grave.

But this average is much higher than it should be. The idea that one-half of the several millions annually arrested must go on and become chronic criminals, has about it something appalling. And when we consider that it is from this throng that the majority of the desperate and vicious criminals come, the question again suggests itself whether there is not something the matter with the system; whether the system is not responsible for a part of this result; whether, in fact, the system we now have, instead of being reformatory and preventive, is not, in reality, debasing and productive.

Having taken a general survey of its size, cost and results, and having seen who are its victims, let us consider its operations a little further, especially so far as the effect on the young, on the innocent, and on the first offenders is concerned. And for this purpose it is important that we have at least some general ideas as to the character of the average police prisons or lock-ups.

CHAPTER V.

Lock-Ups.

Of these, Wines, in his great work on prisons, says:

"There is another class of prisons, little known or thought of, but very numerous and often extremely crowded, namely, the city prison—station houses, or lock-ups, as they are variously called. They almost need a John Howard for their sole reformation. * * * It would seem, at first thought, to be a matter of slight importance, where arrested persons are put for a single night or day, or how treated, or under what circumstances of discomfort kept. It is urged, 'Make the place intolerable and they will keep out of it!' If they would, the case would be different, and there would be less to say. If crime were more effectually prevented by cruel treatment of the criminal, that would be some excuse for it. But all experience proves the contrary. *Brutal treatment brutalizes the wrong-doer and prepares him for worse offenses.* * * * In studying what character to give to a lock-up, we must consider that among the occupants there will always be a number who are there for the first time and the first offense. They have been caught in bad company, or been guilty of some disorder, or found sleeping out of doors, having no in-doors where to sleep; or accused by the blunder of a policeman, or held on groundless suspicion.

"Just at that point not a few of these take their first

step in a downward course. Probably not less than
ten per cent. of all confined nightly in this class of
prisons are there for the first and trifling offense, or for
no punishable offense at all; and the aggregate number
every night shut up in them, throughout the entire
country, can hardly be less than from ten to fifteen
thousand. Think of it! Not less than a thousand
every night in the year locked up for the first time for a
small offense, or for no offense. Not a few of them
children—boys and girls under fifteen years of age,
whose chief fault is that they have never known a
parent's love, never enjoyed the blessings of a home,
never felt the warm presence of Christian care and
kindness. Truly, human justice is a clumsy machine,
and often deserves the punishment which it inflicts."

Dr. Eliot, of St. Louis, contributed, in 1876, a paper
to the New York *Prison Congress*, in which he describes
one of these lock-ups in St. Louis, in which each cell is
twelve feet long by eight feet wide and ten feet high,
with no windows and no ventilation, all the light and
air being admitted through grated doors opening into a
passage. The usual nightly average of occupants to
each cell is four or five, on Sunday nights often going
up to eight or ten. Dr. Eliot says:

" What school-houses of crime are these ! The city's
public schools of vice and profligacy, open for men,
women, and children, every day in the year, with a dou-
bly accumulated crowd for the Lord's day! Go through
the lock-ups of any large city on Sunday night, and you
will see where no small part of the primary instruction
in crime—yes, and advanced instruction, too—is given,
and who the learners are."

I can not add anything to the above, and if any one doubts the correctness of the picture, I simply say to him : Go and see for yourself, and be convinced; and bear in mind that the above condition is not an exception, for these stations, or lock-ups, are very much alike all over the country.   (See *Jails and Remedy.*)

CHAPTER VI.

COUNTY JAILS.

Mr. Chas. E. Felton, the Superintendent of the Chicago House of Correction, who has had a wide experience in prison management, has written the following concerning County Jails:

" If there is a school for teaching vice and crime, it is the ordinary county jail, in which prisoners are herded in cells, and are allowed to congregate in the halls, without the least discrimination being made as to cause of detention, habits of life, physical condition, or previous moral character. This fact as to jails comes from what would be called heredity, if applied to the peculiarities in human character; but as touching jail construction and management, it would be as a resultant of common habit. From the earliest days down to the present time, jails have been constructed without a seeming thought being given to any other end than that of safety from escape of their inmates; and in their management, with few exceptions, there seems to have been but one additional thought, and that was, 'How can the most money be made through the care of their inmates?' Now that is about the status of the jail question to-day. That our jails are nurseries of vice and crime is a recognized fact—one which jail officials seldom, if ever, deny; and in writing thus of them, it is not the intention to point toward any one in particular of the more than twenty-five hundred in this country; nor to exclude but few as being different from the others."

That eminent authority upon prison and reformatory work, Rev. Fred H. Wines, lately said of the jail system:

"It is a system of the association of the clean with the unclean; of the old and the young; of the innocent and the guilty; and, in some jails, of men and women, because men and women are not separated in some jails. In a jail in this State, I have known men and women to have the liberty of the entire jail, without any interference on the part of the jailers. I suppose they were locked up at night; but they were together all the day. Then, again, the jail is a place of absolute idleness. No work is provided for the inmates. In the third place, it is a system in which the State ignores its own responsibility, and throws the men for whom it is responsible into the hands of incompetent county boards. If there is an iniquity in this land to-day, it is the county jail system. I do not know of any greater iniquity perpetrated to-day in the world than the jail system of the United States. It originated in the primitive days of society; and there is no reason for its continuance, except that the people have not awakened to its enormity. There is no reason for it in law, morals or public policy; there is no reason for it, unless, as I have heard suggested, it is kept up, as it is in some cases, I suppose, by the sheriffs, who receive fees for looking after the prisoners, and get an allowance for dieting them, and they are not willing to give up their perquisites."

So much for their character. *As to the remedy:*

The most experienced managers and reformers now agree that none should be confined in county jails except prisoners that are awaiting trial and are charged with offenses of a character so grave as to require confinement before conviction. And these should not be permitted to congregate together, but be kept in separate cells —well-lighted, but so arranged that one prisoner can not see any other—so that those that may be discharged can not contract any contamination while in jail, the prisoner being permitted to converse only with the keeper and with such visitors as may be admitted.

I am informed by Gen. Brinkerhoff, of Mansfield, Ohio, that several jails have been built and are managed on this plan in that State, and the result is found to be so satisfactory, both to keepers and to the better class of prisoners, that the general adoption of the system is most earnestly advocated by all who are familiar with its workings.

I will add that all that can be said in favor of such a plan for a county jail, applies with greater force to lock-ups.

CHAPTER VII.

EFFECTS OF IMPRISONMENT—ARRESTS A MATTER OF PRIDE —PRISON PRINCIPLES — ALL TREATED ALIKE—NO GOOD RESULTS.

What effect do arrest and imprisonment have on those arrested, more particularly on the young?

When we consider the great number annually arrested and imprisoned, and when we realize that of all these a large majority are under twenty-six years of age, that a very large proportion of them are under twenty years of age, and that in some instances one-fifth of them are females; and, still further, that almost all are of the poor—of the class that needs encouragement more than almost anything else—then does the effect of arrest and imprisonment become a most important question.   However great an improvement it may be on the past (and nobody disputes that it is) still it is not a success.

Turning now again to the report of the Chief of Police of Chicago, we find that of the 32,800 arrested, 10,743 were discharged by the police magistrates, to say nothing of those that were bound over to the grand jury and then discharged.   So that during the one year there were in that one city upwards of 10,000 young persons, who, without having committed any crime, were yet condemned to undergo a regular criminal experience.   Think of this a moment.   And if so many in one city, what a multitude must there be throughout the land!

Mind, these were not even offenders. But what was the
treatment which they received? Why, precisely the
same as if they had been criminals. They were arrested,
some of them clubbed, some of them handcuffed,
marched through the streets in charge of officers,
treated gruffly, jostled around. At the police station
the name and a complete description of the person of
each were written on the prison records, there to
remain. Some of the unhappy creatures were bailed
out, while the remainder were shoved into cells and
forced to spend a night, and sometimes a week, there,
forced to stand around with criminals, before they were
discharged. Now, what effect will this treatment have
on them? Will not every one of them feel the indignity
to which he or she was subjected, while life lasts? Will
they all not abhor the men who perpetrated what is felt
to be an outrage? Will they not look on this whole
machinery as their enemy and take a secret delight in
seeing it thwarted? Will they not almost unconsciously
sympathize with those that defy this whole system, and
are they not thus suddenly brought a whole length
nearer crime than they were before? And will not those
that were already weak, and were having a hard struggle
for existence, be farther weakened, and therefore more
liable soon to become actual offenders than they otherwise would have been? Remember, *brutal treatment
brutalizes* and thus prepares for crime.

ARRESTS A MATTER OF PRIDE.

At present, to make numerous arrests is a matter of
pride with many policemen In fact, in many places

their efficiency, their standing as peace officers, actually depends on and is determined by the *number of arrests* they make. And the chiefs of police in many villages, in preparing their reports, take great pride in being able to report a large number of arrests. There often exists even a rivalry in this respect between different police-men on the same squad, each being anxious to get the credit of "running in" some poor wretch. I recently heard a policeman boast of his magnanimity toward a brother officer, whom he allowed to make four different arrests and thus get his standing improved, when the speaker could just as well have made them himself.

Now this is wrong. It begets the wrong kind of efficiency. It encourages unnecessary arrests.

In the enforcement of the law, every unnecessary indignity inflicted, whether by word or act, especially in the case of first offenders, only makes matters worse. The person having to submit to it is thereby made the enemy of the officers and of the law.

In reality, the police and other officers of the law should be protectors and friends of the poor and the weak, and these should naturally fly to the former, as a child to a parent, for assistance and protection. But almost the opposite of this is too often the case. It is the poor and the weak who are afraid of the officers, and avoid them whenever possible. This is not as is should be. The trouble is that too many officers (there are noble exceptions) like to assert their authority when there is no necessity for doing so. They are too anxious to act the master, when they should act rather as friends and assistants. As an illustration, take the following case, reported in the daily papers among the proceedings of the police courts:

OFFICER ———'S ASSAILANT.

"Officer M. D. ———, charged with assault and battery by Addie M———, took a change of venue when his case came up before Justice Prindeville yesterday, and went before Justice Hammer. The evidence was not materially different, from the facts as published the day after the issuance of the warrants by Justice Prindeville, January 3.

" Addie M——— and Rosa L——— were arrested the day before, charged with disorderly conduct, and were discharged January 3d, by Justice Prindeville, on payment of costs. When they stepped outside the court room, Officer ——— tried to arrest Addie M——— for an attempted assault with a deadly weapon on him when he had Rosa L——— under arrest the day before, though he had not known anything about the assault until he was told of it afterward by Officer S———, who took a pocket-knife from Addie M———'s hand. Justice Hammer said he thought it a little singular that a man should have to be told about an assault on himself, and said the arrest at the court-room door, without a warrant, was unauthorized under the circumstances, and fined him $3, the lowest fine for this offense.

"There are some facts in regard to Officer———, and his fight against this woman, which were not brought out in evidence. A few nights ago he arrested her on a charge of disorderly conduct, but, as nothing was proved against her, she was discharged by Justice Prindeville.

Having gained the animosity of this officer, she will have a lively time, for the whole police force is now arrayed against her. A police official said yesterday that she would leave the South Side if she knew what was good for her."

One would think that such an incident as the above would cause the immediate discharge of the police officer concerned; but nothing of the kind is even dreamed of—on the contrary, so trifling is the matter regarded, that the smallest fine possible is inflicted.

Think a moment about this condition of things. Even if it were true that the woman was not of good repute—though nothing of the kind was proven—would her case not be sad enough already? Ought she not, at least, to be let alone until she actually commits an offense? What possible good can result from having a brutal police officer seize her whenever he gets sight of her, and forcibly drag her off to the lock-up and make her spend the night there, for no other reason than that the police officer *thinks* she is not a chaste woman? I repeat, suppose she was disreputable, what possible good can come of such treatment? Is it not alone sufficient to ruin her, even if she were an angel at the beginning? If this were an isolated case, it might not deserve much attention; but it is simply a specimen of what is happening every day in every large city in this country.

Again, every year hundreds of persons, generally boys, are "run in" by the police, simply because they have been found sleeping in sheds, stables and other like places, and have been unable to give a satisfactory account of themselves. When their case is called by the police magistrate, they are charged with being vagrants, or with being disorderly; a fine is imposed, which they, of course, are not able to pay, and then they are sent to the Bridewell to work out their fines. Here they remain from ten days to six months.

See how tenderly we care for the homeless. If a boy who has nowhere to go, when nature is exhausted, ventures to lie down in a shed, we seize him with the strong arm of the law, as if he had committed a murder, and forthwith send him to prison. Now, what effect does all this have? The sentences are short, for, as the unfortunate beings were not charged with anything in particular, the sentence could not well be long. They are imprisoned "for the fun of it," as it were, "just to keep them out of mischief, you know." But what will they do when they get out? Why, nothing is left then but to do the same thing and make the same prison rounds. Would it not be madness even to imagine that any good could come of this? Experience has shown over and over that just the opposite follows; that this process produces exactly those results which society is anxious to prevent.

As early as 1822, the Hon. Hugh Maxwell, District Attorney of New York, speaking of this class of cases, said :

."None of these have actually been charged with crime, or indicted and arraigned for trial. It includes those only who are taken up as vagrants, who can give no satisfactory account of themselves; children who profess to have no homes, or whose parents had turned them out of doors and taken no care of them; beggars

and other persons discovered in situations which imply
the intention of stealing, and numbers who were sleeping in the streets or stables.   These miserable objects
are brought to the police office under suspicious circumstances, and, according to the result of their examina-
tions, they are sentenced as before mentioned.   Many
of these are young people, on whom the charge of crime
can not be fastened, and whose only fault is that they
have no one on earth to take care of them, and that they
are incapable of providing for themselves.   Hundreds,
it is believed, thus circumstanced, eventually have re-
course to petty thefts, and commit the misdemeanors in
order to save themselves from the pinching assaults of
cold and hunger.   That many of these might be saved
from continued transgression, no one can doubt who
will examine the records of the police office.   Many
notorious thieves, now infesting the city, were, at first,
idle, vagrant boys, imprisoned for a short period to keep
them from mischief; a second and third imprisonment
is inflicted, the prison becomes familiar and agreeable,
and at the expiration of their sentences they come out
accomplished in iniquity."

Since Maxwell wrote the above, more than sixty
years have confirmed his observations and shown that
the above treatment defeats its purpose and produces
not only the repeaters for our prisons, but the thieves
and dangerous criminals we so much dread.   Is it not
time to try something else?   The Inspectors of the Penitentiary for the Eastern District of Pennsylvania, in
their report for 1881, say on this head:

"Yearly the crime-cause of youths is developing;

yearly the temptations to crime are increasing; yearly it is more and more apparent that the state has utterly neglected provision for a large number of minors who are moving in the direction of crime, because there is no adequate prevention presented. Congregating youth in a place of detention, more of a prison than a refuge— for loss of liberty by compulsion, and detention by force, is all that a prison pretends to be—is too often making criminals of some who else might be restored to good conduct and made useful citizens. It is congregation under such circumstances that produces the mischief. Congregating, associating youth, deprived of their freedom, as a penalty for some offense of omission or commission, is but training them by such associations for no higher aim in after life. *The stigma—the fact of a* quasi *prison graduation—does not tend to lift up the man out of the degradation of such youthful associations.*"

THE PRISON PRINCIPLE.

The Superintendent of the Michigan State Reform School, in his report for 1880, says:

"The prison principle is hateful to the adult delinquent; to the youthful offender it is abhorrent. The prison principle in reform peculiarly outrages the nature of child life; the shock penetrates his being, and body and soul rise up against it in fiercest antagonism. * * * To the boy, the bolted door, the barred window, the walled yard, and other contrivances of brute force, are enemies that he will resist with all the force of his nature, though he is apparently rendered helpless against them. I believe that these barriers against the cravings of his child nature, instead of tending to his reform, have rather a contrary effect, and will hastily develop any criminal germs which may exist in his nature. The question does not naturally occur to him, 'How shall I reform through these agencies?' but rather, 'How may I escape from them?' and to the solution of this question his best energies are devoted. * * * It frequently causes expressions of surprise to see children of such tender age and innocent appearance brought to our institution, and the question, 'What could he have done?' is asked very often; and yet it is of common occurrence for a powerful officer to present himself at our office, having in his custody a frail lad who has scarcely seen ten summers, bound with handcuffs to prevent him from escaping or from making an assault on his brave custodian."

What is here said about the effect of the prison principle on a boy, applies with equal force to the adult who is not yet inured to crime.

ALL TREATED ALIKE.

At present, so far as personal treatment is concerned, all offenders are treated precisely alike, with the one exception of the length of sentence imposed at the time of conviction. And even herein strange things are done. But, as already stated, the personal treatment is the same in all cases. The man entirely innocent, as well as the boy arrested for some trifling offense, is treated from first to last like the midnight burglar, the highway robber, or the chronic criminal. Arrested on the street, and not infrequently clubbed, often handcuffed, and led in irons to the police station, he is there pushed into a cell as if he were a dumb brute. He spends a night with the vicious of every kind. In the morning the police magistrate goes, as a matter of business—and, if it were a matter of conscience, he could not, under existing laws, do much better—to the station to dispatch the ten to forty cases that have been put on his docket since the previous morning, and, being anxious to get away, he performs his task in the shortest order possible. The cases are called, one after another, in rapid succession, as if they represented so many bundles of merchandise to be shipped, and, as each is called, the police officer, who has made the arrest, makes his statement; the prisoner may say something if he wishes, and this is generally all there is of the trial. In this proceeding, the boy mentioned fares precisely like the old offender with a heinous crime. He takes his position on the sawdust in the bull-pen till his case is called, and, if discharged, goes free (and it appears that in 1882 over 10,000 were discharged in one city by the police magistrates alone, showing that nearly one-third of all those arrested were wrongfully arrested). If not discharged, and the charge be one which the grand jury must consider, he is bound over, and, failing to give bond, is sent to jail. There he is weighed and measured, the color of his hair and eyes is set down—in short, a complete description is taken of him. Then he is hustled off among a number of other prisoners, the iron door is shut behind him, and he stays there for weeks—sometimes for many months—before his case is reached. Then, perhaps the grand jury refuses to find an indictment (for nearly one-fourth of those bound over are not indicted), and in this case he is discharged. Should he be indicted, he is arraigned and sent back to jail. In the course of weeks, sometimes months, his case is tried If then acquitted by a jury, he goes free; if not, he is sentenced to a further period in jail, or is sent to the house of correction, where he is set to work among several hundred prisoners, some of whom are of the most abandoned sort. Having served out his sentence, he is set free. If, however, the offense for which he was arrested is one for which the police magistrate can impose a fine, then, instead of being sent to jail and going the round mentioned above, he is fined; and, having no money to pay, is put, with a great many others, into an omnibus, or "Black Maria," with iron bars at windows and door, and is then driven to the house of correction—a short term penitentiary—to serve out his fine. Of course, if he has friends who will bail him out, or pay his fine, he will escape a part of the imprisonment.

In the meantime, the vicious and hardened criminal, arrested for burglary, for highway robbery, or for some other equally heinous crime, is treated precisely like the boy whose case we have been considering, except that when taken from the jail he is taken to the penitentiary and is sentenced for a longer term of imprisonment.

NO GOOD RESULTS.

Now, does anybody suppose that a boy or a man, either innocent or guilty of only a trifling offense, will be benefited by this kind of treatment? *Does clubbing a man reform him? Does brutal treatment elevate his thoughts? Does handcuffing fill him with good resolves?* Stop right here, and for a moment imagine yourself forced to submit to being handcuffed, and see what kind of feelings will be aroused in you. Submission to that one act of degradation prepares many a young man for a career of crime. It destroys the self-respect of others and makes them the easy victims of vice. Even the morally strong will look back with hatred to the day on which they were subjected to outrage, and, down deep in their souls, they will hate the system, and the men who wronged them.

Every man is sensitive about the treatment of his person, and feels that he is injured when he is rudely jostled about, or forced into humiliating surroundings. Is it, then, reasonable to suppose that the remainder of the treatment above-mentioned—the thrusting into a cell with old criminals, the standing in the so-called bull-pen, or prisoner's dock—will not injure those that are innocent, or that it can possibly have any reformatory influence upon the young man, who, although he has violated some law, is not yet depraved, has not yet lost his self-respect, and is yet desirous of living an honorable life? Nay, if he has any ambition at all, will it not have just the opposite influence? Will he not wish to be avenged? Will he not consider this whole machinery as his foe, and will he not be more ready than ever before to commit crime, if he can but escape detection? I claim, therefore, that imprisonment for trifling offenses before convictions, except in extreme cases, is wrong in principle, and works a great injury not only to those imprisoned, but to society itself.

To save the weak and neglected from becoming criminals, the all-important thing is to develop and to build up their self-respect—their manhood and womanhood. So long as this is wanting, their natural course is downward; and any act that tends to crush this only pushes them lower down.

In October, 1870, there was held at Cincinnati, Ohio, a National Prison Reform Convention. It met in pursuance of a call signed by a large proportion of the governors of the States and upwards of one hundred persons eminent in the cause of prison reform. The convention was composed of several hundred members from all parts of the Union, and was presided over by the Governor of Ohio. Being largely made up of persons familiar with the practical management of prisons, and deeply interested in the subject of prison reform, its proceedings were distinguished for marked ability. It continued in session six days and did a great amount of work. As a result of its deliberations, it formulated and adopted, with almost entire unanimity, a declaration of principles, thirty-seven in number, of which the *sixth* is so apposite to the point now under consideration that I give a part of it here:

"*Sixth. It is essential to a reformatory prison treatment that the self-respect of the prisoner should be cultivated to the utmost extent, and that every effort be made to give back to him his manhood. Hence all disciplinary punishment that inflicts unnecessary pain or humiliation should be abolished as of evil influence. * * * There is no greater mistake in the whole compass of penal discipline than its studied imposition of degradation as a part of punishment. Such imposition destroys* *every better impulse and aspiration; it crushes the weak, irritates the strong, and indisposes all to submission and reform. It is trampling where we ought to raise, and is, therefore, as unchristian in principle as it is unwise in policy."*

If the imposition of degradation has, on actual convicts, the effect described above, what effect must it have on the innocent, and on the thousands who are daily dragged into our police prisons not even charged with a crime, but simply with being *disorderly?* Incredible as it may seem, we now daily take thousands who are not criminals and subject them to almost every kind of degradation—do what we can to crush the weak and to irritate the strong—do what we can to destroy the self-respect of all and send them from bad to worse; and when they finally land in the penitentiary, then we discover that in order to restore them to society we must undo everything we have done.

CHAPTER VIII.

TREATMENT IN HIGHER PRISONS—CRUELTY NEVER EF-
FECTED A CONVERSION—THE WONDER IS THAT ANY
SURVIVE.

Recently there have been some revolts in several
penitentiaries, and precisely those in which, according to
report, the greatest cruelty is practiced—notably in one
of the penitentiaries of New York, in that of Missouri,
and in that of Arkansas. In the last State, the convicts
are leased and the lessees manage the institution as a
close corporation, refusing to give anybody any information in regard to the condition of the convicts.

Concerning this prison, Mr. Wines, in his great work
on Prisons, at page 200, says:

"The lease system of prison labor in Arkansas has been
weighed in the balance by a joint legislative committee,
and clearly found wanting by the evidence as well as by
seven of the sixteen members of the committee. The
evidence, as is commonly the case in such inquiries, was
not a little contradictory; but to my conception the
following points were established: That the prisoners
were not properly nourished, being fed mostly on beef
and corn bread, with vegetables occasionally, but not
commonly—the beef being so poor, so devoid of nutri-
tive qualities, and so indigestible, that its introduction
into the human stomach proves an irritant which gen-
erates the larger part of the diseases, such as diarrhœa,
dropsy, etc., known in the institution. That the prison-

ers are overworked, the hours of labor being usually more than twelve per day, and those who work on a farm five miles from the penitentiary being often forced to walk or trot rapidly, especially in returning after work, thereby inducing over-heat, hæmorrhages, heart disease, and other forms of sickness. That shocking cruelties are practiced upon the prisoners to get work out of them, as well as to maintain discipline, so that many bear marks of violence upon their persons for months after its infliction. That the hospital is unfit for its purpose, being extremely filthy and noisome; sheets and pillow-cases often dirty or wholly wanting; food unsuited to the needs of such persons, proper stimulants deficient and hard to get—the whole being more likely to intensify and even generate disease than to serve as an agent in its cure. And that, to sum up all in a word, the penitentiary is turned into a speculative establishment, in which the convicts are the stock in trade of the lessee, in the prosecution of whose business they are so many mechanical contrivances, to be used for the accumulation of wealth, and operated with little regard to the fact that they are children of the same Father, or even that they are, blood and tissue, vitalized and controlled by the same physiological laws of waste and repair common to all mankind."

On the other hand, in those institutions which have been managed most successfully, where the best results have been achieved, equally in maintaining discipline, in making the prison self-sustaining and in reforming the prisoner, kindness has been the most conspicuous factor in the treatment. Quoting again from Mr. Wines:

"Cruel treatment was once generally esteemed the most sure, just, and only fitting method of penal discipline. But the period is well passed when the interior of a prison is to be the arena for the exercise of brutalizing forces upon erring and wicked men. The thought and action of the present have emerged from the dark shadows of the last century. Surely, all means of penal control which are severally restrictive of the mental, moral and physical good of the convicted criminal, and manifestly tyrannical, simply because an opportunity is afforded or created, do not conserve the high purpose of calm, helpful justice. The government which works out the best results for its subject secures therefrom something more than a machine-like obedience. Submission to rules, and the concurrence in an enforced task, which are not beyond reason, can be secured in the vast majority of cases, in well regulated prisons, by means which are at hand and which are far removed from cruelty. In so doing, the prisoner's self-control is evoked, and habits of industry acquired, which can never be brought about by the crushing process so much lauded by conceited and inexperienced prison reformers."

On this point, the inspectors of the Maine penitentiary say:

"For many years the discipline of the prison has not been as strict as at many other prisons; it has not degraded the prisoners below the brute creation, but has recognized them as men, and taught them to believe that the State had an interest in them beyond their term of imprisonment. For this reason I believe that a large

majority of them have left the prison without bitter
and revengeful feelings, and with a determination to
live better and more useful lives. To this state of affairs
is largely attributable the fact that there is very much
less of crime in Maine, in proportion to its population,
than in any other State."

CRUELTY NEVER EFFECTED A CONVERSION.

In the entire history of the human race there is not a
single instance in which cruelty effected a genuine reformation. It can crush, but it can not improve. It can
restrain, but, as soon as the restraint is removed, the
subject is worse than before. The human mind is so
constituted that it must be led toward the good, and
can be *driven* only in one direction, and that is toward
ruin.

Florian J. Ries, inspector of the House of Correction
of Milwaukee, in the management of which he achieved
a signal success, says, in his report for 1880:

"The subject of reforming convicts is one that ought
to be entitled to the very first consideration in the management of a prison. The idea that a prison is solely an
institution for the *punishment* of violators of the law, is
fast becoming obsolete, and one more humane and in
keeping with our advanced civilization is taking its
place. Experience has taught, and humanity demands,
that the discipline of a prison be directed more toward
the moral improvement of its inmates than to punishment or to torture." And in his report for 1881, he says:
"As to the management of prisoners, I have very little
to add to my report of last year; *my experience has fully
convinced me that by kind treatment and by appealing to the better instincts of human nature, better results can be obtained*

than in any other way." (The italics are mine) He then adds: "Yet all that may be accomplished with the prisoner in this manner, inside the prison, will be of little avail after he is discharged, unless he finds friends who are willing to lend him a helping hand, and encourage him in his effort to lead a better life." But this only demonstrates the necessity of letting him earn something for himself before discharge, so that he can maintain himself, as explained under the head of Prison Labor.

THE WONDER IS THAT ANY SURVIVE.

The real wonder is, not that so large a percentage of those once arrested and imprisoned become hardened and inured to crime, but that comparatively so few do. The wonder is that any are able to outlive and overcome the effects of their degrading experience; and the fact that over half of them do so, shows that human nature is not so depraved. For all these live respectable lives, not by reason of, but *in spite of*, their experience. As the American Colonies prospered in spite of, and not by reason of, the protection Great Britain had given them — the protection having been wholly of a kind that tended to impoverish the Colonies — so the large percentage of men once arrested, who do well, do so in spite of, and not by reason of, their hated experience.

The principle and love of right, the longing to be respectable and to live honorable lives, was so strong in them that it overcame the degrading influences to which they had been subjected. Herein lies one of the objections to our present system. It applies the *crushing process* to those that are already down, while the crafty criminal — especially if he be rich — is gently dealt with.

CHAPTER IX.

Punishment Must Be, First, Necessary; and, Secondly, Calculated to Produce the Desired Result
—Examples Under the Present System.

Society never has claimed, and does not now claim,
the right to punish for an infraction of the moral law.
The right to chastise for an act which has been a violation of the eternal principles of right and justice, has
always been, and still is, conceded to be, the exclusive
prerogative of the Almighty. Society never claimed
more than the right to punish for a violation of its laws;
and this right has always been, and still is, based on the
benefit to be done to the whole.

The fundamental principle upon which man assumes
the right to punish his fellow man, is, that society as a
whole may be protected. It is, therefore, clear that the
imposing of any punishment that is *not necessary for the
protection of society* is unwarranted and wrong; is absolutely indefensible upon any ground whatever; is nothing less than a deliberate injury, done by the strong to
the weak, and is, therefore, in the highest degree, cow-
ardly; and no man can participate in such an act without becoming morally accountable for the injury thus
done to another.

Secondly, it is also clear that any penalty thus imposed, *which does not tend to protect society*, must be indefensible, and, like the other, a wrong inflicted by the
strong upon the weak, for which there can be no excuse.

True, society has to learn by experiment, and it therefore may be excused for some things done in the hope that they will result in protecting the whole. But whenever experience shows that certain things do not answer the purpose for which they were intended, then the right to continue them ceases. That is, whenever it becomes apparent that certain acts done for purposes of punishment do not serve the purposes for which they were intended—*i. e.*, do not tend to protect society—then the right to continue or to repeat them ceases, and any further repetition of them will be simply a wrong done by society to one of its members, an injury inflicted by the strong upon the weak; and it is no excuse to say that the member had first injured society, for one wrong never justifies another. If society has been injured, it may punish the offender in order to prevent a repetition of the offense, either on his part or on the part of others; but it must prescribe a punishment or treatment that will be likely to produce this result, and it has no right whatever to do an act which it has found does not serve this purpose. As an example under the first head, take the case of a cigar-maker in a small, country town, who is arrested by a United States marshal, taken seventy or eighty miles for an examination before a United States commissioner, then bound over to the grand jury, and, being unable to give bail, is put into prison for from one to six months, until that body meets. Then he is indicted and kept in jail some time longer until he can be tried, and when tried he is convicted, is fined from ten to one hundred dollars— and all this not because he is really a vicious man, not because he is a dangerous man, not because he had stolen something or injured somebody, but simply because he had failed to put a dollar revenue-stamp on a small box of cigars which he had manufactured and sold. He may be an industrious, sober man, struggling to the best of his ability to make his family respectable and comfortable. But all this counts for nothing. Some United States detective has been prying into the little shop; a technical violation of the revenue law has been discovered; there is a chance for the detective to win some credit for alertness, and for the United States marshal, United States commissioner, and prosecuting attorney, to make some fees. So the man is arrested, dragged away from his family, who are frequently left without any means of support in the meantime, and is treated precisely as if he had committed a murder or a highway robbery. Could anything possibly be more absurd?

Granting that the law had been violated, and that it was proper to inflict some punishment when the man was convicted, will anybody claim that it was necessary to arrest him and to keep him in jail a long time before he was convicted?—and if it was not *necessary*, then it was not justifiable. As the offense was trivial, and the danger of escape therefore slight, he should not have been deprived of his liberty until convicted. For, mark you, wealthy offenders are never thus dealt with. They are always able to give bail; so that it is only the poor who are thus made to suffer. Cases of similar wrongs are of much more frequent occurrence under the State and municipal laws. Almost daily there are arrests on trivial charges, where, in case of conviction, the punishment generally is only a fine, and therefore there is no danger of escape; yet, as the persons arrested are not able to give bond for their appearance, there is no alternative but to send them to jail, there to remain for weeks, frequently for months, before they can be tried. And when tried, if convicted, they are simply fined, or possibly have a short jail sentence imposed. Now, in nearly all these cases, it is *unnecessary* to make arrests in the first instance, as a civil proceeding would answer every purpose until the trial; then, if the fine is not paid, it is early enough to introduce the jail. Arrests, in the first instance, in this class of cases being *unnecessary*, they are, as above shown, unjustifiable, and are productive of much harm without any compensating good.

Again, things are daily done in the name of punishment which common sense condemns, which all experience has shown to be productive of just the opposite results from those designed and desired, and which society has, therefore, no right to continue doing. Thus, of the 7,566 prisoners committed to the House of Correction at Chicago, during 1882, 4,787 were simply charged with breach of the peace. Granting that some of these had committed grave offenses and the charge was changed, still could anything be more unreasonable than every year to subject over 4,000 human beings to a regular criminal treatment, as heretofore described, simply because they had been guilty of hilarious or disorderly conduct?

CHAPTER X.

Imprisoning Women.

It appears from the report of the Superintendent of Police of Chicago, that in 1882, *6,835 women were arrested and taken to the police prisons in Chicago, and that, during that year, 1,800 women were incarcerated in the Chicago House of Correction, mostly for non-payment of fines, which had been imposed. Of the latter number, 359 were reported prostitutes, 871 were servants, 114 were launders, and all were poor. Now, can any good come of thus treating unfortunate women? What are they to do when released? Can anybody tell? The 359, whom the officers call prostitutes, and think that a sufficient accusation to excuse any kind of treatment, were not the petted children of sin, not those that live in gilded palaces and dress in silks and satins, for these are rarely disturbed; they were the poor, unfortunate and forlorn creatures who, without friends, without sympathy, without money, often hungry, and without sufficient clothing to protect them from the cold winds, wander out on the streets, not so much wantonly as from necessity, literally trying to sell their souls for a morsel of bread, dealing in shame, not from choice, but because every Christian door is shut against them, because there is no place where they can work and find shelter. Now, in what condition are they when they

* The number has been increasing every year with the number of arrests.

have gone through the above experience? What are they to do when again set at liberty? Experience has answered this a hundred times. They return to their old ways, because there is nothing else that they can do; the only difference being that they have become more degraded, more brutalized, by the treatment which they have received, and from which no good ever has or ever can come. Is it, therefore, reasonable to continue it?

Take the other 1,450 women who in 1882 were incarcerated in the Chicago House of Correction; what is to become of them when released? What can they do? For what has the prison fitted them? Some of them, no doubt, have homes to which they can go; but they will enter these more degraded because of the experience they have had, and instead of being better prepared to resist temptations than formerly, they are weaker and more liable to go downward than otherwise. As to the remainder—those that have no homes where they can be received and taken care of—what are they to do? Where will they be admitted? How can they make an honest living? There is no answer to these questions, and the probability is that the great majority will be literally driven to get their bread by the wages of sin, and go down the path of vice and misery, dragging out an existence that will long for death. Now, wherein has society been benefited or protected by the above treatment? Clearly, in no way. On the contrary, it has done to itself an injury, and to the wretched beings, who were charged only with slight offenses, a great wrong.

It is both *unnecessary* and *unsuitable*.

In the reports of the proceedings in the city police courts, as published in the daily papers, you can see, almost every day, items like the following:

"The seventy vagrant and disreputable women corraled in the basement pen of the Desplaines Street Police Station, Wednesday night, were brought before Justice C. J. White yesterday in a lump. Sin-hardened, sad, poor and unhappy, the haggard crew presented a sickening sight. Most of them escaped with light fines, the justice recognizing that these wrecks of human beings deserved merciful consideration."

"Bridget Smith, a poor woman whose path through this world has led her through several terms in the Bridewell, was found drunk, in the snow, Sunday night, at the corner of Desplaines and Adams streets. For this mistaken idea of getting enjoyment out of life, Justice C. J. White sentenced her to another short term in the said institution and a $10 fine."

And at another time the following:

"There seems to have been a general raid by the West Side police on the disreputable women found on the streets. At all events, twenty of the poor creatures were before Justice White yesterday, and fourteen were arraigned in Justice Woodman's court. They were mostly a dissipated, worn-looking lot, most of them shabbily dressed, but three of them were young and rosy, and one was a mere child, hardly fifteen years of age. Fines ranging from $1 to $5 were inflicted, and the poor, misguided mortals passed out of court."

Reflect on this a moment! Was it necessary to drag in these unfortunate creatures every few weeks and cor--

ral them like cattle? And wherein has society been benefited by the whole proceeding? What object was there in all this? Certainly none can be perceived, except to make a large amount of fees for the police justices. Several dollars cost, in each case in which the fine is paid, extracted from these miserable people, may be satisfactory to the police justice, but what is to become of the women? One of the accounts says, "they passed out of court." Of course they did, but where? Where did they go? Whither? Why, a great many of them to the Bridewell, because they did not have $3 or $5 in the world, nor any friend to pay the amount for them. And when they get out of the Bridewell, what are they to do? Is there any other course open than to make the same round? Mind you, they were not the gay and luxurious sirens, for these, though numerous, were not disturbed.

Now, if it were even conceded that some measures were necessary in the matter, it certainly can not be claimed that the proceedings given above were necessary, much less that society is benefited by them. This being so, where is the justification for these proceedings?

Take the woman found drunk in the snow. She is sent to prison time after time—simply to lie down again in the snow. The very frequency of the sentences shows that they only aggravate the case, and serve no good purpose; then, why continue repeating them?

Take the following item from the police court proceedings:

"The officers of the Humane Society brought William

Hogan, his wife and four children into Justice R——'s court yesterday for disposition. They had been existing in a hovel at the corner of Stave street and Armitage avenue, in the most squalid poverty and destitution. There was no food or fuel in the place, and little or no bedding. The family were in rags, were dirty, and were all covered with vermin. Their condition, as they appeared in the court-room, was at once disgusting and pitiable. Mr. and Mrs. Hogan were sent to the Bridewell, and the children, aged five, seven, nine and eleven years, were sent to the Home for the Friendless."

Think of a system that will send a woman to a penitentiary simply because she is the mother of four small children and has a husband who either can not or will not support her! As to the husband, if he was unable to do anything, he should not have been sent to the Bridewell; and, if able, then he should be required to earn something for his family. We have already too long kept up the practice of crowding our prisons with those that ought not to be there, and, as a consequence, we find that prisons no longer have any terrors for those that should be there.

CHAPTER XI.

THE PRESENT INDISCRIMINATE FINING LEADS TO NO GOOD RESULTS.

If any person wants an accurate idea of the manner in which this system is carried on, let him attend one of our so-called police courts on some morning when from ten to thirty miserable beings, many filthy and squalid, are "trotted through." The charges are usually of the minor sort—"drunk," "disorderly," etc. Generally a fine of from five to one hundred dollars is imposed; and what then? Well, if the unfortunate creatures can not pay it they are packed into the omnibus and taken to the house of correction, as already mentioned, and there they "*work it out*," as heretofore explained, the time required for this purpose being from ten days to six months; and when they get out, the conditions in which they lived before having in no way improved, on the contrary, generally having become worse, they almost immediately make the same rounds again, and then again, getting a little worse every time until they land in the penitentiary.

But in many cases the fine is paid, often even after commitment to the house of correction; and of course the prisoner is discharged.

But who generally pays this fine? Here is the vital question. Usually the prisoner does not pay it, for as a rule he has nothing but the rags on his back. Well, then who pays it? Why, generally his squalid family. The wife pawns whatever she may have left in order to get her husband out; or more often it is the mother who already is unable properly to feed and clothe her smaller children, and who is suffering from the ailments, both physical and mental, that a life of poverty and misfortune entails, but who will yet, by heroic effort, scrape together enough pennies to pay her child's fine and get him out. Well, the fine being paid, then what? Why, the conditions being all the same, the companionship the same, there having been nothing reformatory or elevating in the experience through which the offender has gone, he is in no wise better, is no more industrious, no more sober; and, instead of being morally stronger and better able to overcome the weakness that got him into trouble, his prison experience has, if anything, lowered him; he is less able now to cope with the world than he was before, and the almost invariable result is that he goes the same round time after time, becoming constantly more vicious, and in the end swells the number of hardened criminals. Take the hundreds of poor women fined in the police courts; if they themselves pay their fines, it takes usually their last penny, and not infrequently the very money with which they pay the fine is the earnings of shame. *So that while the law with one hand prohibits vice, it pockets the earnings of vice with the other.*

Now every time a fine is paid in any of the cases mentioned, the crime-producing conditions have been aggravated; the want existing before has been intensified; the offender has not been benefited, while his family has been injured. Fines should therefore be imposed only in exceptional cases, where nothing of a reformatory character is required.

CHAPTER XII.

FORMALITY—INEQUALITY OF SENTENCES.

The present system is *formal, iron-bound and superficial;* every case has to go through the same steps, no matter how much the circumstances may differ; the proceedings must be the same, no matter how trifling the charge; the accused must be *arrested,* must then either *give bond* or be *locked up* until he can be tried and the fact be ascertained whether he is even guilty of the trifling offense charged or not, and, if found guilty, then no matter what the condition of the accused may be, whether old or young, vicious or merely weak, male or female, there is but one course open, and this for all alike; that is, to impose a fine, and, if this is not paid, to send the accused to the jail or to the Bridewell. The magistrate is not to blame; it is the law, the system, which is at fault.

If the State were to enforce a system of medical practice, and were to provide that but one prescription should be given for all the ills that afflict the flesh, it would not be more absurd than is the present system of treating offenders.

INEQUALITY OF SENTENCES.

In the Fifth Biennial Report of the Michigan State Board of Corrections and Charities, 1879–80, the subject of " Inequality of Sentences " is thus considered:

"Having still in view our analogy between crime and mental disease, which analogy we do not claim to be one that is perfect and holding at all points, yet holding sufficiently to justify what we have said and what we shall say, we shall conclude this paper by a few moments' commentary upon the sentences of the courts.

"We can stay but for a single example of the inequality of sentences, growing out of qualifying circumstances and the inability of judges to see things alike, or, as in the case of the one referred to, form opinions even for themselves.

"Assault with intent to commit murder, *intention* being the gauge of crime, necessarily implies the *guilt* of murder.

"In Michigan, during the year ending September 30, 1877, there were eight convicts sent to the State prison for assault with intent to commit murder—one for forty-five years, one for twenty-five years, one for fifteen years, one for nine years, one for six years, one for five years, one for two years and one for one year.

"It is supposable that these eight men, so sentenced for the same technical offense, may have been seen in prison working in the same department, eating at the same table, listening to the same prayers in the chapel, with occasional opportunities for surreptitious exchange of notes as to their respective allotments of justice and their progress in reformation—reformation being agreed upon, in all such conferences as this, as one of the chief ends, if not the chief end, of punishment.

"This inequality of sentences runs through all the courts. Cases like this (an actual case) occur somewhere in the United States every month in the year. At the same term of the court a bank teller, for a theft of $500 from his employers or from a customer, is released on nominal or suspended sentence, while a boy of seventeen is sentenced to prison for three years for stealing a second-hand suit of clothes worth less than $20; producing in appearance distortions of justice a little like Lord Dundreary's distortion of proverbs when he says, 'one man is hanged for looking a gift horse in the mouth, while another may see the whole animal over a hedge and get clear.'

"The damage to society of a given offense can be approximately estimated; the guilt of the transaction is beyond man's power of measurement.

"Then why not better to cut the Gordian knot and proceed for the good of society; estimate the offense according to its damage and danger to society, and at once remove the offender, not for one, two, ten, or forty-five years, but until he is apparently restored to such condition, whether mental or moral, or both, as will give the public reasonable assurance of safety?

"If there were high courts or commissions in lunacy, and they were to commit eight maniacs who had attempted murder, from one State, in a single year, to an insane hospital for terms varying from one to forty-five years, it would at once be apparent to all that the high court itself was wildly insane. If, on the contrary, the would-be murderers were sent to a hospital until wholly restored to reason, the conduct would appear to be reasonable.

"But, if the criminals are put under restraint by a

similar seclusion in buildings suitable for the purpose, that is, in prisons properly provided and graded, it may be asked: How shall it be ascertained with certainty when they are so far reformed as to make their enlargement safe to society?

"The answer is, that we can not know with certainty, but it can be known at least equally well in this case as in the cases of insanity. Some insane patients are discharged apparently cured, three, five or ten times, but are found still dangerous to society, and have to be returned to the hospitals, and ultimately die without recovery. There will be mistakes, incident to imperfect human knowledge.

"Criminals sentenced for limited terms are discharged and re-committed over and over again, with this difference against the good sense of the proceeding, that there is, in the majority of cases, no appearance of reformation, but, on the contrary, perfect knowledge on the part of the authorities that they are turned out more and more dangerous to society at each successive time."

The following table, taken from the Report of the Commissioners of the Illinois Penitentiary at Joliet, for the year ending September 30, 1882, shows what incredible difference there is in the length of sentences imposed for the same offense in the State of Illinois:

Comparative Table of Sentences and Crimes, showing their relative connection with the number of convicts in the Illinois State Penitentiary, September 30, 1882.

CRIMES.	One year.	Between one and two years.	Two years and fractions.	Three years and fractions.	Four years and fractions.	Five years and fractions.	Six, 7, 8 and 9 years and fractions.	Ten years and fractions.	Eleven to fourteen years & fractions.	Fifteen to twenty years inclusive.	Over twenty years and less than life.	Life.	Total on hand.
Abduction....................			1			1							2
Arson	1		2			1	3	2					9
Assault, etc................	2												2
Assault to commit burglary....			1			1							2
Assault to commit felony...						1	1						2
Assault to commit larceny......	1			1									2
Assault to do bodily injury.....			1	1									2
Assault to kill................	5		4	2	1	6	7	2					27
Assault to murder............	2	2	6	4	3	6	4	6	2	1			36
Assault to rape......		1	3	1	1	2	7	1	3				19
Assault to rob.............			3	2		1							6
Attempt to procure abortion....			1	1									2
Being found in postoffice with intent to steal................				2									2
Bigamy................	2		1										3
Buggery....................						1							1
Burglary....................	73	16	87	49	19	33	33	10	4	11			335
Burglary and larceny..........	42	5	45	39	16	22	15	5	2	2			193
Burglary and larceny and arson.			1	1				1	1	1			5
Burglary and larceny and assault to kill......................										2	1		3
Burglary and larceny as bailee..			1										1
Burglary, murder & assault to kill										1			1
Burglary with intent to steal.....				1									1
Confidence game..............		1	3	4	3	2		2					15
Conspiracy....................			3	4									7
Conspiracy and larceny........				1									1
Conspiracy to commit offense...				1									1
Counterfeiting				2		1	1	1		1			6
Crime against nature..........				1									1
Cruelty to children............	1												1
Embezzlement................	1		1			1		1					4
False affidavit to procure money				1									1

CRIMES.	One year.	Between one and two years.	Two years and fractions.	Three years and fractions.	Four years and fractions.	Five years and fractions.	Six, 7, 8 and 9 years and fractions.	Ten years and fractions.	Eleven to fourteen years & fractions.	Fifteen to twenty years inclusive.	Over twenty years and less than life.	Life.	Total on hand.
Felony..............						3	5						8
Forgery..............	13		7	10	2	4	3		2	2			41
Forgery and larceny. ...													2
Grand larceny	6	1	8	8	4	3	1	1		1			35
Grand larceny & burglary										1			1
Having in possession burglars' tools					1	1							2
Horse stealing..........						3	5	5	1	1		1	16
Incest.................							2	2	2	1			7
Larceny	82	10	64	75	13	31	23	10	3				311
Larceny & confid'ce game						1							1
Larceny & Embezzlement				1									1
Larceny from postoffice .				1									1
Larceny and receiving stolen property........						1							1
Larceny and robbery....		1								1			2
Making and uttering fictitious notes..........	1	1	2			1							5
Malicious mischief	1		1	2	1								5
Manslaughter	1	2	2	2	1	8	4	4	1			2	27
Mayhem.................	1								1		1		3
Murder						2	4	5	26	31	20	52	140
Obstructing railroad ...	1												1
Obtaining money by false pretenses	1												1
Passing U. S. cont'fit coin						2							2
Perjury		1	1	3			1						6
Personating another	1		1										2
Rape.				3		1		5		2	2	2	15
Rape and assault to rape										1			1
Receiving stolen property				1	2		1						44
Robbery..............	11	7	12	15	15	11	16	10	5		2		10
Robbery and burglary ..							1	2					3
Robbery and larceny.....			3						1	1	2		7
Sodomy						1							1
Total...............	249	48	265	239	85	155	138	70	56	59	29	56	1,449

A glance at this table shows that sentences imposed for the same offense range all the way from one to twenty years. Of course, allowance must be made for the fact that some of the crimes were committed under more atrocious circumstances than others of the same class; still, the great diversity, after all, is due to the fact that the different cases are tried before different juries and different judges. For it not infrequently happens that in the same court a man who has deliberately committed a crime under circumstances showing great depravity, will be sentenced for a much shorter term than another who has committed the same offense under circumstances showing far less depravity. So that, practically, we have the same law sentencing the hardened offender to a short term, and the less dangerous to a long term for the same offense. Now, if fixed sentences were entirely abolished and indeterminate sentences (to be presently discussed) were substitued, this would not happen so frequently.

CHAPTER XIII.

REMEDY.

I am aware that it is difficult for one man to see all sides of a complicated question, and that all new remedies are apt to prove crude and more or less impracticable when attempted to be applied—for the perfect remedy is the outgrowth of experiment. Still, every improvement must have a beginning, crude though it be; therefore, I venture to give my views freely, and leave it to those who have examined and considered the subject more thoroughly to suggest something better.

In discussing a remedy, it is important to keep in mind the exact difficulties to be remedied, or that are capable of being remedied, which in the present case are:

1st. That many are imprisoned, before trial and after, and broken into the prison life and brought into contact with the criminal atmosphere, and thus started on the downward road, who ought not to have been imprisoned at all, and who, had they been differently treated, might have made good citizens.

2d. That the pole star of the present system seems to be *punishment*, whereas the protection of society should be its sole object, and as punishment never made a sincere convert, and as the multitude of first offenders comes from the weaker class, they should be treated rather as *wards*, whom it may be necessary to confine, but whom it is yet necessary to train and educate, if possible, into good citizens.

3d. That at present our prisons do not, as a rule, reform the prisoners, but turn them loose, at the expiration of sentence, in a condition which soon returns a great per cent. of them to prison.

4th. That the really vicious and dangerous criminals are treated like the good-intentioned, but weak, are not, at the beginning, convicted with promptness; are discharged after short terms of imprisonment when they ought not to be, and that in a condition which almost precludes their doing anything but committing crime.

Keeping the foregoing in mind, I would suggest:

First. The abolishing of the fee system, so that no petty officials will be directly interested in having arrests made for the sake of earning a few dollars of money; the State should pay all officials a salary for discharging their duties.

The Maryland Legislature, by acts passed in 1880 and 1882, substantially abolished the *fee system* in criminal cases, so far as it related to proceedings before magistrates in the city of Baltimore, and the result was a falling off in the number of arrests in that city from upwards of twelve thousand to about seven thousand, or almost half, in one year.

Second. Arrest and imprisonment before conviction should be permitted by law *only* in those instances where it is shown that the offender is a dangerous person, or that the offense with which he is charged is of a character so heinous as to require his arrest and incarceration, or the placing under bonds until he can be tried.

This would reduce the incredibly large number of improper arrests by police and other officers. As heretofore shown, of the 32,800 persons arrested by the police of Chicago in 1882, over 10,000 were discharged because they were not shown to have been guilty of any offense whatever. It would also prevent imprisonment for trifling offenses, as is now the practice. Thus, of the 7,566 committed to the Chicago House of Correction in 1882, 4,787 were simply charged with a breach of the peace, 1,171 with drunkenness, 673 with vagrancy, 169 with being inmates of disorderly houses, 222 with the violation of miscellaneous city ordinances, and 354 with violating village ordinances. The remainder of the 7,566 were charged with the following offenses: Robbery, 12; burglary, 29; horse stealing, 1; assault with intent to kill, 21; assault with intent to do bodily injury, 3; conspiracy, 1; rescuing prisoners, 1; obtaining goods under false pretenses, 1; passing counterfeit bank notes, 4; vagabondage, 4; larceny, 113. So that it will be seen that out of a total of 7,566 committed, only 190 were charged with crimes; and of these 190, the large number of 113 was charged with larceny, or petty theft, whether the thing stolen was worth fifty cents or ten dollars.

But the great majority were not criminals, and society would have been better off if it had not arrested and incarcerated them.

Deducting the 190 charged with offenses that are considered criminal, it leaves 7,376 that should have been differently dealt with. No blame is attached to the officers, for they simply carried out existing laws. But these laws should be changed. There is no doubt that in very many cases of drunkenness and of disorderly conduct, if the parties were taken directly to their homes by the officers, and nothing further done for the first offense except a memorandum of the fact made by the officers for future reference in case of a repetition, it would have a better effect than arrest and incarceration. And where proceedings are had, there she 'd, except in extreme cases, be no arrest until the trial is ended and a sentence is imposed. This treatment of first offenders would have all the benefit that can be got from a scare or the terror of the law, and none of the degrading and hardening effects that produce stolidity and hatred. I refer more particularly to the young and to those charged for the first time with any offense. Hardened cases would, under the plan about to be discussed, soon be weeded out and be situated where it wa , at least, possible for them to reform.

In this connection, the city should be divided into small police districts, with a competent man in each, who should acquaint himself with the condition of every offender, and use his best efforts to induce him to quit bad associations, and who should also find out the homeless and try to have them cared for. This would be a great preventive of the small offenses which are the initiatives of criminal careers. Every one knows how valuable is a little timely encouragement. This system of a public agent to look after all cases of first arrests for minor offenses has been tried for a number of years in Massachusetts, with most satisfactory results. A gentleman who once filled the position of agent, and is now

at the head of one of the excellent reformatory institutions of that State, recently stated that they had found
it necessary actually to imprison only a little over one-
fourth of those who fell into the hands of the police. In
most cases they procured better homes for the young
offenders, and found that they did well thereafter.
In Baltimore, as I am informed, the same plan has been
tried on a smaller scale, but with most gratifying results.
The present neglect is productive of crime. In those
cases that prove incorrigible, and in which something
must be done, and it becomes necessary to try a party
for the commission of further offenses of a light character, the suit should, except in extreme cases, be begun by
civil process. Then, this man should either directly assist
the magistrate by sitting with him, or at least should
testify to the result of his efforts in the case, giving fully
the character, habits, surroundings, history and associations of the accused, and also show whether, from all the
information obtainable, there is a reasonable prospect of
the offender's yet reforming and living an industrious,
orderly life, if the sentence were suspended. And if the
magistrate is of opinion that there is yet a reasonable
prospect of reformation, sentence should be suspended
and the offender let go, with the understanding that he
is, to a certain extent, under the supervision of the superintendent of the district, and that he can at any time be
taken into custody.

BUT FEW WOMEN WOULD BE IMPRISONED.—It is safe
to say that under such a regulation very few women
would ever have to be incarcerated, and the present diabolical practice of annually arresting thousands of friend-

less and helpless creatures for trivial offenses—in many
cases for no offense at all—and locking them up like so
many cattle in cells, and then fining them and sending
them to the Bridewell, would cease.

If, however, the magistrate is of opinion that from
all the information obtainable, there is no prospect of
reformation, then the offender should be sentenced *generally* to the House of Correction, not for a few days or
for a few months, as is now the practice, from which
no good comes, nor can come, but simply to the
House of Correction, the maximum time of confinement there to be fixed by law, and to be not less than
several years, but the actual time of confinement to be
determined in each case by the conduct of the offender,
as hereafter explained.

The House of Correction should be conducted with
some modifications upon the principle obtaining in the
Reformatory at Elmira, N. Y.   This institution, as a
reformatory, appears to be far in advance of any institution of the kind in this country, and to be productive
of the most gratifying results.   The principle upon
which it is conducted, and upon which offenders are
confined there, is, in brief, this: The prisoner enters for
no definite time, except that the maximum time is fixed
by law, and that he must stay at least one year.   And
while treated with firmness, he is yet treated kindly,
and an effort is made to develop his self-respect; he is
given to understand that it is largely for his own good
that he is confined, and that the length of confinement
will depend on himself; that as soon as he shows that
he is able to govern himself, and that he can safely be

trusted to make an honest living and live an orderly life, he will not only be given his liberty, but an effort will be made to find him employment. Then, as a part of his prison duties, every prisoner must attend a school conducted within the prison-walls, and take a regular course of instruction, while, at the same time, he is required to do a given amount of work every day; thus, in fact, a great many acquire there a good education, and a preparation for the duties of life which they never would have got elsewhere. The conduct and development of the prisoner are watched from day to day, and when the board of inspectors, who at the same time are put in possession of all the facts relating to the previous history and condition of the prisoner, are of opinion that he can maintain himself against his evil propensities or surroundings, they secure him employment, and send him out, as it were, on a probationary parole, they continuing, for at least six months, to look after him, by corresponding with his employer and otherwise. Should he do well during his probationary period, he is dropped; if not, then the inspectors have the power to take him again into custody. So different is the treatment of prisoners in this institution from that in the ordinary prison, that such a thing as an attempt to escape is almost unknown, although the prisoners are trusted to an extent which could not be even thought of in other institutions. And in several instances where probationers were unlucky in losing their jobs, and were not able to get other work, rather than commit crimes, they came back and voluntarily entered the prison until another job was secured, when they again went out and got along well.

In connection with such a system as this, the prisoner should be not only permitted, but required, to earn something for himself while in prison, over and above the actual expense of keeping him, as will be more fully explained in discussing Prison Labor.

Under this system none would be subjected to the prison influences except those whose character, vicious inclination, or confirmed habits rendered their restraint necessary for the best interests of society; and this number would be reduced to a minimum; and these being the vicious, could be held in restraint until it was thought safe to liberate them, or until the maximum time fixed by law expired.

Thirdly. As to the lighter offenses that are yet classed with crime, such as petty thefts, etc., the treatment, instead of being alike in all cases, as at present, should be varied to meet each particular case; instead of being bound over to the grand jury, as now, they should be tried at once by magistrate and jury. The treatment described under the last head should, to a great extent, be followed. The superintendent should investigate the previous character, habits, condition, and associations of the offender, and the magistrate or jury should determine, in each case, first, whether the accused is guilty of the offense charged, and, secondly, the magistrate should determine whether sentence should be suspended as discussed above.

There is no doubt that offenses of the character now under consideration are often committed by parties who are not criminals, and who, if properly treated, would never again be guilty of any offense, the simple detection alone being sufficient for all purposes of reform, while additional prison treatment would only harden and debase.

Fourthly. As to those guilty of the graver offenses, and all those cases that show a deliberate criminal intent, they should be tried at once, directly upon information of the prosecuting attorney, or upon warrant sworn out by private parties, instead of being sent by the circuitous grand jury route as now. And on the trial all that can be learned about the previous condition, character, habits, etc., of the prisoner should be shown, not simply by his friends, but by the prosecution, the jury to determine whether the prisoner is guilty of the offense charged, but nothing more. In fixing sentence, the prisoner, if young and the offense is his first, should be sentenced generally to the House of Correction. If not, or if he has shown strong criminal propensities, he should be sent to the penitentiary under an indeterminate sentence; the maximum as well as the minimum time of confinement being fixed by law. There he should be not only permitted, but required, to earn something to be carried to his credit before being again discharged, as will be explained hereafter; so that when again set free he will not be in a condition in which he can scarcely do anything except beg, starve or steal.

NOTE.—The law of Massachusetts, just referred to, provides for the appointment of probation officers, who shall examine the conditions of every person arrested, and, if they think best, endeavor to save him from imprisonment. This law has produced results so astonishing that I here give its most important features, and also a summary of the results of the first ten years' experience under it in and about Boston. Having provided for the appointment of probation officers—one in each district—and for the manner in which notice shall be given them of every arrest, among other things, it says:

SECTION 75. Such probation officer shall carefully inquire into the character and offense of every person arrested for crime in his city or town, for the purpose of ascertaining whether the accused may reasonably be expected to reform without punishment, and shall keep a full record of the results of his investigations.

SECTION 76. Such probation officer, if satisfied, upon investigation, that the best interests of the public and of the accused would be subserved by placing him upon probation, shall recommend the same to the court trying the case, and the court may permit the accused to be placed upon probation, upon such terms as it may deem best, having regard to his reformation. [When probation is recommended by the officer, the prisoner is practically released on his own bond.]

SECTION 78. He shall attend the sessions of the courts held within said county for criminal business, investigate the cases of persons accused or convicted of crimes and misdemeanors, and recommend to the courts the placing on probation of such persons as may reasonably be expected to reform without punishment. He shall have a place in the office of the superintendent of police. When he deems it advisable for any person placed on probation to be sent out of the State at the expense of the city, the city council may make the necessary appropriation for the purpose, to be expended by him, under the direction of the superintendent of police, and he shall render an account of such expenditures, with the items, quarterly, to said superintendent. He shall, also, as far as practicable, visit the offenders placed on probation by the court, at his suggestion, and render such assistance and encouragement as will tend to prevent their again offending. Any person placed upon probation, upon his recommendation, may be re-arrested by him, upon approval of the superintendent of police, without further warrant, and again brought before the court; and the court may thereupon proceed to sentence, or may make any other lawful disposition of the case.

The law was passed in 1878, and on January 1, 1889, Mr. Edward H. Savage, probation officer for the central district of Boston, made a report of his work for the year 1888, showing that during the year there had been referred to him 1,056 cases in his district, which were disposed of as follows:

Done well and were dismissed.................. 473
Sent to their country homes.................... 329
Sent to charity homes........................ 138
Sailors sent to sea........................... 49
Died before term of probation expired.......... 3
Did not improve and were surrendered for sen-
    tence...................................... 52
Ran away..................................... 12

Total................. 1,056

Of these, 880 would have been imprisoned, except for the provisions of this law, and the minimum time of imprisonment in all these cases put together would have amounted to 2,334 months, or nearly 200 years, which was practically saved to both the persons arrested and to society, for, had the accused been imprisoned, they would probably not have earned anything for themselves or for society. Besides, there was saved to the public $22,978 in prison expenses.

The offenses charged ranged from forgery to vagrancy. Under the head of work done by agent, appears the following:

Visits to homes of persons on probation......... 1,061
Visits at office by persons on probation.......... 1,467
Reports from persons sent to country homes...... 337
Reports from persons sent to private charity homes 208
Investigations for persons charged with crime.... 3,673
Places of employment secured for persons on pro-
    bation.................................... 64
Temperance pledges taken by persons on proba-
    tion...................................... 557

Investigations on applications for release from prison.................................... 53

(In reference to the last item, it should be stated that this law provides that persons already imprisoned, may, under certain conditions, be released.) A summary of the ten years' experience is also given as follows:

	1879	1880	1881	1882	1883	1884	1885	1886	1887	1888
Whole number taken on probation..	430	376	418	549	788	846	797	852	827	1056
Did well and were discharged	375	335	377	489	718	757	742	790	784	992
Proved incorrigible	55	41	41	60	70	89	55	62	43	64

The report also shows that, had there been no probation, all those that were saved must have been sentenced and imprisoned, and their sentences during the ten years, when put together, would have amounted to 1,715 years and ten months, or an average of 171 years and seven months of time each year, all this having been saved to the accused and their families, as well as to society; for in prison their time would have been substantially a dead loss, while the extra prison expense to the public during the ten years would have been $210,856. But all this sinks into insignificance when compared with the loss which would have followed when the imprisonment was over. For in most cases the discharged convict would have been unable to make a living; in fact, he would have been a ruined man or boy, who would never do much for himself or for society, but in many cases would be almost forced into a criminal career to prey upon society.

I have thus far given only the results in one probation district, but the results in other districts in and about Boston were of the same gratifying character. Mr. George N. Parker, the officer for the South Boston district, summarizes his report as follows: "About 93 per cent. of the persons placed under my care have done well and have been discharged. On account of their poverty all would have had to go to prison had they been sentenced on the day of trial. But, as probation was intervened, many of them have since lived good, orderly lives; have been a blessing to their families; have kept their homes from being broken up and their children sent to charitable institutions. So that the workings of probation have in many cases been twofold, viz.: Reformed the parents and saved the children."

In his report for 1889, Mr. Savage says: "In the 1,125 cases disposed of during the year, 1,065, or 94 per cent., were accredited with doing well, while 60, or less than 6 per cent., proved incorrigible. * * * Of the 315 persons sent home, a majority were strangers in the city—had been convicted of some minor offense and were without means. They were sent home to save them from prison. Among them were 49 young women convicted the first time, and were sent to parents or relatives to save them not only from prison, but a probable life of infamy. * * * Probation, by securing opportunity for hundreds of unfortunate specimens of human frailty, who show an honest desire to reform; by restoring to destitute and suffering families those on whom they were dependent for the necessaries of life, and by aiding to stay the increase of the criminal classes—ren-

ders a service that outweighs any pecuniary consideration."

Mr. Wm. F. Reed, probation officer for the Roxbury
district, closes his report for the year 1888 as follows:
"*Probation has saved many of both sexes from exposure,
shame and loss of situation, in cases where they had committed
their first offense, and not only saved them for the time being,
but for all times.*"   I will simply add to the above that I
am informed that boys and young women have almost
entirely disappeared from the prisons of Massachusetts.

THE METHOD OF PROCEDURE is simply to continue a
case for three months, and then to continue it again as
often as may be deemed necessary.   If the accused does
well, he is finally discharged.   If he does not do well, he
can be sentenced at any time.

FEW RUN AWAY.—It is a most remarkable circum-
stance that so few run away.   Thus, out of 1,056 placed
on probation in one district in one year, only 12 ran
away, and, on the whole, the average of runaways is
scarcely one and one-half per cent.

CHAPTER XIV.

INDETERMINATE SENTENCES.

The idea of having the maximum length of confinement fixed by law, and then sentencing offenders *generally* and letting their actual confinement be determined by certain conditions, though comparatively new, is meeting with general approval by men who have given this subject much thought. W. D. Patterson, superintendent of the Cleveland House of Correction, in his report for the year 1881, says on this point:

"It is worse than folly to attempt or expect the reformation of such old-time chronic offenders as frequent our police courts every week or every month when they are out of confinement, by the infliction of such penalties as an imprisonment of five, ten or thirty days, or by the imposition of a fine and costs. The object sought to be accomplished by such a course, however good the intention of the law, or however correct the motives of those whose duty it is to enforce the same, must end in an expensive failure, and the offenders continue in their degradation and debauchery and bestial inebriety, notwithstanding the law and the courts and the prison. Instead, as now, let them be committed as children are to the House of Refuge, or as prisoners are now committed to the New York State Reformatory at Elmira, until their reformation is accomplished. An imprisonment in such cases as the above would not only be wise and beneficial to the offenders, but would be of especial advantage to the community financially."

In the report of the committee on prisons, made in 1881, to the Legislature of California, with some reflection on prison discipline and management, the question of "indeterminate sentences" is thus discussed:

"By indeterminate sentences is meant that all persons in a State who are convicted of crimes or offenses before a competent court, shall be deemed wards of the State, and shall be committed to a Board of Guardians, until, in their judgment, they may be returned to society with ordinary safety, and in accord with their own highest welfare. If this principle be adopted, the confinement of a prisoner will depend upon his own exertions to earn promotion and eventual freedom. The duration of confinement is placed under the control, and is determined by the conduct, of the convict himself. The advantages of an indeterminate sentence are:

"1. It supplants the law of force by the law of love.

"2. It secures certainty of restraint and continued treatment, which operate to prevent crime, as severity does not.

"3. It makes possible the arrest and right training of that whole brood of beginners, before great depravity is reached, and character is irretrievably fixed.

"4. It utilizes for reformatory ends the motive that is always the strongest—the desire to be released, the love of liberty.

"5. It removes the occasion, and so mollifies the feeling of animosity usually felt toward the law and its officers, puts the personal interest of the prisoner plainly in obedience to the rules of discipline, and leads him to co-operate with those laboring for his welfare."

Again, under the head of "classifications," the report continues:

"It is self-evident that the young offender should be disassociated from the old criminal; that the person who has committed the first offense, perhaps venial, should be separated from the hardened villain; that the comparatively innocent should not be associated with the pronounced guilty. The real classification is one based on character, conduct and merit, as shown in the daily routine of prison life."

In the report of the special commission of the State of Connecticut on contract convict labor, with accompanying papers, 1880, the Reformatory at Elmira, N. Y., is thus commented upon:

"There are several peculiarities about this prison, which, so far as your committee is aware, are not found at any other in this country, and which tend largely to its success. It is strictly a reformatory, and as such is graded into three classes. No prisoner is received over thirty years of age, and all only for the first offense. Special laws have been enacted, all of which are in the interest of reform, and to enable the proposers of this experiment to give the plan a full and fair trial. The prisoners are not sentenced to a definite fixed period, but for a maximum term. Upon entering the prison they are received into the second grade, from which they are promoted to the first for good conduct, or degraded into the third for bad. * * * As a reformatory, the prison, so far, is a success. All the power of hope, love, ambition, pride and shame is brought to bear upon each individual; every possibility of a speedy liberation and success in the future is held up to the prisoner—of places of respect and honor in society and confidence in business, if by well-doing they deserve respect and confidence; or shame, poverty and a prison, if, by a return to criminal practices, they again forfeit their right to liberty. Such treatment can have but one result. Whenever, in the opinion of the superintendent and board of managers, a prisoner has shown, by long-continued good conduct, that he is fit to be trusted with liberty, he is given a leave of absence, during which time he must keep the superintendent informed of his whereabouts, and of his condition and prospects, until, after a time of trial, having proved his reformation by his conduct, he is given a full discharge. Out of twenty-four liberated on parole, twenty-two earned their discharge by showing their fitness for liberty—one was returned to prison to serve out the full length of his sentence, and one left the country. The same motives which induced these prisoners to strive for the highest grade, also induce them to do the most and best work."

The following extract is taken from the message of Governor Hoyt to the General Assembly of Pennsylvania, January 4, 1881:

" What can be done for the very young, up to the age of sixteen years, who, by commitments by courts and magistrates, have fallen into the hands of the law, for various offenses, has been well exemplified by the House of Refuge in Philadelphia and the Pennsylvania Reform

School at Morganza. Amid some controversy over these schools, and the methods at the bottom of them, it is too late now to question their value and service, although neither has as yet reached an equipment necessary for the best work. The purpose of their existence, and the aim of their managers, is to rescue their inmates from the evil associations out of which they have come and to reform them. Few of these waifs have responsible parentage or guardianship. They are quite sure to become State charges. The State, co-operating with private benefactors, proposes to return them, self-supporting, to society, under the best auspices the case will admit. Within the limits of the school they are moulded, intellectually and morally, by competent, careful teachers, and instructed, trained, and drilled to some trade or industrial pursuit. The effort is to reproduce, within the enclosure, the exact condition of society they will encounter when they return to the world. This requires time, and the inmates are retained until the work is more or less completely done. The process goes upon the correct and safe assumption that it is impossible to reform the conduct of a child or man without first measurably reforming his nature. The scheme is no longer an experiment, as it has been faithfully worked out in England, France, Germany and many of the States of our Union. This leads up to an extension of the general method, which, in the judgment of political economists of the very highest authority, promises the most beneficial results. This will include all the first offenders, except of the most brutal type, under the age say of thirty years. The purpose of the process is also to return them to society, with the preparation and discipline best fitted to enable them to earn an honest livelihood, permit them to retain their self-respect, and fit them to resume their places among their fellow-men, if they so choose, without the brand of infamous punishment or penal servitude upon them. The aim and scope is to give the convict intellectual, moral and industrial training, systematic habits, and definite purposes, in a reformatory school, and not in a penitentiary; to afford him another chance in life; in short, to help him to help himself.

"In the discretion of the court rendering the sentence, defendants convicted of a first offense of such magnitude as to justify adequate imprisonment, and under the age of thirty years, are committed to such an intermediate prison. They go without a determinate sentence, but can not be held for a period longer than the maximum term fixed by law for the offense. Under a proper system of grades and classes and marks, every motive to shorten the period of detention is presented. That period will lie in the discretion of the proper officers of the institution. Positions in life are found for them, and they may then be conditionally discharged on parole, reporting from time to time thereafter their behavior and surroundings; or, in default thereof, or of good conduct for a prescribed period, they may be liable to be returned to the institution. It has been found by experience that the prisoners thus discharged have been well received again by society, and in one of the largest institutions of this kind in our land, it is officially reported that less than seven per cent. of the number discharged have failed to maintain their promise of good conduct. I refer to the Reformatory at Elmira, New York. The acts creating it, and the practical management there carried out, are worthy of attention and study."

In accordance with Governor Hoyt's recommendation, a committee, composed of members of the Senate and House of Represenatives, visited Elmira, made a thorough inspection of the practice pursued at the Reformatory, and subsequently submitted a report, unanimously advising the erection, in the State of Pennsylvania, of buildings in conformity with the principles there in operation.

A commission from the State of New Jersey also inspected the Reformatory at Elmira, and made a like recommendation to the legislature of that commonwealth.

The " Tenth Annual Report of the Commissioners of Prisons of Massachusetts," January, 1881, devotes considerable space to the consideration of " Indeterminate Sentences," in the following language:

" Whatever plan may be adopted to afford the best opportunities for accomplishing the reformation of criminals, the highest results can never be attained while the present system of imposing definite sentences for crime is in force. This was long ago recognized as true in the treatment of young offenders, and for many years children have been sentenced to the reform schools for their minority, no time-sentences being imposed, the power to release them when they are deemed to be reformed being given to the authorities in charge of the schools.

" There are many reasons for applying the same principie in the treatment of adult criminals. The present system holds out no inducement to the convict to reform. His sentence is a fixed one, and expires on a day certain, regardless of his conduct or of his character. The one thing he keeps more constantly in mind than any other is the day of his release. He knows that this will not be much delayed by anything he may do, and can not be materially hastened by good behavior or by any change of character. He learns to look upon his punishment as wholly retributive; and, when he comes out of the prison, he feels that he has 'wiped out' the record against him, and is to begin again. During his trial, his main effort, and that of his counsel, is to secure as light a sentence as is possible, and often, with no conception of the gravity of his offense, he harbors a spite against the government for punishing him too severely.

"It may be necessary to continue for the present this system for most offenders, as a change from fixed sentences to indefinite ones involves a change in the whole system of prison management and discipline. But for an institution whose first aim is the reformation of criminals, indefinite sentences must eventually prevail. Under such a system, a convict would be confined until he was deemed to be reformed, be it a short or long time. This throws around the prisoner every possible inducement for self-improvement. He realizes that his future is in his own hands. He sees that the State is not punishing him arbitrarily for his crimes, but is interested in his welfare; that he is deprived of his liberty not so much on account of his *acts* as on account of his *char-*

acter; and that his right to freedom is dependent upon his reformation, which in turn depends upon his own use of his opportunities.

" With such a view of his offenses, of the results they have brought, and of the way of obtaining his liberty, he has every inducement to do his best. Some, with their future thus in their own hands, will speedily change their habit of life, and make resolute endeavors to build up better characters, and can soon be released. Others will come to such endeavors very slowly, and some, possibly, not at all. Some of those who begin the struggle will fail; but, as a rule, they will try again and again, until they attain some degree of success.

" In determining when a convict has reformed, a great responsibility rests upon those who have his training in charge. They will sometimes be deceived; and sometimes one who has within the prison really reformed, will fall under temptations in a life of freedom, and return to a criminal life. But this is equally true of other wards of the State. A large percentage of those discharged from our asylums for the insane, as cured, return again for treatment; the physicians having been mistaken in regard to the cure, or having over-estimated its permanency when the patient came in contact with the world. But these mistakes would not lead any one to suggest a fixed term of confinement for the insane with a discharge at its end, regardless of the condition of the person.

" If an indefinite sentence, to be ended only by his own reformation, be deemed too severe, the indeterminate sentence now imposed in New York upon those who are sent to the State Reformatory at Elmira, ought certainly to be tried. A convict is there sentenced to the reformatory for the longest period for which he could possibly be sentenced for his offense. For instance, under our criminal code, a person may be sentenced to the State prison for five years for larceny from the person, or he may be sent to jail for a lesser term. Under the New York statutes, a person sent to the reformatory for this offense would merely be sentenced to that institution, and regardless of the amount stolen, or of the circumstances, he could be held for five years, unless sooner reformed. In the reformatory he is subjected to the closest surveillance and the most careful training. He wins his release by his deportment and by his character. Whenever he is thought to be reformed, he may be released upon parole. He continues under the control of the Board of Managers until the expiration of five years, unless they sooner discharge him, precisely as minors released from the reform schools in this State do. He may be returned to the reformatory for misbehavior at any time during his sentence.

"It will be seen that this plan holds out to the convict the strongest possible inducements for reformation, both in confinement and after release. If anything in the way of legislation will secure a change of life, this will; for it takes advantage of every motive which usually moves a rational being, and makes full use of the means which are most likely to change a criminal into a good citizen. The system has produced excellent results in the Elmira reformatory; and we recommend that it be adopted in sentences to the reformatory prison for women, and to the reformatory for men, which we have suggested, if it shall be thought wise to send a part of the prisoners to it directly from the courts, instead of transferring them from the county prisons."

In the report from the Joint Committee of the Senate and Assembly, appointed to investigate the affairs of the New York State Reformatory, submitted April 27, 1881, to the questions, "Is the reformatory doing the work for which it was intended? Is it reforming young men? Is it a success?" the following reply was presented:

"We take pleasure in commending the management for the excellent condition in which the buildings and grounds are being maintained, and for the skill, thoroughness and efficiency with which the work of reforming and reclaiming the inmates is being carried on. The prisoners are all young men, between sixteen and thirty years of age when sentenced and convicted of their first offense. The prison was suggested, planned, and is erected and operated, with a view to the reformation of this class of offenders. We are convinced that its object is being attained to a greater degree than its best friends anticipated. The structure has cost nearly, or quite, a million and a half of dollars, but the State has something to show for its money. The buildings are large and substantial, well lighted and ventilated, and models of cleanliness and good order. The 500 cells are of good size and comfortable, each being furnished with a bed, a chair, a small cupboard or bookcase, and a crude writing-desk; and each is lighted with gas. The food supplied to prisoners appears to be plentiful and wholesome, and the clothing is all that is required.

Books and writing materials are supplied as needed. In the arrangement of the buildings, as well as in the management of the prison, every thing compatible with reformatory discipline seems to have been done with a view to the comfort of those who are so unfortunate as to be incarcerated within its walls. The prisoners are kept hard at work throughout the day, and attend school during three alternate evenings of each week; the intervening evenings being occupied in study. It was the privilege of the committee to attend the schools, which we found in the hands of competent instructors. The work bore every evidence of substance and thoroughness, while the advanced studies taught, and the brightness and proficiency of the pupils, quite surprised us.

"As is well known to the legislature, if not to the people, the inmates of the reformatory are sentenced to the institution for an indefinite period of time, the law only providing that they shall not be imprisoned for a longer period than already authorized by law in a State prison or penitentiary for a like offense. Aside from this provision, the time of their imprisonment depends upon their industry, good conduct, and proficiency in studies. They are made to understand that they can regain a place in society by deserving it. The pride, self-respect and ambition of the inmates is encouraged and stimulated by a system of marks most skillfully arranged, which results in classifying them into different grades, thus entitling them, as they advance, to enlarged privileges, greater confidence, and better and more attractive clothing, and, finally, to release upon parole.

The committee were struck with the frankness, cheerfulness,
and manly conduct of the inmates, and the entire absence of
that sullen and dogged indifference and abandonment so univer-
sal in prison life.

"In general, we have none but words of commenda-
tion for the *reformatory* work of the State reformatory.
The experiment is being proved a success. Young men
who have fallen into bad ways are being saved to homes,
friends and society, instead of being crushed in spirit
and prepared for deeper shame and greater crimes.
The principle upon which the reformatory is conducted
should, in our judgment, be persevered in, developed,
and extended into the other penal institutions of the
State."

In 1881, Mr. Langmuir, inspector of prisons in Canada, in company with a number of Canadian officials,
visited the prisons in several of the States of the Union,
and, on his return, in an interview published in the
Toronto *Globe*, gave his opinion of the system in vogue
at Elmira, as follows:

"*Q.* Did you see any new methods which might be
introduced here in whole or in part?

"*A.* Yes, we did. At the New York State Reformatory for adult males, at Elmira, I found certain features
of prison management decidedly in advance of our
views. The system has been in operation five years.
The building is a fine one, and is furnished throughout
with all the modern conveniences of prisons. Instead
of the prisoners being associated together, as they are,
without regard to the differences in their character and
conduct, there are four large dormitories which provide

242 OUR PENAL MACHINERY AND ITS VICTIMS.

sleeping room for four different classes of prisoners. The distinction made is not on account of the offense for which they were committed, or the length of the term of imprisonment to which they are liable. There are three grades, and entrance to the higher of these depends entirely on the conduct of the prisoner while in prison. Offenders sent to this prison are not sentenced for definite periods, as with us. The State law provides a maximum period of confinement for the different classes of crimes, and no minimum. This applies only to the Elmira prison. What the real duration of the sentence shall be, depends on the prisoner. All enter in the same grade, and their conduct is observed carefully from the very first, and marks of merit and demerit are given. By good conduct a prisoner may earn promotion to the first grade, which has certain privileges attaching to it. Here good conduct still further promotes the interest of the prisoner, and if the signs of reformation which led to his promotion from the second grade are still manifest, the superintendent and prison managers may release him on a probation, which generally lasts six months. The friends of the prisoner are corresponded with, and their wishes consulted. Arrangements are also made with farmers and others in a part of the State where the prisoner is not known, and there he is sent to earn his living. Great care is exercised in securing respectable employers, who, of course, are confidentially informed of all the antecedents of the prisoner. The employer makes a report at the end of the time, on the probationer's conduct and sincerity in his efforts for reformation. The prisoner also reports every month. A comparison is made between

these reports, and the superintendent and board of managers may then decide on an unconditional discharge.
In this way a prisoner is encouraged to reform, by the
prospect of shortening his term of prison life, which
may in some cases last ten years, to five or six years, or
even to two or three. Good conduct ensures confidence
and promotion. Some of the prisoners are even employed
as monitors, and some are entrusted with the keys to various apartments. * * * I never saw a prison in which
the inmates had less of a convict expression. They were
cheerful, and wore an expression of openness and candor
I have never seen in any other penal institution. The
great encouragement given to right conduct has a very
salutary effect, both in securing good conduct and
encouraging good habits and desires. A prisoner told
me that he could scarcely sleep at night, thinking what
he could do the next day to merit a good mark. There
are other excellent features associated with the system.
The superintendent, instead of addressing the prisoners
as a mass, must become personally familiar with the
disposition and conduct of each man. He is brought
into contact with each, and this contact has the effect of
individualizing the prisoner. Of course, no pains are
spared to make each man, while retaining his manliness,
submit his will to subordination." I have cited at
length from the reports relating to the Elmira Reformatory—not for the purpose of praising it, however excellent it may be—but to show the opinion our leading
public men, who have examined the subject, entertain
in regard to indeterminate sentences.

Sir Frederick Hill, who obtained great reputation in

the successful management of Scottish prisons, said that the chief reliance of a prisoner is on hope. "This," he says, "secures the hearty co-operation of the prisoners, without which there can be little expectation of real reform. I set a high value on the arrangement in convict prisons by which it is granted to a prisoner, by great self-control, industry, and exertion for moral improvement, to materially abridge the length of his confinement."

Dr. Despine, an eminent physician and philosopher of France, made a profound study of the criminal from the standpoint of psychology, and, after showing that criminals are, as a rule, morally weak and in an abnormal state, says:

"If these men who are the subjects of a real moral idiocy are dangerous, they are, at the same time, deserving of our pity. To shield ourselves from danger we have to separate them from society. This is in itself a punishment. But the treatment which aims only to punish, is dangerous both to society and the criminal. It rarely improves the latter, but often makes him worse. In France it produces from forty to forty-five per cent. of repeaters. This is because, having taken as our guides only fear and vengeance, and not scientific data, we have never studied the moral state which leads a man to crime; we have ignored this abnormal condition. If the criminal is different, in a moral point, from other men, the best way to prevent crime is to cause this difference to cease—not wholly, which is impossible, but near enough to render him a safe member of society. In this view, it is the first duty to segregate them, not, however, for a fixed period determined in advance by the nature of the crime com mitted. It is rather the moral state of the criminal that is to be taken into account.

" Here we have the first point in reference to the treatment of criminals, that of the time of sequestration established by science, which is thoroughly in accord with what is demanded by common-sense. Under the system which fixes the time in advance, we see daily set loose in society a multitude of malefactors who are known to be dangerous. Does not such a mode of action wear absurdity on its face?

" In taking, as a starting-point, the principle that we have here to deal with persons afflicted with a moral anomaly in the nature of a disease, it is evident that to cure, or, at least lessen this malady, should be the supreme aim in their treatment. It is to this end that all the means employed ought to converge. Further, as the moral anomaly with which criminals are attacked varies almost indefinitely, it is as irrational to treat all these varieties in the same manner as it would be to treat all the ail-ments of the body alike."

To what is said above about indeterminate sentences, I will add that, in my opinion, the convict should be required to earn some money for himself, as explained hereafter, before he is permitted to leave the prison, in order that he may not be absolutely dependent, should he fail in either getting or keeping work.

For, *granting that he has completely reformed, and is anxious to lead an honorable life, he is then still no better, nor can he possibly be morally stronger, than the honest man who never was in prison; and even such a man would be in great danger of becoming a criminal should he suddenly be left with-out money, without work, without friends, with nothing to eat, and nowhere to go when night comes.*

So long as a man is able to pay his way, he preserves his self-respect and is comparatively free from danger.

CHAPTER XV.

Grand juries should be abolished. They work a great injury to the innocent, and greatly assist the guilty. For, the delays incident to the action of the grand jury keep hundreds in jail, who are, on examination, discharged. At the same time, the great delay incidental to their action is of the greatest advantage to the real criminals. They thus gain time, frequently many months, till the public has lost interest in their case, and further delays have become easy to procure.

At present, there is an examination before a justice of the peace, where a number of continuances are generally obtained. Then the offender is bound over to await the action of the grand jury, and, if he can not give bail, he has to go to jail, and the worst criminals often are able to give bail, while the poor, wrongfully arrested, frequently are not. Owing to the number of cases, trifling and otherwise, requiring their action, it frequently takes a number of months before the grand jury reaches the case. Then the prosecution is required again to produce all its witnesses. If an indictment is found, it again takes months before it can be reached for trial, when the whole agony has once more to be gone through with. Surely, no system better calculated to defend criminals and injure the innocent could well be devised.

Courts should always be open for the trials of criminals, so that a continuance would be but for a few days, and not for a number of months to the next term, as now. Then the accused should be tried on information, so that a trial could take place immediately after the offense. This would protect the innocent, and, at once, bring to justice the guilty. The speedy trial is what the guilty always dread.

PART SECOND.

PRISON LABOR.

CHAPTER I.

PRISON LABOR—KIND OF WORK DONE.—EARNINGS AND
COST OF PRISONERS—LOSS TO SOCIETY—INNOCENT
SUFFER WITH GUILTY—REASON OF LOW AVERAGE
—NO INTEREST IN LABOR MAKES POOR WORKMEN
—LEAVES HIM IN HELPLESS CONDITION—INDUS-
TRIES LIMITED.

There are in vogue four methods of working prisoners: By the first of these, called the Public Account
System, the State furnishes material, and then sells the
goods made. By the second, which is known as the
Contract System, the services of a specified number of
convicts are hired out or contracted to one contractor
for a fixed time, and at a fixed price per day, and the
money thus made goes to the State; by this method the
State keeps control of the prisoners and feeds and
clothes them. The third is the Piece Price System, by
which outsiders supply the material, and often some of
the machinery, and the State manufactures the desired
articles at a fixed price per piece. These three systems
are in vogue in the Northern States, except Delaware;
in that State the prisoners do not work. By the fourth

method the convicts are leased out, and, as they are thenceforth clothed and fed by the lessee, they receive from the State scarcely any further attention. This system prevails in many of the Southern States, and is, by far, the most objectionable of all. Under it, there is scarcely a possibility of the reformation of a prisoner. The lessee wants to make as much money, and give as little in return, as possible; and, in some cases, the condition of the prisoner is said to be far worse than that of the most cruelly treated slave.

KIND OF WORK DONE.

The work done in prisons varies. In the Northern States it is generally confined to manufacturing; the making of boots, shoes and chairs being carried on to a greater extent than the making of any other article, though a great many prisoners work at stone-cutting. In some of the Southern States mines are worked and plantations managed by prisoners.

EARNINGS AND COST OF PRISONERS.

The average earnings of prisoners in the best managed State prisons is 50 cents per day for every man engaged in what might be called productive labor, skilled and unskilled. The average for all, including those that do prison duties, is about 35 cents per day per man. Thus, in the penitentiary at Joliet, Illinois, which, in this respect, is one of the best managed in the country, the average contract price, per man, per day, for year ending September 30, 1881, was $46\frac{83}{100}$ cents, and for year ending September 30, 1882, was

$52\frac{52}{100}$ cents; and the average earnings, including working days, Sundays and holidays, was $33\frac{91}{100}$ cents and $39\frac{12}{100}$ cents, during said years. It will strike any one at a glance that this is an exceedingly low average; that it is less than half what a man should earn and less than half what a free laborer will earn on an average.

But, notwithstanding this, many prisons in which the inmates labor are self-sustaining; some require appropriations by the State, while some actually have a surplus; the total average cost of keeping (including guarding, clothing, etc.) each convict in the various penitentiaries being from 28 to 35 cents per day.

LOSS TO SOCIETY.

It will be seen, by the above, that in the case of every convict there is an actual dead loss to society of over half of his productive powers. That is, over half of his ability to support not himself simply, but others, is absolutely lost. His time is passing, he has so many less months or years to live. But he is contributing less than half of what he should contribute as a free man.

Society is so constituted that it requires every able-bodied man to contribute a proportionate share toward the support of the whole. This he usually does in supporting his family or those depending on him. And whenever, from any cause, he fails to do this, there is a loss to society, and the burden of the remainder is proportionately increased. This increased burden is felt in various ways, and is just as real as though the whole of the loss had to be collected in increased taxes every year. In fact, to a certain extent it is, for as the number of those

paying taxes is diminished, the burden of the remainder
increases, and what is paid directly and indirectly for
charitable purposes, to feed and clothe those that are
dependent for support on those confined in prison, might
as well be paid in the shape of taxes. Further, in so far
as those dependent on a convict are more poorly cared
for, though not actually objects of charity, they become
poorer citizens, and are more likely to be a bill of
expense than a source of assistance to society in the
future. Even in the case of the convict who has absolutely no one depending on him, society sustains this
dead loss, for his time is lost, his best days are passing,
he is accumulating nothing, he is not equipping himself
for the struggle of life that is before him; he can not,
therefore, after he becomes free, accomplish what he
otherwise might have done — nay all the chances are
against him, and his life liable to be a failure; thus society
will lose not only his assistance, but will actually find in
him, at some time in the future, a burden.

INNOCENT SUFFER WITH GUILTY.

Under the present system, the innocent are punished
with the guilty. The law intends that its penalties
shall fall only on those that actually violate it; but, at
present, in many cases the consequences of a conviction
fall with equal severity upon the innocent and dependent,
for it, in effect, takes away their bread. When, therefore, a man is convicted, those dependent on him are at
once left without support, besides having to bear the
terrible social blight which settles upon families of convicts, isolating them from the rest of mankind and

making them objects of aversion, for which it is hard to suggest a remedy, and which can not well be avoided. But to be deprived of the means with which to procure the necessaries of life is an uncalled-for hardship; for the man is not dead, his strength is not destroyed, he is as able as ever to work, and in very many cases would gladly work harder than ever before, if thereby he could do anything for those he leaves behind. And why should he not be permitted to do so—nay, why should he not be actually required to do so? He has violated the law, it is true, but his family have not; he ought to be punished, but they ought not to be. While, therefore, he must be deprived of his liberty, must be isolated from society, and bear the hardships of prison life, he should still be not only permitted, but required to contribute to the support of those that are absolutely dependent on him. True, the State may require that he first work enough for it, to pay the expense of feeding, clothing, guarding, and superintending him; but this, in most penitentiaries, is only from 28 to 32 cents per day, while he is capable of earning, perhaps, three times as much. Upon this subject, W. Searles, Chaplain of the Penitentiary at Auburn, N. Y., in his report, says:

"An agreeable and profitable intercourse with the inmates of the prison, which I enjoy, arises out of their social correspondence, which it falls to my lot to conduct. The prisoners are permitted to visit my office during the week to obtain permission to write, or for advice, or to transact such necessary business, or ask for such favors as rules will permit. I read, record, and direct all letters that go out, and also read all that come in. This opens up my way to their most tender and susceptible moral feelings and family sympathies. The letters received by the prisoners from their almost broken-hearted wives, mothers, sisters and friends, enjoining upon them repentance, reformation and obedience to the prison rules, that they may the sooner be reunited, must have a great influence upon them, both for their present and future good. And, sir, it is the perusal of these letters from the poor old mother, the broken-hearted wife, the suffering children, the grieving brothers and sisters, that enforces upon my mind the lesson that no man liveth to himself alone. In the vast majority of cases, these mothers, wives and children are poor, and were dependent upon the son, the husband and the father for the actual necessaries of life. In consequence of his imprisonment *they* must suffer. While it is the duty of society to protect itself against the inroads of the criminals, let me inquire, is it not equally the duty of society to protect from want and suffering the innocent wife and child? As I have heretofore suggested, permit me again to express the hope that the incoming legislature will make some provision by which *a portion, however small, of the convict's earnings, may be set apart for his own or his family's benefit.*"

This system, therefore, works a great injustice to the innocent, and, in the long run entails a heavy burden on society; for where the family of a convict is left without support, the burden of providing falls directly on society. It is immaterial whether this burden be discharged in taxes or in charity, or in the loss of goods stolen; it still comes from the public.

Further than this, the children of a convict thus situated, having no regular source to look to for bread, are liable to grow up violators of the law, from the sheer force of their surroundings; for squalor and misery are hot-beds of crime.

So that, instead of extirpating crime by the punishment inflicted, we create anew the conditions out of which it grows—that is, we constantly create the conditions that will be certain, in due time, to bring forth new criminals, with all the expense to the public that is incident to arresting, prosecuting and confining law-breakers. In fact, it would be much cheaper for the public, and certainly much better even to charge the convict nothing for guarding, superintending, feeding and clothing him, than to pursue the system now pursued; for the results just described will, in the end, cost the public much more than thirty cents per day. But as already stated, if given an opportunity, he could pay the State and contribute toward the support of his family besides; and as thirty cents per day is as little as he could be clothed and fed for at home, he could in reality pay the State for his keeping and contribute almost as much to the support of his family as if he were free. In fact, in many cases he could be required to contribute much more than he would if free. But I shall consider this subject hereafter.

REASON OF LOW AVERAGE.

The chief cause of the low average earnings of convicts lies in the fact that it is unwilling labor. A man while free will earn more than double what he will earn as a convict.

Of course, much depends on the skill of the foreman in managing the prisoners, and getting much work out of them. But the chief reason of a low average is apparent.

NO INTEREST IN LABOR MAKES POOR WORKMEN.

A convict has no interest whatever in his work. It does him no good to do a large amount of work in a day, for it will benefit neither him nor any one dear to him. Men are generally impelled to work by a desire to benefit themselves or those dependent upon or dear to them. But the convict has none of these incentives. He may be anxious to earn and save a pittance, so that when he regains his freedom he will be able to support himself for a time even though he fail to get work. Or, he may be eager to earn something for the assistance of those that are without bread because of his acts and absence; but all in vain. If he does more work than he is required to do, the profits go generally into the pockets of wealthy contractors, while he is simply wearing himself out. In short, he has no heart in his work. It is involuntary servitude, which rarely accomplishes more than half what voluntary service will.

At present, the convict's work is to him a treadmill affair, from which he is to get no benefit. He goes to his task because forced to go; works only while forced to work; studies to slight his work rather than to do it well; tries to get along by doing as little as possible. Indeed, how could it be otherwise? Outside of prisons men study to do as little as possible of that in which they feel no interest and from which they are to get no benefit, and surely we can not expect to find more virtue inside of prison than out.

The effect is, therefore, to make a man a slow work-man, and in many cases an indifferent and careless one; and in time these habits will become natural, especially where they are long continued. Therefore, instead of becoming an expert and skilled workman, he is more apt to become a slow botcher, and is, therefore, not well equipped to make an honest living when he regains his liberty. And if the effect of his confinement has been to make him a poor workman instead of an expert, the chances are against his being able to get along, and the probability is increased of his drifting, with his family, among the criminal classes. Few have any conception of the expense entailed on the public by the relapse of a convict, especially when the depredations committed before he is again incarcerated are included. In 1872 Mr. Tallack, at the request of the Howard Association and of the Central Committee of the International Prison Congress, collected a vast amount of information on the subject of prison management, prison labor, and the reformation of prisoners; on this point he says: " Prisoners, if discharged untaught and untrained, soon relapse, and cost the public £159 per annum (nearly $800), at a low estimate, by their robberies."

LEAVES HIM IN HELPLESS CONDITION.

But by far the most serious defect in the present sys-tem lies in the fact that when a man has spent years in prison, on again going out into the world he is abso-lutely dependent; he has no money and generally no friends who will help him; he may be anxious to work and earn an honest living, but often can not get work. Now, what is to be expected in such a case—bearing in mind that in the first instance he succumbed to evil influences and violated the law, and, that a man not a convict and with friends, but who has nothing but his labor on which to rely, has a very hard lot of it? I ask what can with reason now be expected? .He is under a ban. He is an outcast. Everybody's door is shut against him. He may be full of good resolves, but he can not live on them. He may again long to be respectable and independent; but he must be housed, fed, clothed, and if work is not to be had, what can he do?

Florien J. Ries, one of the most successful prison managers, in his report of the Milwaukee House of Correction for 1880, in speaking of this subject, says:

"Many, doubtless, leave the prison with a strong determination to lead honorable lives in the future; but here the question arises, how will they accomplish this? With all boasted philanthropy and all pretended kindly feeling toward these persons, how does society meet them when the prison door has closed behind them? As long as people *demand* that prisons must be self-sustaining, these persons will receive but a pittance upon their discharge. With this they venture out upon the world, seeking employment; and, if they are frank, and admit that they have just been discharged from prison, who will employ them? Without employment, without money, without friends, what are they to do? Is it not perfectly natural, under these circumstances, that they should seek and find their former associates in crime? Here, then, is a wide field for humanitarians, a field in which, perhaps, the practical reformation of many of these persons could be accomplished. What can the prison officials accomplish by assuring those prisoners that if they will only show the good will to reform, society will receive them and forgive past transgressions, when, after their actual discharge, there is no one to extend a helping hand? I believe that a 'prisoners' aid society' could do an incalculable amount of good in the way of advising and assisting such persons. This is a subject which should receive the earnest consideration, not only of our legislature, but of all true humanitarians."

The following forcible remarks are from the report of William H. Hill, moral instructor of the California State Prison. In enumerating the conditions necessary for the reformation of prisoners, he says:

"*Second.*—The prisoners must desire and determine to reform.

"*Third.*—The officers in charge should help in the work of reformation.

"*Fourth.*—Christians and philanthropists in the world outside should also help, and not by cold looks and colder actions drive the discharged prisoners again into crime.

"As to the second element, there is a great misapprehension on the part of the people generally. It seems to be taken for granted that all who are here deserve their punishment, and should be kept from further harm by indefinite imprisonment. This is a great mistake.

Some of the inmates here are undoubtedly innocent, having been the victims of perjury or mistaken identity. These may be few in number. The great majority of the prisoners, however, are here for the first time —at least three-fourths of the whole number. A mistaken impression is abroad as to this. It is not true, as often asserted and believed, that a large, or even any, majority return for the second, third or fourth time. Not one-fourth do so. This would seem to be proof positive that the majority not only resolved to lead a different life after release, but carried their intention into practice. And facts are always more conclusive than fiction.

"As to the third requisite, I can bear testimony that the officers do their duty, and wish to help the prisoners to do well, not only in the prison, but out. And if their efforts were as earnestly seconded by outsiders, there would be little necessity to ask any of the above-named questions. And right here is met the greatest obstacle in the way of reform of prisoners; for I must answer the question involved in the fourth position, by saying that Christians and philanthropists outside, though plentiful in lip service, do not help the prisoners to reform, but passively, if not directly, lend their influence to drive them back to crime and punishment. This is a bold charge, I know; but unfortunately it is true. No matter how well an inmate may conduct himself while in prison, nor how sincere he may be in his efforts and determination to reform and lead a better life, he goes out with the prison taint upon him. He applies for work, and honestly tells where he has been. With very few exceptions, he is immediately rebuffed. In vain does he plead his reformation and determination, and show his certificate of good conduct from the prison officers. 'I pray thee, have me excused,' is what he hears on every side. Tempters to crime are neither scarce nor fastidious; and thus repulsed by those who claim, morally, to be the better class, it is not strange if he is again drawn aside from the right path, and returns here more hardened than ever, on account of his repulse by those from whom he had a right to expect better things. That is one obstacle in the way of his reform.

"But suppose, to avoid this, he simply conceals the fact that he has been an inmate of the State prison. He secures work as a mechanic, or clerk, or laborer, and is honest, industrious and faithful. A short time only elapses before he is 'spotted' by some depraved ex-convict, and 'blackmail' is demanded on threat of exposure. If he resists the claim, and is still trusted, notwithstanding the exposure made as threatened, it is well. But how often is that likely to be the case? Not one time in twenty, I am sorry to say. If he submits to the demand of the ex-convict, then he is at his mercy, and will be driven to desperation, if not to suicide, by further and still more exacting demands. Nor is this the other side of the picture. Can he escape Scylla and not fall into Charybdis?

"And I am sorry to say there are some—not all—of the police in San Francisco and other large cities, who seem to take a delight in pointing out these poor unfortunates as 'State prison birds,' and thus drive them from honest work into crime. What wonder, then, that the percentage of real and permanent reform is not as large as could be desired? I feel like saying to these outside, fault-finding philanthropists, 'physicians, heal yourselves,' ere throwing upon the prison officers or directors the blame of failure in efforts to reform. Let outsiders do their duty as men and Christians, and I believe that nearly all of those sent here for the first time would reform and lead honest, if not true, godly, Christian lives, when restored to liberty. I hope to live to see the day when this shall be the actual fact, and not merely a picture of the imagination."

Upon the same subject, W. C. Gunn, chaplain and teacher of the Iowa State Prison, who has interested himself greatly in the welfare of discharged convicts, says, in his report:

" What becomes of the discharged convicts, is a question that is frequently asked. That depends very much upon how they are treated after they are discharged. And here let me emphasize what I said two years ago. Perhaps none, unless connected with a prison, and but few even of those, have the remotest idea of the difficulties which a discharged convict, without friends, has to meet before he obtains employment. Many, when liberated, do not wish to return to the place from which they were sent; why, I know not, unless realizing their disgrace, they are unwilling to go back where it is known. Many have no friends or relatives, and, as a rule, not only prefer to go, but do go, where they are unknown. The stigma of the penitentiary resting upon them, the strength of public opinion against them, and nearly penniless, they are almost compelled to do one of three things; beg, starve or steal; and, alas for the weakness of good resolutions, the latter at times is resorted to. What are discipline and teaching and reformation in prison, unless society sustains the effort outside of the prison? Can not society afford to try the discharged convict once more? I know that the cloud of the penitentiary hangs heavily over him. But what if it does? Should not Christian men, philanthropic men, and especially neighbors, do what they can to save the erring? Let the following letter, received from one of the 'unfortunates,' tell, and it is only one out of several in my possession:

"'M——, IOWA, January 28, 1881.

"'REV. GUNN, DEAR CHAPLAIN:—I am encouraged to address you by the remembrance of the kind and undeserved interest you manifested in my welfare during my stay in Ft. Madison. I have been at home now five months, and I am beginning to experience the difficulties which attend a man in his effort to regain the position he held in the estimation of his fellows before departing from the path of rectitude. My professions of intent to lead a life of honesty are distrusted, and I am tempted to relinquish any other life than that almost forced upon me by my treatment at the hands of my neighbors. Your appreciated efforts to reclaim the fallen emboldens me to turn to you for advice and encouragement, etc.'

"While that unfortunate man was in the penitentiary, he was bolted *in;* now that he is on the outside world he is bolted out—bolted out from the sympathy and confidence of his neighbors, bolted out from the workshop, bolted out from farm labor. I therefore most heartily recommend that a State Prison Aid Association be organized, with a branch in every county, and that persons with large sympathy and warm hearts be encouraged to assist in this noble enterprise, thus procuring, for all who desire to reform, places to work, where they can earn an honest living, by this means shielding them from idleness and from the merciless attacks of unkind and evil disposed persons.

"Kindness oftentimes may be scarce towards a discharged convict, but it is not wholly dead. There are some who are not afraid to take them by the hand and succor them in time of need. During the three years and one month of my chaplaincy, I have found good homes for three hundred and five out of the six hundred and forty-six discharged. Only *two* of these were discharged by their employers on account of dissatisfaction—one in Des Moines county, for not earning his wages, and the other in Marshall county, for smoking too frequently. Both have done well since. But what became of the three hundred and forty-one for whom no homes were found? As far as I am able to learn, thirty-nine of them are in the penitentiary, seven are living by gambling, and two are 'fugitives from justice.'"

The Prisoners' Aid Societies mentioned above, which have in late years been formed by kind-hearted and philanthropic people, are doing a great good, but they have, after all, the nature of a palliative and not of a cure.

INDUSTRIES LIMITED.

Keeping all prisoners entirely within prison-walls, as is now done, greatly limits the industries which they can pursue, and the result is, that too many are forced to take up particular trades, which they would not have taken up as free men, and this is a direct injury to the honest free laborer swho, with their families, are dependent for their living upon that particular trade. These laborers have no right to complain of men working at a particular trade in prison, provided it appears that the parties working at such trade in prison would have worked at it had they never been imprisoned, and, provided, further, that the effects of this prison labor do not reduce their wages any more that they would have been reduced had the prisoners remained free men and followed the same trade as they do in prison. For every one has a right to follow any trade that he may wish. A free laborer can not object to other men choosing whatever trades they prefer. A fair competition between parties similarly situated is not objected to, but the overcrowding of certain trades by purely arbitrary and unnatural means is doing an injustice to those that have voluntarily selected those trades as a means of livelihood.

If the prisoners could be divided, and those that have long sentences to serve, or that are guilty of heinous crimes, be kept within prison walls and divided among such trades as can well be carried on there, the number assigned to each would be small, and, probably, not in excess of the number that would have selected the same trades as free men. And, if a system were adopted whereby the temptation to escape would be greatly reduced, then the remainder of the prisoners could be taken out to labor at such work as they would, to a great extent, have chosen had they labored as free men. By this means, prison labor could be assigned to many more branches of industry than is possible at present. Besides, the moral effect would, under proper regulations, be much better. As it is, a great number of men are set at the same kind of work, without regard to their adaptation for it. Instead, therefore, of learning trades or occupations which they could follow when again free, they find, upon regaining their freedom, that they have, in fact, no occupation at all, as the work at which they have been engaged was not the kind for which they were adapted or which they could successfully follow.

Further. The objections to convict labor now so strenuously urged in so many quarters, could be removed without increasing the burdens of the public. It will be noted that the objection is more to the method of conducting the convict labor, and of bringing it into competition with free labor, than to the working of convicts at all. In fact, no objection could be urged against this, for every man has a right to pursue some kind of labor. Nay, it is his duty to do so. When, therefore, convicts work in prisons, they are doing no more than they would have done, or at least should have done, as good citizens.

But, besides the forcing of large numbers of men to perform a particular kind of labor which they otherwise would not have performed, the objection to convict labor, as now managed in most prisons, is, that it is contracted out at such figures that the honest free laborers are reduced to starvation in the necessary competition which ensues; or, in case the convicts work under the public account system, that their products are sold cheaper than the same kind of goods can be made by free labor at living wages.

That goods manufactured on public account for the

State are sold at lower prices than the like goods manufactured by free labor is, I believe, not generally true,
and certainly ought not to be permitted, for the State
ought not to enter into competition with its own citizens. But that convicts are contracted out in great
numbers, at average prices (40 to 55 cents per day) that
appear on their face to be ruinous to free labor, is true.

At present there is much ground for complaint,
especially in regard to certain ·kinds of skilled labor
that can be carried on in a prison as well as elsewhere.
Thus, there is no doubt that the making of shoes, sad-
dlery, cigars, and a number of other articles requiring
skilled labor, by convicts, under the contract system, at
present injuriously affects the free laborers in these
branches of industry, and it effects them most injuriously
in dull times, for in good times, when the demand is equal
to the production of the entire country, all find employment, and that the contractor of prison labor is making
excessive profits, is not generally noticed. But when
times are dull and the demand limited and prices low,
then, inasmuch as the product of the convict labor must
continue to be the same—as the contracts usually run
for a term of years—free labor has to suffer; for, should
the demand be no greater than can be supplied by the
prisons, then free labor would either have to seek other
employment or accept such wages as would enable it to
compete with convict labor. Of course, wages would
still be greater than the convict's wages, for, being much
more productive, free labor would inevitably command
higher wages; but still they would be lower for the
prison competition. On the other hand, the prison

contractor also finds his profits reduced in dull times, for he pays the same wages as when times were good, and must pay these right along, whether he can sell his products or not.

Now, if a system were introduced by which convicts could be converted into voluntary laborers, and paid something near the wages paid voluntary laborers, convict labor would never undersell free labor, and the prisoners could be set at labor for which they are adapted, and thus the overcrowding of certain branches of industry by convicts could be avoided. True, it may be said that by changing involuntarily into voluntary labor, the products would be greater than at present, and must still more affect prices. But the answer is, that there are no more men at work than would be, or at least should be, at work if there were no convicts at all; and, as their labor would not undersell free labor, there could be no moral ground of objection. And further, the real trouble now with convict labor is, not that all industry is affected by it, but that a few branches of industry are overstocked by it.

CHAPTER II.

REMEDY.

If the practice recommended in Chapter thirteen of Part First, page sixty-eight, were adopted, it is safe to say that after a short period, in which the more hardened characters would be weeded out, the annual commitments to prison would be diminished by more than half, and the prison labor question would thus be solved to that extent. Then, if those in prison were permitted to earn something daily for themselves, so as to give them an interest in their work, and thus remove the temptation from all except those confined for long terms, to desert, most of the prisoners could be set at work outside of prison walls, so that comparatively few would be crowded into the trades where they come into competition with skilled labor, who would not otherwise have pursued the same calling. It is safe to say that there would soon be no question of prison labor to agitate the public.

The idea of working prisoners outside of prison walls is not new. It has been tried, successfully, even under existing laws, which, by depriving the prisoner of almost all hope, may be said to encourage desertion. But unfortunately the only States where this plan has thus far been tried, are those in which the lease system prevails, under which the most shocking barbarities have been practiced, on account of which many good men have become prejudiced against the idea of letting prisoners work outside of prison, at all. It must, however, be borne in mind that cruelty may be practiced as well under one system as under another, and that there is no more excuse for its infliction where prisoners work outside of prisons than where they do not.

The Warden of the Northern Penitentiary of Illinois —an institution having nearly sixteen hundred inmates —recently stated to the writer that he was in favor of the purchase by the State of a large tract of land lying near the prison, which would enable him to carry on farming and gardening with the prisoners, for the purpose of supplying the prison with farm and garden products, and he added that he believed the project to be entirely practicable.

To carry out the foregoing, and also to overcome the objections to the present system considered in the last chapter, it will be necessary to change *involuntary* into *voluntary* labor, which can be done by paying each convict wages nearly equal to the current wages paid to free men for like work, and then to charge the convict with the total expense of his keeping, including guarding, superintending, clothing, feeding, etc. As the average cost of keeping a convict is usually not much over thirty cents per day, and as he could, if laboring voluntarily, earn much more, there would soon be a surplus in his favor. This surplus should be placed to his credit and be applied toward the support and education of his family or other dependents, if there are any, and if there are none, then to be held on deposit until his discharge; and when he is discharged he should be paid a small

portion of his money—say enough for transportation to
the point which he may desire to reach, and for his support for a month or longer, until he shall have again
become accustomed to the ways of the world and have
had time to determine what he shall go at for a living,
and then he should be paid the remainder. He will thus
have saved something out of the years of his confinement, and will have something to start on. He will not
be driven at once to beg, steal or starve, and will not be
likely soon to find himself again on the way to the penitentiary.

This would be salvation to all those that really wanted
to live respectable and useful lives, and it would have a
good influence on even the abandoned; for nothing is so
adapted to steady a man as first-training him to work
and then letting him accumulate some property. As
soon as he has something to call his own, he begins to
grow conservative; there is aroused in him a desire to
better his condition, and he will avoid the vicious from
a sense of self-protection, if for no other reason.

Under this system almost every convict would become willing and eager to work, and the present stolid
indifference of some prisoners, who care for nothing but
to drag through the weary days, the hopeless despair of
others, and the desperation of still others, would give
way to hope in most, and to comfort and satisfaction in
all; for even they who know that their days must end
in prison would feel that they could make some beings
comfortable, if not happy, by contributing something to
support those to whom they should have been protectors.

I am aware that the State can not carry on business as economically as private individuals—or, at least, rarely does—but it will be noticed, the State has very much of an advantage to start with. It is not required to pay rent or interest on the investment in buildings, machinery, etc., for even in those institutions, which under the present system boast that they have become self-sustaining, no allowance is made for rent or interest on investment. This is certainly a large item, and one would suppose it alone would be sufficient to enable the State to pay the same wages (not necessarily per day, but for work done) that is paid by private parties, and come out whole.

But as shown heretofore, under the present system the State annually loses, directly and indirectly, very large sums of money, besides the loss, both financial and of a higher character, that will result from the evil effects upon a large proportion of her citizens; so that if the State were, under the proposed system, to lose money, it is doubtful whether she could by any possibility suffer as much in the long run as she now suffers. However, as there would be at least twice the amount of work done as there is now, it is difficult to see how the State could possibly lose anything.

Should the contract system be preferred to the public account system, the matter can be easily arranged by requiring the contractor to pay the prisoner for what he does — that is, in all cases, where possible, to pay him by the piece; where this can not be done, to pay him for a full day's work when he does it. All the contractor asks is to have the work done. If, therefore, a convict is willing and able to do as much in one day as he formerly did in two, the contractor should not hesitate to pay him double the wages. Nay, he could, in that case, pay more than double the wages, because he saves the expense of superintendence and of furnishing power, and of other incidentals for one day—that is, in that case one-half of what he now pays for the last-named items would be saved to him, and he could afford to pay more than double the wages he now pays. Besides, the work would be done better, for a willing man always does his work better than an unwilling one, and his goods will therefore command a higher price in the market. But the " piece price" system of managing convict labor is the best thus far devised. Under it, the contractor simply furnishes the material and agrees to pay a stipulated price for having it manufactured. Ilis agents have nothing to do with the prisoners, as now, and the State neither buys material nor sells manufactured products.

CHAPTER III.

The Objection that Criminals will not Work—Make Time of Discharge, in Part, Depend on Surplus Earnings—Aids in Preserving Discipline—Too Much Prison Labor—Working Outside Prison Walls—Waste of Sentiment—Labor as a Part of the Punishment—Results.

It will, however, be objected by those with whom the reformation of criminals is no object, who see nothing worthy of consideration about any person in prison, that the criminal classes do not work except when compelled, that the chance of earning some wages, over and above the expense of their keeping, would not induce them to make any extra effort; and that, therefore, the proposed system would fail.

To this I reply that, supposing the objection to be good, supposing it to be true that many convicts would not do any more than they were compelled to do, and consequently would not earn anything over and above the total expense of their keeping, then there will still be nothing lost. Society will still be as well off as now, for that is all that the best are now made to do, on the average.

But the objection is not well taken, for it has been found that the majority are eager to earn something, if only given a chance. Thus, in the Michigan State Prison, where the contract system prevails, and where no provision is made for giving the convicts an opportunity to earn something for themselves, but where, nevertheless, those that worked by the piece were not prohibited from overwork, it appears from the report of the inspectors, that during the year 1881 this class of convicts earned, over and above what they had to do, $9,485.85; and during the year 1882 they earned $11,154.75 by voluntary overwork. Referring to this, the inspectors say:

"This sum has been paid by the contractors to the prison, and been credited to the convicts in proportion to their several earnings. This money is in many cases remitted by the convict to his family, and what remains, if anything, is paid to him at the expiration of his term. It is not unreasonable to suppose that some, at least, have in this way done more for the comfort of their families than they would have done had they remained outside."

This was earned in spite of the fact that no provision had been made for them to earn anything for themselves. Will anybody deny that had there been regulations permitting, nay, requiring all convicts, including those that were not assigned to piece-work, to earn something for their families or for themselves, that they would not have done it, especially if they had known that they could not be set at liberty until they had made certain provisions of this kind?

In the inspectors' report of the Western Penitentiary of Pennsylvania, I find the following:

"In the shops we aim to have order and silence; unruly conduct is punished, and excellence of labor performed is rewarded by a proportionate division of profit with the prisoners, in the shape of overwork. In this way many of the convicts are enabled to make weekly or monthly remittances to their homes, thus contributing toward the support and comfort of the dependent ones, made so by their indiscretions. During the past two years, $26,080 have been earned in this way, and for the most part distributed as stated."

In Minnesota the convict in the State Prison is allowed, for good conduct, six days every month, for which he receives the same rate that is paid by the contractors to the State. The money thus earned may be paid by the prison authorities to the convict's family, if needy, and when not thus paid, it is given to the convict on being discharged; many convicts on leaving the prison have had upwards of $150 to their credit, with which to start again in life. Are these not more likely to do well than if they had not a cent?

In 1876 Mr. Richard Vaux, president of the board of directors of the Eastern Penitentiary of Pennsylvania— one of the very best institutions of the kind in this country—in speaking of the work done there, said:

" Manufacturing material is bought at market prices, and the goods manufactured are sold at the same; so that there is no unfair competition with manufacturers who employ honest men. The convicts are allowed pay for over-time. *One man supported a wife and family outside of prison by over-work done in prison.* The prisoners cost about thirty-four cents a day, *per capita.* Labor is not farmed out, nor let out by contract. We are not self-supporting, and I trust we never shall be. When a prison becomes self-supporting, it is just what prisons are not intended to do." (The italics are mine.)

The inspectors of the same prison, in their report for 1881, say:

" As a reformatory agency, intended also to stimulate the self-respect, strengthen and preserve the ties of father and husband and family, the system of over-work has been adopted in this institution. The task of each prisoner, able to work after he has been taught, is fixed. All the prisoners are included in this provision. When the task has been completed, then whatever excess of work is done by the prisoner is divided; one-half is given to the county sending the individual, and the other half is credited to him on the books of the clerk. He can give orders for his share to his wife and family. These orders are in printed forms, signed by the prisoner and attested by his overseer, and entered into a separate account kept for each prisoner. When these orders are presented to the clerk, they are paid, and the receipt endorsed on the order. If no orders are given, the prisoner receives his share on his discharge. During the year, over $10,000 have been gained by the convicts and paid to them or their respective families. It is believed that decided good results from this plan, and even in an economic view, it is of decided advantage. Labor thus applied * * * gives to convict labor a phase that neither degrades the laborer nor adds a stigma as an inflicted punishment."

William Kunz, Superintendent of the St. Louis Work-house, says:

" By carefully studying the habits and inclinations

of the prisoners, I arrived at the conclusion that a greater amount of work could be obtained from them by offering a reward to the industrious prisoners, than by exacting work from them under the threat of punishment. With the consent of the Board of Public Improvements, and the approval of his Honor, the Mayor, I established task-work for all such labor as the possibilities would allow, whereby a prisoner inclined to be industrious has the opportunity afforded him of materially shortening his imprisonment by making overtime. Of this a great many prisoners have availed themselves. To others, to whom, from the nature of their employment, no regular task could be assigned, I have held out the promise of executive clemency as a reward for their industriousness, and it has frequently been earned, and, after a proper investigation, has been granted by his Honor, the Mayor. The system works very satisfactorily; the foremen in charge of the various gangs have fewer complaints of indolence of prisoners; cases of punishment for failure to perform the amount of work expected are becoming rare, and the production of the institution has been materially increased."

Wines, in his exhaustive treatise on Prisons, in referring to America, says:

"In a few of our prisons, the convicts are allowed some small share of their earnings; and the influence of this is admirable, indeed, almost magical." Again, he says: "The practice of allowing prisoners a share of their earnings has not been extensively adopted in America. But whenever the principle has been introduced, its effect has been excellent. Let me cite an

example: The Allegheny County Workhouse, at Clare-
mont, Pennsylvania, a correctional prison for persons
guilty of minor offenses, has introduced this principle
into its administration. Its chief industry is the manufacture of kerosene oil barrels, which is carried on in
two large work-shops, in the same building, one above
the other. At a certain point in the manufacture, the
casks are passed from the lower to the upper shop,
and the prisoner receiving them at this point is required
to finish seven for the institution, without any gain to
himself, after which, for each additional barrel completed he gets five cents for himself. The average day's
work outside, for a free laborer, is about fourteen.
Under this stimulus, I saw prisoners making twenty-
four barrels a day, and the average daily production is
from sixteen to eighteen, equal to one and one-fifth
day's work of ordinary workmen in free shops outside.
At first the proprietors of the petroleum refineries
laughed the superintendent to scorn for thinking that
he could utilize the labor of his short-term men on such
a manufacture at all, the average sentence being a little
over two months. But the laugh is now on the other
side, for the prison-made barrels actually command five
cents apiece more in the market than those made in the
outside factories. Most of the work done in the lower
shop is unskilled, and for a time the prisoners working
there received no part of their earnings. At length the
superintendent hit upon the plan of giving to each prisoner against whom there was no complaint at the end of
the day, a credit of ten cents for that day. The effect
of this was magical. I visited the establishment three or

four months after the plan went into effect, and not a
man in the shop had received a single black mark. All
had regularly gained their credits of ten cents a day.
The daily amount of work performed in that shop had
also very sensibly increased."

The same author has traced the history of the struggle of prison reformation in Europe, amid the corruption,
brutality, and officialism of the past, and cites several
instances of success, that merit attention. Speaking of
Belgium, he says:

"Near the middle of the eighteenth century, all
Europe was desolated by the scourge of innumerable
tramps. * * * Out of this fact grew a remarkable
reform in penitentiary science and practice in that part
of Europe which now forms the kingdom of Belgium.
* * * Prince Charles, then (1765) Governor-General
of Flanders, called attention of the privy council at
Vienna to the inefficiency of whipping, branding, and
torturing for the repression of the evil. * * * But
the most important agent in this work of reform was
Viscount Vilain XIV. * * * He was the founder
of the Great Central Convict Prison at Ghent. * * *
Here, then, we find at Ghent, already applied, nearly
all the great principles which the world is, even to-day,
but slowly and painfully seeking to introduce into prison
management. What are they? Reformation as a
primary end to be kept in view; hope as the great regen-
erative force; industrial labor as another of the vital
forces to the same end; education, religious and literary,
as a third essential agency; abbreviation of sentence
and *participation in earnings* as incentives to diligence,

obedience, and self-improvement; the enlistment of the will of the criminal, etc." The result of this management was a remarkable success. Again, he says, that: "Among the most remarkable of the early experiments in prison discipline was that of Colonel Montesino in the prison of Valencia, Spain, containing from 1,000 to 1,500 prisoners. This experiment covered the period from 1835 to 1850. Previously the re-committals had run up to forty, fifty, sixty, and even seventy per cent. For the first two years no impression was made upon these figures, but after that they fell rapidly, coming down in the end to nearly, or quite, zero. To what was this remarkable decrease owing? Mainly to the use of moral force, instead of physical, in the government of the prison. He introduced a great variety of trades, about forty in all, and allowed the prisoner to choose the one he would learn. * * * He seized those great principles which the Creator has impressed upon the human soul, and molded them to his purpose. He aimed to develop manhood, not to crush it; to gain the will, not simply to coerce the body. He employed the law of love, and found it the most powerful of all laws. * * * *He excited the prisoners to diligence by allowing them a by no means inconsiderable portion of their earnings.* He enabled them to raise their position, step by step, by their own industry and good conduct. * * * Mr. Hoskins, an intelligent English traveler, after giving an extended account of the prison, adds this conclusion: "The success attending the reformation of the prisoners in this establishment seems really a miracle.'"

Wines also records one other remarkable case, and

that in a country where it was least to be expected—
Russia. It appears that Count Sollohub introduced a
system in the House of Correction in Moscow, similar in
its general features to that last described. So long as
a convict remained an apprentice, he got no part of the
product of his labor; but as soon as he was adjuged to
be a master workman, he received a proportion equal to
two-thirds of his entire earnings, the greater part of
which was reserved for him as a little capital to begin
life with again after his liberation. So effectual was
the power of hope thus applied, that in some instances
the convict apprentices learned their trade and became
master workmen in two months. Nine-tenths of all
learned their trade so thoroughly that, on their release,
they could fill the position of foreman in other shops.
And further, there were scarce any relapses; so that of
2,128 persons released during the first six years, only
nine were returned to prison.

But the times were not ripe for such a reform in
either of the countries mentioned. Corrupt and rapacious officialism, which sought only to make money out
of the prisoners, soon managed to get other men in
charge of the prisons, with whom reformation was no
object; and as in each case the systems which had been
productive of such good results were not supported by
law, but had depended on the overseer alone, they retired
with him, and the old order of things continued.

MAKE TIME OF DISCHARGE DEPEND IN PART ON SURPLUS
EARNINGS.

But as a most powerful incentive to work that can be
thought of, if such a thing is necessary to induce some

prisoners to work, *let the law provide that no prisoner shall be set free or given his liberty until he has earned a certain sum with which to start out again in life*—except where he has been supporting his family out of extra earnings.

There is no doubt that this would transform almost every convict into a most anxious and energetic laborer. For no matter how averse the worst man may be to labor, the anxiety to get free again, which is powerful with all prisoners, would overcome the aversion.

AIDS IN PRESERVING DISCIPLINE.

Under such a system, it would be a comparatively easy matter to keep up the strictest discipline. Corporal punishment, or confinement in dark cells, etc., would rarely, if ever, need to be resorted to; for the fear of having his surplus earnings diminished by very small fines, as well as having his term of imprisonment lengthened, would make almost every prisoner willing and obedient.

TOO MUCH PRISON LABOR.

If it is objected that there would then be too much prison labor performed, by which free labor would be injured, I answer that, in the first place, there would be no more men at work than there would be, or at least should be at work, if there were no prisons; and, as the prison labor is no cheaper than the free labor, no injustice would be done to the free laborer. In fact, one great cause of complaint that now exists—viz., the cheapness of prison labor—would be done away with.

And further, as the temptation to desert would be but slight, the prisoners could be divided; so that while the vicious, and those that had long terms to serve, were

kept within the walls, the remainder could more generally be set at work for which they were adapted, both
inside and outside of the prison. Instead of being confined to the few trades that can be successfully carried
on inside prison walls, prisoners could be set at almost
every kind of manual labor; and, instead of having to
crowd them all into a few branches of industry, as is
now done, thus overstocking them, they would be distributed more nearly as they would have been had each
selected work from choice as a free man. Surely no
fault can be found with this. In all cases in which a
young man who is imprisoned for a term of years, desires
to learn a trade by accepting lower wages for a time, he
should be permitted to do so. In other cases the prisoner should, as nearly as may be, be set at such work as
they are adapted for, or as they followed before conviction, and can successfully follow after they are again set
free. Especially should those that had no honest voca-
tion before conviction be set at work which they could
successfully follow when again set free; for it is idle to
expect a man to be industrious and make an honest living, if he has no means of becoming the one, or of doing
the other.

WORKING OUTSIDE PRISON WALLS.

The idea of working prisoners outside of prison
walls, when possible, has been tried and found to be
highly beneficial. In fact, this is about the only thing
that is urged in favor of the *leasing* system which now
prevails in many of the Southern States, under which
prisoners work plantations, work mines, build railroads,
etc. True, there it has been marred by the brutality

practiced; the lessees, and not the State, having charge of the prisoner, and feeling no interest in him except as a machine, to be worked as hard as possible, at the least possible outlay, so that the convict soon becomes worse than a slave, and almost destitute of hope; for the master of a slave had an interest in his preservation as so much property, and saw to it that he was at least properly fed, housed, and cared for. But not so with the lessee of a convict. He has no interest in the convict, except for the work he can get out of him. But if the State were to keep charge of the prisoner, and give him an interest in his work, the whole would be changed. Not many would think of deserting, and perhaps the majority of all those now confined could be set to work at various things outside.

As some convicts (working at skilled labor) would get higher wages than those that worked at unskilled labor, it would, perhaps, be proper to charge the skilled laborer a little more for his keeping than the common laborer, in order to prevent too great a difference between them in this respect. But, as heretofore stated, in all cases of young convicts they should be required to learn a trade, and that a trade, if possible, that they would have selected as free men. But, in any event, the employments should be diversified as much as possible.

In this connection, I quote from the report of the Bureau of Labor Statistics, made to the Legislature of Illinois for the year ending January 12, 1881, which is a remarkably full and able document. The Bureau had availed itself of the reports of the committees appointed by different States, particularly Massachusetts and

New York, to investigate the question of prison labor. Among other recommendations are the following:

"*Fifth.*—Increased diversity of employment in penal institutions tends not only to lessen whatever competition now exists, but has an excellent reformatory effect on the prisoners."

Again, the same report recommends: "That, whenever possible, farms shall be carried on by the prison administration for the supply of the institution."

WASTE OF SENTIMENT.

But there are some who will pronounce all talk about humane treatment of convicts a waste of sentiment, because, say they, "these fellows are criminals, and are not entitled to any consideration, and would neither do better nor reform if they could." This objection is ill-considered; for, as heretofore stated, the most of them are weak rather than criminal, and, secondly, experience has shown that the great majority of convicts are capable of reformation, and that the chances of their reforming are always in proportion to the humane treatment received. Under the old system and in the old prisons, as in the existing prisons of this country, where brutality is still the reigning deity and cruelty the only disciplinarian, there is no hope for the prisoners; few if any of them ever reform. Even if they possessed both self-respect and a desire to do better at the time of entering the prison, the treatment received either forever breaks their spirits or makes them desperate; and they leave the prison, if they survive at all, either total wrecks or desperate enemies, bound to be avenged upon that soci-

ety which they feel has not simply punished them for
their misdeeds, but has greatly wronged, if not ruined
them. (See Chapters VII and VIII, of Part First.)

LABOR AS PART OF THE PUNISHMENT.

Again, it will be objected by some that the labor of
the convict is a part of his punishment, and, therefore, to
give him the benefit of a part of his labor would be to
reduce his punishment. This objection grows out of a
misapprehension of the objects for which labor was
introduced into the larger prisons. This was not as a
punishment, but as a sanitary and humane measure.
Its object was to benefit the prisoners, to give exercise
to the body, and to employ the mind. For it was found
that when men are doomed to a long period of enforced
inaction, they break down, both physically and mentally,
so that the death-rate in the old prisons was fearfully
large, and what may be called the *insanity rate* was still
larger. There are prisons for the convicted where the
prisoners do not work. Yet in the eye of the law the
punishment is the same. The punishment consists in
the disgrace of conviction, and in the imprisonment, *i. e.*,
being deprived of their freedom. The idea of the State
making money out of the earnings of the prisoners was
an after-thought, and it is only in recent years that this
has been considered. While in some States it has been
thought quite an achievement to make the penitentiaries *self-supporting*, in others, where the subject was more
carefully considered, this has been made a secondary
matter, and the reformation or moral development of
the prisoners is considered the matter of greatest mo-

ment. Thus, Governor Hoyt, of Pennsylvania, in his last message to the Legislature of that State, expressed himself, as follows, on this subject:

"In neither of the penitentiaries of this State has there ever been an attempt yet made to administer them on the vulgar, wicked, unworthy consideration of making them self-sustaining. In neither of them has it been forgotten that even the convict is a human being, and that his body and soul are not so the property of the State that both may be crushed out in the effort to re-imburse the State the cost of his scanty food, and at the end of his term what then is left of him be dismissed, an enemy of human society."

But all that could possibly be claimed for the State in any event, is that it should be paid out of the earnings of the convict the actual cost of keeping him. It has no right to make a slave of him. It has no right to take his services from him without paying him, any more than it has a right to take his property from him without making compensation for it. When, therefore, as at present, the State prohibits him from earning anything over and above the expense of keeping him, it is forcibly taking something valuable from him without making compensation. For it might as well take his property as his time. While it has the legal right to take both to an extent sufficient to make good its outlay, it has no right to take any more. This is no part of the legal punishment. The idea of the State trying to make money, over and above the outlay, out of its convicts, is monstrous; and the right to do so has never

yet been claimed. See report of inspectors of Pennsylvania penitentiary on this subject as follows:

" There is a broader, more scientific, and far more
important view to be taken of the duty society owes to
itself, and to those convicted for crimes against its security and welfare, than that narrow, selfish and pecuniary
consideration which is satisfied in proclaiming that the
State has made a money profit out of the crimes of its
citizens."

The plan suggested gives the State everything it is
entitled to; and, I will add, it is a serious question
whether the State would not better forego even the
right to deduct the cost of keeping, in some cases, in
order that the prisoner may be the more certain to be
self-supporting when again free, than to take the chance
of having to re-arrest and re-incarcerate him.

RESULTS.

I therefore claim that by the proposed change

First.—Discipline could be easily maintained.

Second.—There would be no loss in productive labor
to society; in fact there would be an increase, for those
that have never been taught to work, and consequently
prey upon the community, would not only be compelled
to work as much as they are now, but most of them
would, under the conditions mentioned above, work to
the best of their abilities, so that in effect there would be
restored to society a vast amount of productive labor
which is now lost.

Third.—The innocent. *i. e.*, the family and dependents
of the convict, would not be punished by being deprived
of his support, as they now are, but would be supported

by his earnings—not only as well as, but in many cases, where he was dissolute, very much better than when he was a free man.

Fourth.—The kinds of labor that could then be carried on being greatly increased, the convict being put to work at something for which he was adapted and which he could follow when again released, would, as a rule, learn to do his work well; and, further, would learn to work rapidly, and, thus, instead of being turned out a stolid and desperate man, who for years has trained himself simply to put in his time without regard to results, and is, consequently, not prepared to do a full day's work, he would be able to do as much work as anybody, and therefore much more likely to get along.

Fifth.—When again set free, if his money has not been used to support his family, he would, in many cases, be comparatively independent; he would not find himself without money and without friends, shunned by everybody and unable to get work, and thus at once driven to beg or steal; but would have money enough, not only to support him for some time, until he could find something to go at, but in many cases, where the best years of his life have been spent in prison, he would have means enough to enable him to do a small business for himself.

Sixth.—All convicts would not then be forced into a few trades, and the present objections to convict labor would be at least in part removed.

Seventh.—All the chances of reformation and development of moral character would be in favor of the convict, instead of being almost entirely against him, as now.

APPENDIX.

UNNECESSARY IMPRISONMENT.

An Address Delivered Before the National Prison Reform Association, at Detroit, Mich., Oct. 21, 1885, by John P. Altgeld.

Early in this century Sir Samuel Romilly, after years of disappointment, succeeded in affecting what was regarded as a great reform in the criminal law of England. But his reforms were limited in their scope, and related only to the punishment to be inflicted after trial and conviction in certain classes of felonies. He stopped the practice of inflicting inhuman barbarities in the name of punishment in certain cases; and so great was the opposition that it took all his life to accomplish this. He had no time to insist that the punishment inflicted on the poor, who can not pay a fine, and are guilty, say, of a breach of the peace, should differ not only in degree, but also in character, from that meted to those guilty of heinous crimes—that the former should be treated rather as moral patients who needed treatment, than malefactors to be punished. He had not the time to point out that it was monstrous to treat all that may chance to be taken into custody precisely alike until after trial and conviction (unless they can give bail) whether they have committed a felony or simply shouted too loud upon the streets.

In these two particulars, at least, the criminal law has undergone but little, if any, change; it stands to-day substantially as it did centuries ago, and may be said to be mediæval not only in origin but in character. And the various criminal codes of this country are, with some slight modifications, simply enactments of the criminal law of England as left by Romilly; and most of the cities and municipalities, in framing their ordinances in relation to minor offenses, have blindly followed the codes in this respect. So that young men and boys, and even girls, accused of violating some city ordinance, are treated by the police and the police magistrates, in the first instance, in the same manner as the hardened criminal. They are arrested, not infrequently clubbed, sometimes handcuffed, marched through the streets, in charge of an officer, to the station, which in many cases is worse than a jail, where a full description of each is written down opposite their respective names, and then they are required to give bail for their appearance at some time in the future when the magistrate can hear their case. If they can not furnish the bond instantly—and generally they can not—they are shoved into a cell, and frequently occupy the same cell for a night, and sometimes for a week, with the most desperate of criminals. The station-keeper is not to blame for this, for the law has made no other provision and left no alternative but to lock them up.

Attend a session of the police court in any of our large

cities, on almost any morning, and you will see on the saw-dust in the prisoner's pen a miscellaneous crowd of human beings of both sexes, ranging from middle life down to tender years, nearly all from the less fortunate class in life—poor, more or less ragged, with misery stamped deep into their faces, weak, with little or no training, no steady habits, without homes worthy of the name, and raised in an atmosphere destitute of good, and pregnant with vicious influences. As their cases are called, you learn that about one out of twelve is charged with a serious offense, about five-twelfths are charged with minor offenses, but there is something about the appear-ance of the accused which tells you they have made this round before. The remaining half are also charged with minor offenses, such as drunkenness, disorderliness, etc., but you soon become satisfied that they are not yet thoroughly depraved; that while they may have violated some ordinance, they yet have the stuff in them to make good citizens if given a little better chance; and, as you look at them, the conviction settles in your mind that it was unnecessary, and therefore wrong, to drag them in and corrall them like so many cattle, and that neither they nor anybody else will be benefited by such treat-ment. If you ask the magistrate why they were thus treated before they had even been tried to see if they were guilty, he will tell you that the law required this; that under the law no other course was open.

You sit down while their cases are heard, and to your surprise find that about one-third are discharged by the magistrate because the evidence fails to show that they were guilty of any offense whatever. (The police reports show that nearly one-third of all that are arrested are discharged by the magistrate.) Turning then to those not discharged, you find that a few, being shown to be probably guilty of the graver offenses, are bound over for the action of the grand jury, while the great majority are shown to have violated some ordinance, and are fined; and as the fines are not paid at once in many cases, you see men, women, and often children, crowded into an omnibus with iron grating at windows and door, and driven to the work-house or to the Bridewell (which may properly be called a short-term Penitentiary) to work out the fine, or, in the absence of a work-house, they are led back to jail to serve out the fine at so much a day.

Dismissing from your mind those bound over for the action of the grand jury, and calming your feelings by saying that the security of society requires that those shown to be even probably guilty of serious offenses against property or human life should not be permitted to roam at large, you turn to consider the omnibus-load of ragged humanity—some thoroughly vicious, some simply besotted, some almost innocent. Children, women, men, all thoroughly wretched, going to the Bridewell—some for twenty, some for sixty, some for ninety days, and a few for even a longer time, for having violated some city ordinance; and as you wonder what is ultimately to become of these people, you find yourself both asking and then answering questions after this fashion:

" Will these people be any better when they regain their liberty?"   " No; for there is nothing in this treat-

ment that is adapted to make anybody better." "Will
they be more intelligent or better educated?" "No."
"Will the idle be more industrious?" "No." Will the
industrious be more able to get employment?" "No;
on the contrary, this stigma will be in their way."
"Will the untrained be masters of a trade?" "No."
"Will they have better homes?" "No." "Better
friends?" "No." "Better surroundings?" "No; if
anything, poorer surroundings." "Will those that
now have no homes then have places to which they
can go?" "No." "Will society extend them a helping
hand?" "No." "Will there be any Christian door
open to receive the women and children on their return?"
"Scarcely." "Will the self-respect of any be raised
and they, therefore, be stronger?" "No; on the contrary, the self-respect of all will be lowered and they
will, therefore, be weaker." "Will the good-intentioned,
but weak, be better off?" "No." "Will the viciously
inclined be more subdued?" "No; on the contrary
they will be a little more desperate." "Will those without homes have any money when they leave the prison,
with which to maintain themselves until they can find a
home or something to do?" "No; not money enough
to pay for a night's lodging." "If men who have not
been imprisoned find it very difficult to get employment,
will these people find it easier?" "No; on the contrary,
they will find it harder." "Then what are many of
them to do?" "Well, they can beg, starve, or steal."
"How will the police treat them?" "Well, the police
call them jail-birds, or Bridewell-birds, and seem to take
delight in 'running them in' again at the earliest possi-

ble opportunity." "Then will many of these people make this round again soon?" "Yes; experience teaches that they will, and that they will become a little more vicious and desperate as they do so."

"Referring to those not yet vicious or criminal— the boys, the women, and first offenders generally— whence does society derive its power thus to incarcerate them?" "From the right of self-protection." "Was it, then, necessary for the immediate protection of society thus to treat these first offenders?" "Oh, no; but this is done to enforce respect for the majesty of the law, and thus prevent others from violating it." "How long has this been going on?" "Oh, several hundred years." "Well, then, how has it worked; does this practice actually deter others, and are there really fewer arrests now in proportion to population than formerly?" "No; to tell the truth, there are more." "Can this practice, then, be truly said to protect society?" "Well, no." "But suppose that arrest and imprisonment had a repressive influence on outsiders; would you not get enough of it by the arrest and incarceration of the actual criminals and hard cases, and do you not destroy the efficacy of your remedy—in fact, rob it of its influence— by applying it so indiscriminately and making it so common?" "Well, the results indicate that this is so." Finally: "Does society get any benefit from this treatment of its first offenders?" "On the contrary, to say nothing of the expense, it is a question whether this practice of imprisoning people for trifling offenses does not constitute the training which crushes the self-respect, and, by degrees, forms those desperate characters whose crimes all over the land make men shudder."

Now, I ask, if—instead of this superficial, and, in a sense, unjust system, which requires a conviction if a technical offense be proven, and after conviction allows some that can pay a fine to escape incarceration, while it sends the poor to the Bridewell, no matter what their physical or moral conditions may be, and no matter what the past history of the accused may be, and without reference to the question as to whether such a course is necessary for the well-being of society—it would not be better in all minor offenses to adopt a practice which would require, not only proof of a technical offense, but also an inquiry into the moral condition of the accused, his habits, associations, etc., and then, except in extreme cases, permit, if you please, a suspension of sentence, and release the accused with the understanding that if his conduct in the future gives no offense he will not be disturbed, but that otherwise he will be taken into custody? This would have none of the degrading influence of actual imprisonment, while at the same time it would be a most powerful incentive to good conduct. Then it should be the duty of some officer to assist the delinquent. as far as possible, in getting employment, finding a home, etc. This latter plan has been tried both in Massachusetts and in Baltimore, with the most happy results.

And in extreme cases, or cases in which repetition of offense requires a sentence of imprisonment, would it not be better to adopt the indeterminate sentence system, whereby the maximum time of imprisonment would be fixed, but the actual term would be determined by the conduct of the accused, and his probable ability to become a law-abiding citizen? And supplement this, not only with educational influences that shall develop his character, but also with a provision requiring him to work, and, at the same time, giving him an interest in his work, so that a certain per cent. of what he earned every day shall be carried to his credit, and be applied, either to the support of his family or paid to him, not at, but after, the time of his discharge. And further provide that in no case shall a prisoner be discharged until he has earned a sufficient sum to his credit, so that on regaining his liberty he will not be an outcast or in a position in which about the only alternative he has is to steal or starve.

The experiment of giving prisoners a part of their earnings has worked almost like magic where it has been fairly tried, and if the provision were added requiring them to have something ahead before they could be set at liberty, almost every prisoner would be a willing laborer, which is the very first requisite effecting his reformation and developing character. Under such a system only the incorrigible would ever need to be imprisoned, and, when they are imprisoned, instead of being discharged in twenty or sixty days, as is now the case, simply to make the same round again, they would be held for such a length of time and under such conditions as would make it at least possible to create habits of industry and develop character, so that, when finally released, there would be at least ground to hope for reform. The large class of repeaters, loafers, and known hard cases, would soon be weeded out and subjected to a course of training, which would not only tend to make them steady and self-supporting, but would free society from their presence and put an end to the farce of perpetual re-conviction.

THOSE DISCHARGED BY THE MAGISTRATE.

Turning now to those that were discharged; what about them? Well, most of what has been said about those not discharged will apply, if possible, with greater force to these; for most of them were innocent, yet they have been imprisoned; their names and a complete description of their persons are on the prison records. They have been wronged, and will feel the indignity to which they were subjected as long as they live. They have been shoved down in the struggle to rise. They will hate and keep out of the way of the police. Many will sympathize with those that circumvent and defy the police. They will be more ready to slink into dark places; and as they become accustomed to dark places, they will become familiar with dark deeds, and many of them will soon make the round with those in the omnibus, and in time form a part of that ubiquitous horde against which we bolt our doors at night, and whose nocturnal visits we dread worse than the plague. Society, in making war on these people without cause, has wronged them, and, at the same time, made enemies of such as are certain to be avenged.

But some one will ask whether there is enough in all these things to make much fuss necessary. In reply, I will refer to the Report of the Superintendent of Police of Chicago, for 1884; and I take this, because, in Chicago, the present system is found at its best, Chicago

having one of the finest and best-managed police forces
in the country, and the proportion of arrests to population is, if anything, smaller there than in other large
cities. According to the report, the whole number
arrested in that city by the police, to say nothing of the
arrests by State and county officials, during the year, was
39,434. Of these, 16,260, or considerably more than one-
third, were discharged by the magistrates; about 2,000,
or five per cent. of all arrested, were held for the action
of the grand jury on criminal charges ; about 900, or one
out of forty, were sent to hospitals or asylums ; and
about 20,000, or a little over half of all arrested, were
fined by the magistrates ; 8,547, or about one-fifth
of all arrested, were females ; 17,566, or nearly half of
all arrested, were without any occupations. Of the whole
number arrested, over, 23,000 or considerably over half,
were originally only charged with being either drunk or
disorderly ; and the fact that out of nearly 40,000
arrested, only about 2,000 were held on criminal charges,
shows that 95 per cent. were arrested for the minor
offenses. Of these, 6,532 were sent to the Bridewell for
non-payment of fines, which shows that they were of
the very poor.

As already stated, in many sections of tne country
the proportion of arrests to the population is greater
than in Chicago. It is, therefore, safe to say that during that year there were, including repeaters, nearly
two millions and a half people arrested in the United
States, of whom about three-fourths of a million were
discharged by the magistrates because it was not proven
that they had violated any law, and, therefore, should not

have been arrested. Notwithstanding the appallingly large number of arrests, crime seems to be on the increase, and careful observers are asking the question whether our penal system, instead of being a success, is not, through the needless arrests and the blind application of brute force, actually swelling the number of criminals in the land. We fancy that the Constitution of the United States is a great bulwark of liberty, but you would be astonished to see with what ease a policeman and a police magistrate will brush it all away when dealing with the poor.

The question may now be asked: "Why should people be arrested and locked up before there has been an examination to see if they are guilty of any offense?" In reply, we say that it is right that persons charged with crimes which indicate a wanton disregard of human life or of the property-rights of others, on the part of the accused, should be restrained as long as there is even a probability of their guilt; that the safety of society may require this. But I submit that in all those cases where the offense charged is simply a misdemeanor, and where there is nothing to indicate that society will in some way suffer or be endangered before a trial can be had, unless the accused is placed in custody or put under bonds, he should not be deprived of his liberty until shown to be guilty.

"O, but," says some one, "if that were the practice, every one in danger of being convicted of a misdemeanor would run off, so that by the time you had your trial there would be nobody to be fined or to collect costs from." Well, suppose for the moment that this were true, who would suffer by it? Mind you, those that we are considering are not criminals. There is nothing in their case to indicate that if they were to go away and settle in some other community, they would endanger the lives, or property, or even the peace of others. And this is the only ground upon which society has the right to deprive a citizen of his liberty before conviction.

Furthermore, if those charged simply with the more trivial offenses were to leave the country before conviction, never to return, would not this, of itself, be as severe a punishment for them as could be inflicted? The thought of being obliged suddenly and forever to leave the community in which one has his abode, is, to most people, horrible—so much so, in fact, that the probability of escape before conviction would be slight. Society derives its power in the matter solely from the necessity of protection; therefore, in all cases of this grade in which the safety of society does not require the confine. ment of the accused before trial, society has no right to deprive him of his liberty until after conviction.

The practice of imprisoning before trial, in cases where some trifling offense was charged, never came into existence as the result of a careful consideration of the best interests of society, but had its origin in that mediæval barbarism which regarded every kind of violation of law as a source of profit—a source of revenue at first for the feudal lord, and later for the magistrates, jailers and other small officials. The more numerous the charges and the more protracted and complicated the proceedings, the fatter these officials got. And yet they were more consistent than we are. They understood that the liberty of an Englishman meant the liberty of the rich, and that the term was merely a beautiful fiction when applied to the poor; while we incorporate lengthy provisions about liberty in our fundamental laws, guar. antee it to every man, woman and child, and then we adopt a system and permit a practice which robs the fiction even of its beauty—a system and a practice which gave more suffering, more misery and more degradation to the poor of England than all her wars. Strange as it may seem, we not only still follow medi- æval ways—blindly make local applications of brute force for ills that require constitutional treatment— but we still make the failings and wrong-doings of a part of our people a source of revenue for others. In almost every city and town there are men who expect to support their families on the toll to be collected in the shape of fees from those that may, from time to time, be accused of some violation of law. Think of a band of officials, men in good standing in the community, directly interested in having the law violated, and who would starve if there should suddenly be a cessation of wrong- doing! Many of them watch with whetted appetites for an opportunity to have some wretch brought before them, no matter on what charge. If he gives bond, there is an extra fee for the bond; if he is sent to jail, there is an extra fee for the magistrate, an extra fee for the constable, and an extra fee for the jailer. What is it to them that they are crushing the self-respect of a man and casting on him and his family a stigma which may ruin him? The law permits it, and they are making money out of it, and that is enough. I am informed that the Legislature of Maryland, in 1882, abolished the "fee system," in so far as it related to Baltimore, and the result was a falling off in the number of arrests for minor offenses in that city, in one year, from 12,000 to 7,000, or almost half; thus showing that the "fee system" had been responsible for nearly half of the arrests theretofore made.

In addition to this there prevails too widely the notion among policemen that their standing and efficiency as peace officers are to be determined by the number of people that they run in. Hence the eagerness of many policemen to make arrests, especially in cases where they do not apprehend much danger. There was a time in the history of education in this country, when some people seemed to think that the efficiency of a school-teacher was to be determined largely by the number of pupils he flogged—as if flogging and not teaching was the main object of the school—and when there was in many schools a suppressed but constant hostility between pupils and teacher, and a perpetual effort on the part of the pupils to deceive or outwit the teacher, and on the part of the teacher to detect the pupils; and as a result, offenses of all kinds against the rules of the school were frequent, and flogging was a matter of daily occurrence. But now we have got to a point where we consider *teaching*, and not *flogging*, the chief end of the school, and we have discovered that to have a feeling of confidence, and even affection, between teacher and pupil, is productive of far better results, and that a very little use of the rod is sufficient in most cases.

Now, society demands protection to life and property

and a preservation of the peace. That is all that it has any right to ask. It has no authority to sit in judgment on the sins of its members. This is a function which the Almighty has thus far reserved to Himself. It is with a view to protection solely that peace officers are created, and their chief object should be to keep the peace; but, owing to the fee system and the false notion with reference to efficiency, a practice just the opposite in spirit has always prevailed. *Arrests* appear to be the prime object, and to *protect life and property* seems a secondary matter.

Read the report of some chief of police, and see with what genuine satisfaction he speaks of the large number of arrests; it shows that the force has been doing something. There is something spectacular, something almost brilliant, about our system; it makes a large showing so far as numbers are concerned. Sir Astley Cooper, the great English surgeon, when once in conversation with another surgeon, who boasted of his own brilliant performances, was asked how many *brilliant* operations he, Cooper, had performed in his professional career—that is, operations requiring a rare union of nerve, dexterity and skill—to which Cooper replied that he had performed thirteen operations which he considered of that character. "Thirteen," exclaimed the other surgeon; "why, I have performed one hundred and fifty most brilliant operations; how many did you save out of your thirteen?" "Well," replied Cooper, "I saved the lives of eleven out of the thirteen; how many did you save out of the one hundred and fifty?" "Oh," was the answer, "they all died; but the operations were very brilliant."

Now, our peace-keeping establishment points with pride to millions of annual arrests, but when we ask how many are saved to society by reason of these operations, we learn that all the patients grow worse, except such as have sufficient moral vitality to recover in spite of the treatment they receive.

If we think most of that teacher who can teach a good school with but little flogging, why should we not think most of that policeman who can keep the peace, can protect society, and yet make but few arrests? We have found that mutual confidence and affection between teacher and pupil, which follows kind treatment, is productive of better results in the school than mutual hostility. Can anybody doubt that a kindly feeling between the police and, not the criminals, but the poor and the outcast, would produce better results than the mutual hostility which now exists?

"Oh, but," says some one, "there is too much sentiment about this; those people are violators of the law and ought to be punished; they have done wrong and ought to suffer, and it doesn't make any difference what becomes of them."

To this I first demur, and then answer: I demur because it does not lie in the mouth of any person not possessed of a perfectly white soul to raise this objection, and if none other raise it, we shall hear little of it in this world, for none of us are perfectly pure, and none other has a right to sit in moral judgment on his fellow-man; very likely even the objector, if judged by the principles of eternal justice, would himself be in the lock-up. And I answer that, in the first place it is not

correct, because, as already shown, over one-third of all
arrested by the police are discharged, because not
shown to be guilty of any offense whatever, and, further,
. if it is true, as competent observers assert, that notwithstanding our numerous arrests, crime is on the increase,
that our present system makes criminals of many that
would otherwise not become such, then it should be
changed; and, as we have been trying brute force and
the crushing policy with such unsatisfactory results,
let us stop locking up the young before conviction, and
dispense with a little of the brute force, and in those
cases in which something must be done, try a system of
development, which, while it will protect society better
than the present system, will also make it at least possible for the accused to come out with more character,
moral strength, and self respect, than he had when
taken into custody.

WHAT SHALL WE DO WITH OUR CRIMINALS?

[An address delivered before the Sunset Club, of Chicago, March 27, 1890, by John P. Altgeld.]

No man can examine the great penal system of this country without being astounded at its magnitude, its cost, and its unsatisfactory results. There are in the United States upward of 2,200 county jails, several hundred lock-ups, or police-stations, between fifty and sixty penitentiaries, with work-shops, machinery, etc. The first cost of the erection of all these buildings and shops has been estimated at upward of five hundred millions, which is dead capital. The interest, at 5 per cent., upon which sum alone, would annually amount to $25,000,000. To this must be added the sums annually appropriated out of the treasury to feed the prisoners, pay the officers, judicial and executive, and keep up and maintain all these institutions, which sums have been estimated at upward of $50,000,000, to say nothing of the costs paid by the accused; there are, in addition to the many thousands of policemen and detectives, about 70,000 constables in this country, and about as many magistrates. There are upward of 2,200 sheriffs, and in the neighborhood of 12,000 deputy sheriffs. Then come the grand juries, petit juries, judges and lawyers; next the keepers and their numerous assistants for all these prisons. On the whole, there are about a million of men partly or wholly, supporting their families from this source, and as I am on the list, I may speak with freedom, and say that, as a rule, they are comfortable, are anxious to hold on, and ready to defend the system which gives them and their families bread.

A glance at this system almost suggests the question whether society has any other object to care for, or mission to accomplish, than simply to maintain this machinery. Looking at its workings, we find that there are in the neighborbood of 75,000 convicts in the various penitentiaries. As the average sentence is about two years and one-half, the whole number, on the average, is, therefore, renewed once every two years and one-half; so that there are in the neighborhood of three quarters of a million of men living in our midst who have had a penitentiary experience. We next see that upward of 5 per cent. of the entire population is arrested by the police and other officials every year; so that there are about three million people arrested and " run in " every year. Assuming that one-third of them are what are called " repeaters "—that is, have been arrested before — it would still leave two millions who are for the first time each year broken into what may be called a prison experience; and yet, notwithstanding the vast army of men employed, the millions annually expended, the numerous arrests, the large number imprisoned, crime is said to be increasing, and our whole penal system is pronounced to be a failure, both in this country and in Europe, where they have similar systems.

And the question is asked by thoughtful men: What shall be done? Society must be protected. If the present system is a failure, what shall we substitute? It has been but a few years since the general public gave this question any consideration. Heretofore the only remedy ever suggested or thought of was the application of brute force. In all the past centuries, and in every country on the globe, methods of punishment for the prevention of crime have prevailed which were the embodiment of brutality and of fiendish cruelty. The prisoners were often transformed into either raving maniacs or wild beasts, while the keepers of prisons became fiends in human form; and in all times, and in every country on the globe, this system of human torture was a failure. Brutality never yet protected society or helped humanity. There was a time in England when men were hanged or burned for trivial offenses; but instead of deterring, the very shadow of the gallows seemed to produce a crop of fresh offenders, and the glow of human embers invited new victims to the stake.

One difficulty with our system is that it proceeds on the idea of expiation, that is, paying for having violated the law. In feudal times every violation of law was a source of revenue to the feudal lord, or to the king. The fine was paid to him, or whatever penalty was paid, went to him, the more serious of offenses being followed by a confiscation of property. The imposition, then, of a fine was one of the means employed by the strong to plunder the weak. Now we have advanced until theoretically we declare that crime should not be a source of revenue, and that it is only for the protection of society that punishment can be inflicted; yet when we come to impose penalties, we proceed upon the theory that if the offender pays for or expiates the violation, then that ends all. He can go right on and violate the law a second time, and if he pays the penalty all is wiped out. Instead of inquiring into the history, the environment and the character of the offender, and then applying a treatment which will in reality protect society, we simply fix a price upon each infraction; and we treat those who are not vicious, but have been unfortunate, and have been guilty of some slight offense, in almost the same manner that we treat the vicious who have been guilty of graver offenses; and we put both in a condition in which it is next to impossible for either to make an honest living when they have been once imprisoned.

I desire to consider the subject rather from a practical than from a theoretical standpoint. The first important question that arises when we are brought face to face with the workings of our system, is, where do all these people who are arrested come from? What is the environment which produces them? As we have not the time to inquire extensively into home-conditions, or the training of the youth, we will start at once at the point where they are first brought to our view, and that is in the police court, and we will soon see where they come from.

The report of the superintendent of police of Chicago for the year 1888 shows that in that year the police officers of Chicago alone arrested and carried to the lock-up 50,432 people, 40,867 of whom were males, 9,565 of whom were females. The great majority of them were under thirty years of age; nearly 9,000 were under twenty years of age; a little over 30,000 of them were American born; the others were made up of various nationalities. The same report shows that 10,263 were common laborers; 18,336 had no occupation; 1,975 were housekeepers. Some of you may ask: What were these people arrested for, and what was done with them? Well, the same report shows that upwards of 15,000, or nearly one-third, were discharged in the police court, because it was not proven that they had violated any law or ordinance; and, out of the whole number arrested, only 2,192 were held over on criminal charges. The rest were fined for a violation of some ordinance, generally on the charge of disorderly conduct. The police magistrate having no power to try a charge of crime or grave misdemeanor, it follows that every case of that nature had to be sent to the grand jury; and I repeat that, out of the whole 50,000, only a little over 2,000 were held over; and the records of the criminal court show that, of these, more than two-thirds fell to the ground because no offense could be proven.

Bearing in mind that those arrested were young; that they come from the poorer classes, from those who are already fighting an unequal fight in the struggle for existence, I ask you what effect do you suppose the act of arresting them upon the street, possibly clubbing them, then marching them to the lock-up, and shoving them into a cell—what effect did all this have upon the 15,000 who were not shown to have been guilty of any offense, who had violated neither law of God nor statutes of man? They were treated while under arrest as if guilty of highway robbery. Did this treatment strengthen them, and make them better able to hold their heads up, or did it tend to break their self-respect, to weaken them? Did it not embitter them against society and a system which had done them this wrong? Will they not feel the humiliation and degradation as long as they live; and will that very treatment not mark the beginning in many cases of a downward criminal career?

But we will follow the subject a little further. You are aware that when a fine is imposed in the police court, if it is not paid the defendant is taken to the House of Correction, that is, the Bridewell, which for all practical purposes is a penitentiary. It has for many years been in charge of Mr. Charles E. Felton, who is one of the most experienced and most intelligent prison managers in the United States. In his report for that year he says: "In the year 1888 the number of prisoners was 10,717, the average daily number imprisoned was 764½, the average duration of imprisonment was but 26$\frac{1}{10}$ days. Of the above who were received during the year all save ninety-six were convicted for petty offenses, the executions under which they were imprisoned showing their offense to have been chiefly disorderly conduct, or other violation of municipal or town or village ordinance, mere petty misdemeanors, punishable by fine only, the imprisonment being the result of the non-payment of the fine."

Reflect upon this a moment: 10,717 were imprisoned during the year, and out of this number only ninty-six were convicted of criminal offenses. The others, in the language of Mr. Felton, were guilty of mere petty misdemeanors, punishable by fine only, and they were imprisoned because they could not pay this fine. Of these 10,717, 1,670 were women and girls.

Speaking of their social relations, Mr. Felton's report says that 2,744 were married; 7,184 claimed to be single; 2,121 had children. It also shows that nearly 4,000 had no parents living; upwards of 1,600 had only mother living, and 822 had only a father living, showing that one-half were without proper parental supervision.

Several years ago Mr. Fred L. Thompson, chaplain of the penitentiary at Chester, Illinois, made a personal inquiry of 500 convicts in regard to their early environment, and the result showed that 419, or upwards of four-fifths were parentless, or without proper home influence before reaching eighteen years of age. Also that 218 never had attended school. Mr. Thompson sums up an interesting report in these words: "I have come to the conclusion that there are two prime causes of crime, first, *the want of proper home influence in childhood, and,* second, *the lack of thorough, well disciplined training in early life.*" I will only add, it is the boy and girl who grow up on the streets or amid squalor and misery at home whose path seems forever to wind toward the prison door, and whatever system will train the youth, or will let light into the hovels, cellars and garrets where children are growing up, will reduce the ranks of criminals.

The fact that all save ninety-six of the inmates of the Bridewell for that year were there because they could not pay a fine, shows that they came from the poor, the very poor, the unfortunate. And as they had not been charged with any serious offense, and as the treatment which they got in the Bridewell in 26$\frac{1}{10}$ days would not build up or strengthen character, could not educate the mind or train the hand; and inasmuch as the treatment there, as in all prisons, of necessity tends to weaken self-respect, and as all these had to go out of the prison absolutely penniless and friendless—for they were sent there because they were penniless and friendless—I ask what were these people to do when they came out? What could they do to make an honest living? Take the 1,670 women and girls who were sent there because they had not the money with which to pay a small fine, and had not a friend upon earth to pay it for them; can any of you suggest what they could go at when they were turned out of the Bridewell and found themselves on the corner of Twenty-sixth street and California avenue? There was absolutely nothing left for them except to go back to their old haunts—go anywhere where they could get something to eat, and a night's lodging. And the prison experience they had had only degraded them, weakened them and sank them lower into depravity.

The same may be said of the men and boys confined there. The city is full of men who have not been imprisoned, and who, during a large part of the year, can get nothing to do. It was estimated that this winter there were 60,000 men in Chicago out of employment. This being so, what show is there for a boy, or a young man, coming out of the Bridewell, to earn an honest living? And if imprisonment in the Bridewell has not helped them, but, on the contrary, has, as a rule, injured them, wherein has society been benefited by the fact that it imprisoned 10,717 people on an average of twenty-six and one-tenth days, because they had committed trivial offenses? But some of you will ask, Well, what have you to suggest? Society must be protected. We must preserve order. To which I reply, unquestionably society must be protected at all hazards, and we must preserve order and protect life and property. But I insist, to begin with, that it is unnecessary to arrest and lock up people who have committed no offense, merely to preserve order; that the 15,000 who were not shown to have committed any offense in that year, should never have been arrested and "run in" by the police; that arresting them neither tended to protect society nor to preserve order, but was a wrong — in many cases an outrage — for which society, in the end, must suffer; that the trouble is, that there has grown up in our police force a feeling that their efficiency is to be determined largely by the number of people they run in, which is all wrong. Again, police officers too frequently feel that when they have arrested somebody, that it is then incumbent upon them to make a case against him, and hence are reckless in their swearing; so that it frequently happens that juries in criminal courts decline to give much credit to the testimony of a policeman. Policemen should feel that their standing is not to be determined by the number of people whom they may happen to arrest, but rather from their ability to preserve law and order; to protect life and property, by making but few arrests.

I am satisfied, further, that it would have been better if a great majority of the 28,000 who were fined in the police court had been let go, the offenses being so trivial that, in fact, it would have been better for society in the long run if no arrest at all had been made.

Then, in my judgment, we should adopt here a system which has been in operation in Massachusetts for over ten years, whereby the city is divided into districts, called probation districts, and in each district there is appointed a probation officer, whose duty it is to visit the prison every day in his district; get the name of the prisoner; go to his residence; see his family; acquaint himself, as far as is possible, with the history and character of the prisoner, his home influences and general environment, and if it is found that he is not vicious, and if the charge against him is not of such a heinous character as to require that he be confined, the probation officer recommends to the justice or to the judge, as the case may be, that if the accused is guilty, instead of sentence being pronounced, the case be continued from term to term, for the period of a year, sometimes more. This done, he is released; the probation officer assists him in getting employment, where this is practicable; assists him with counsel and advice; keeps a supervision over him for the period of a year, requiring him to report from time to time, and if he does not do well, the probation officer orders him arrested, and he is then sentenced.

This system has been in operation in Boston for upwards of ten years. The city of Boston was divided, as I understand it, into three districts, and I have here the reports of the probation officers covering a period of ten years. In one district during the year 1888, 1,139 prisoners were taken charge of by the probation officer. Of this number, twelve ran away, or about one per cent.; fifty-two had to be surrendered, because they did not do well; but all the remainder did well—led sober and industrious lives. During ten years in one district, 7,251 prisoners were taken charge of by the probation officer. Of this entire number, during the ten years, only 107 ran away, a very remarkable fact, which is to be borne in mind in considering the best method of dealing with people who have violated the law. Only a little over one per cent. ran away. Of the 7,251, 473 had to be returned for sentence. All the remainder did well. I will simply say that the results in the other probation districts of Boston were of the same character.

In speaking of the saving to both the prisoner and to society by this method of treatment, the officer reports that, had the lowest sentence possible been imposed, the aggregate time of all the prisoners which must have been spent in prison during the ten years would have amounted to 1,715 years, which was saved to society and to the accused, while the saving in expense to the public by not imprisoning amounted to many thousands of dollars per annum. The fact of having an intelligent and humane man acting as probation officer, visiting the home of the accused and assisting his family with counsel and advice, can scarcely be over-estimated; in many cases it will save not only the children, but also the parents from a criminal career. One of the probation officers of Boston, in speaking of those who were saved from imprisonment in his district, says: "Generally they have since lived good, orderly lives, and have been a blessing to their families, and where they were married, kept their homes from being broken up, and their children from being sent to charitable institutions. In many cases they have changed from lives of vice and crime to become good citizens."

If we were to make our system what the law really intends it should be, and that is, protect society against crime, and would put a stop to the practice of arresting and breaking into prison experiences those who have been guilty of no offense, and would, further, put a stop to the practice of "running in" all who may have been guilty of some trivial offense, and would apply the Massachusetts system of probation in cases where the officer felt it could be safely done—for in many cases it could not be done—we would so greatly reduce the number who would have to be sent to prison that they could then be detained, not for twenty-six and one-tenth days in the Bridewell, or from one to three years in the penitentiary, and not under the conditions that exist now in our prisons, where reformation and instruction are almost impossible; but they could be detained until, in the judgment of a competent board, the accused had acquired such habits of industry and had developed sufficient strength of character to go out and make his way in the world, and then he should be assisted in getting a position, so that he would not at once find himself penniless, friendless and homeless. They should be sent to prison on an indeterminate sentence, nearly in accord with the system that has now for a number of years been in vogue in the Elmira prison in the State of New York, where prisoners must remain at least a year, and can be kept a number of years if, in the judgment of the board, it is not safe to let them at large. Here prisoners go through a regular course of instruction, having regular hours of labor, and the treatment is of such a character as is calculated to develop and build up the man. And the management, instead of knowing nothing about the man, as is the case now with us, is put in possession of his whole history, all the information that can be gathered in regard to it, and whenever it becomes satisfied that the accused can with safety be given his liberty, the management first secures him employment, and exercises, for a period of at least six months, a sort of general supervision over him. If he does not do well they can take him back. If he loses his place they assist him in getting another; and if he does well for a period of a year, he is discharged. And at different times men who have been discharged and then suddenly found themselves out of employment, rather than beg or steal, voluntarily came back to the institution and asked to be taken in until they could get another job; and here again, there were scarcely any desertions, by those who were on parole.

Under such a system as this, hardened and dangerous criminals would not be set at liberty every two or three years, as they are now, to go out and prey upon society; but they would be kept confined until they could be safely set at liberty; while, on the other hand, the good intentioned who had got into trouble would not need to be confined behind brick walls until they became hardened, stolid and desperate, as is now the case.

In addition to this, there should, in my judgment, be given every convict in prison an opportunity to earn something over and above the cost of keeping him. I know this involves difficulties, but none that can not be overcome. He should be not only permitted to earn something, but he should be required to earn something to carry to his credit before he is again set at liberty; so that when he leaves the prison doors, he will have something to sustain him for a while; and this should not be paid him at once, but in installments, so that he can not lose it at once; or, if he has a family to support, he not only should be permitted to work, but required to earn something while in prison for the support of his family.

You will see, by such a system as I have outlined, the number whom we would have in the end to imprison would be greatly reduced; and these, too, could be so separated that the great majority could be set to work, if necessary, outside of the prison. They could farm; could be made to work the roads; could be made to do any kind of work, because the temptation to desert would then be practically taken away. I must say, however, that the temptation to desert is not so great at any time as many people suppose.

Major McClaughrey, who was for many years warden at the Joliet Penitentiary, several years ago told me that he was then carrying on a small farm near the penitentiary, and working it with convicts, and they had had no trouble at all upon this point, and that he had repeatedly urged the State to buy him three or four hundred acres, and said if it would do so, he could work the farm with the prisoners, and could raise not only what was needed for his institution, but for other State institutions, and that he had no fear at all of desertion.

If that is true at present, then under a system whereby the prisoner was made to feel that he was doing something for himself instead of simply wearing his life out for the benefit of some wealthy contractor, very little would need to be feared upon that point, and the number of prisoners who were serving long sentences, and who would be or were considered dangerous, and therefore have to be kept at work in the prison, would be so small by the time they were divided up among the various industries which are now carried on inside of the prison, the number in each industry would be so small that we would hear no more about prison-made goods coming in competition with free labor. The question of prison labor would solve itself.

We would thus save thousands of boys from a prison experience, and a possible criminal career. We would put an end to the practice of degrading and breaking down women and girls by repeated imprisonments for trivial offenses, which never does any good. We would prevent the really vicious and hardened criminals from being turned loose upon society every year or two. Both the convict and society would be the gainers.